REALITY BYTES

architecturaltheory.eu

REALITY BYTES

Selected Essays 1995–2015

BART LOOTSMA

Birkhäuser
Basel

SELECTED ESSAYS 1995—2015

Contents

ACKNOWLEDGEMENTS

Acknowledgements

The essays in this book have been selected because they deal with more general aspects of the architectural discourse as it developed over the last twenty years. More classical architectural criticism dedicated to one building, practice or protagonist was not taken into consideration, unless the immediate occasion for the essay really functioned as inspiration for speculations far beyond the occasion itself. There are no images in this book, even if the essays may originally have been illustrated. Not using images is, for those who know me, not typical for what I do. For most publications, I consider image editing as least as important as the editing of the text. This, and not my text, turned my book SuperDutch into an international bestseller.[1] Here, for once, I hope the themes of the essays come out stronger than the work they refer to, how indebted I may be to the architects and theoreticians they feature.

I realize I have been extremely lucky that I could not just write but also publish about such incredibly interesting people and projects from the very beginning of my career on. This certainly has to do with the fact that when I started publishing in the nineteen eighties, the architectural discourse was still largely bound to nations and therefore to language. I could introduce international subjects for a Dutch audience. There was so a real curiosity and hunger for this. Later on, I could use the authority I gained by publishing about renowned international architects in the Netherlands to introduce unknown Dutch architects, designers and artists.

I am grateful that through Geert Bekaert and Hans van Dijk, the Dutch magazine Wonen/TABK (the predecessor of the more internationally oriented ARCHIS and Volume) offered someone with hardly any noticeable experience in writing like me the opportunity to fill a complete special issue on the Poème Électronique by Le Corbusier, Xenakis and Varèse in 1984 – the traces of which still haunt some articles in this book.[2] It should be said that I'm not a natural writer. Writing is something I have to work hard on and I still depend heavily on final editing. This is increasingly the case since about twenty years I no longer write in my native language, Dutch, but either in German or in English. Therefore I am extremely grateful to all the final editors I have worked with: I could simply never do without them.

1   Lootsma, Bart. *Superdutch: New Architecture in the Netherlands*. New York; London; Stuttgart-München; Nijmegen: Princeton Architectural Press; Thames & Hudson: Deutsche Verlags-Anstalt; SUN, 2000.

2   "Le Poème Électronique, Le Corbusier-Xenakis-Varèse," Special issue, *Wonen/TABK*, no. 2, 1984.

That editing a magazine is more than text editing I was able to learn when, not long after my publication in Wonen/TABK, on the initiative of Madeleine Steigenga and Peter Loerakker, I was invited by the Dutch association Architectura et Amicitia to join the board of Forum. Ever since, I have loved editing magazines. Even if or maybe just because the nineteen eighties and nineties were a period in which most magazines wanted to work thematically, I am very aware that a magazine is something different than a book. A magazine can never compete with a book and a book can never compete with a magazine. A magazine is not just an editorial board with an idea, but the publisher, the authors and the readers are integral parts of the vessel one must try to steer. This is only possible when it moves. Different from a book, a magazine has a rhythm of deadlines one has to dance to. A magazine is something that moves in time. In German it is called a Zeitschrift, a writing in time or maybe even a writing of time. It should develop like a character in a good novel or like the protagonist in a good television series, which returns regularly. Only then the readers will subscribe and remain loyal, which is the basis for the existence of a magazine. They should be eager to know how the story goes on, otherwise it can only be financed retrospectively and every issue can be the last. This is something I learned from Janny Rodermond when I was working as an editor for the Dutch magazine de Architect in the early nineties.

The articles collected in this book were published not for one but for different smaller international architectural magazines, such as Forum, hunch, Daidalos, ARCH+, and increasingly in exhibition catalogues and books. They were never written with a larger plan of a larger book in mind, in which they could carefully find a place. Still they deal with clusters of similar themes, they touch and sometimes even overlap, because originally they appeared in completely different contexts and even in different languages.
The first three magazines I mention above (and ARCHIS) no longer exist, and even though wonderful new magazines come and go all the time, there is no question that the disappearance of magazines, first in the nineteen nineties, had to do with the changing structure of publishing companies demanding a minimum profit from every title, and second, in the first decade of this century, with the rise of the Internet. The first is problematic, the second I do not just see negatively. The Internet develops it's own magazine-like formats and blogs which, because of the global nature of the Internet, can address much larger reader groups worldwide than the old magazines and I am sure we can

develop formats that will be richer and more satisfying than books. Suddenly, there are even individual architects and authors who, like myself, have 5,000 friends on social media like Facebook or even more followers. These are not only mouth-watering numbers for most magazines and books, what makes the Internet and social media so different and appealing is that it is much easier to have a feeling or even an idea what these people think, because they can react to publications. This interactivity, how sceptical people may be about "likes" on Facebook, is a breakthrough. Until recently, this was only reflected in cold boardroom statistics. I realize very well that in terms of financing, there is an ever-increasing divide between commercial professional magazines and blogs, more culturally oriented magazines, and academic magazines. We will see how to solve that. We are at a moment in history that the Internet offers new opportunities and challenges for critics and editors but it also poses a risk for architectural discourse –as it does for any discourse. Therefore I think that if 1995 was the year for me that globalization of the architectural discourse offered new opportunities, 2015 is the year that the new opportunities and challenges offered by the Internet become more dominant and ask for new roles and new initiatives, which I am happy to try to develop at the University of Innsbruck on the webzines http://txt.architecturaltheory.eu/, and architecturaltheory.tv, in synergy with social media like Facebook. I have to thank Jan Willmann, Christian Rapp, Christoph Planer and Olaf Grawert for helping us create and develop these websites.

1995 and 2015 may be years as arbitrary as any other, but they are good enough brackets for this book. 1995 was also the year I was invited by Wiel Arets to teach thesis at the Berlage Institute, first in Amsterdam and later in Rotterdam. I am extremely grateful for this, as the Berlage developed under Wiel's leadership into one of the most exciting schools worldwide – even if it was officially not even a school. The constant debate with the regular professors Winy Maas, Raoul Bunschoten, Elia Zenghelis and not to forget staff members Vedran Mimica, Roemer van Toorn and editor Jennifer Sigler of hunch produced the most creative and productive climate I have ever worked in. It deeply formed me. It attracted the most talented participants from all over the world, who were instrumental in producing high-quality content. Several of them have leading practices today or became professors themselves at important international universities. The weekly lectures read as a Who is Who of international architecture. As one of the first architectural schools largely dedicated to research it opened the perspective to a new practice as a critic: a practice not based on immediate reactions to the actuality of work produced, but a practice before, next and after it, which allowed for a more profound way of dealing with architecture in the context of other spatial and cultural practices. Even if I had been teaching before, The Berlage opened the door to a new, different, international, academic architectural world.

It is no secret that from the nineteen eighties on, it was impossible to escape the influence of Rem Koolhaas in the Netherlands. His name regularly appears in this book and I am greatly indebted to Rem in many different ways, but not necessarily in the way most people would expect. Even if I met Rem only when I was twenty, I hear his name from that I was six, because he was the best friend of my stepbrother Rene Daalder. Rene, always so far away, has been a great inspiration for me all my life, the brother I did not have to look up to. Rene, being already eighteen years old when I was six, driving cars, drinking beer, making movies and music, would come home sometimes to have discussions with his father and they almost always ended with discussions about this mysterious Rem I had never met, who was a journalist and a screenplay writer and apparently producing all kinds of scandals I did not understand. It was Rem who advised Rene to tell me to study in Eindhoven and certainly not in Delft in 1975. It was also Rem who, more directly this time, pushed me to become an architectural critic. In 1984 I was sent by the editors of Forum to do an interview with Rem, who had just finished a series of groundbreaking projects with OMA. Not knowing who I was, Rem received me in the offices of OMA but made clear that he was not interested in giving interviews any more. He had done so many projects, written so much and had held so many lectures that now others should write about his work. So, with my specific knowledge I did and was immediately asked to stay at Forum.[3] In the decades to follow, Rem became one of the central figures of Dutch and international architecture, a figure impossible to avoid and almost equally difficult to be close to for a Dutch critic slowly entering the international discourse. There has always been a critical distance.

There are other people that may not be mentioned in this book, but who nevertheless have deeply influenced me. Only lately, I realize that Geert Bekaert, the professor for architectural history and theory in whose institute I studied

3   Lootsma, Bart. "The Strategies of OMA." *Forum* 29, no. 3, 1985.

in Eindhoven influenced me more than I thought, notably in the pleasure I have in writing essays rather than complete monographs. With Laurids Ortner, a highly original architect, writer and curator, first as a founding member of Haus-Rucker-Co, later of Ortner Architects, who gave me my first job as an assistant at the Art University of Linz, we had weekly intense discussions. He encouraged me to write and continue the editorial work for Forum in the Netherlands even if I was working for him in Austria. I would equally like to mention Wolf Prix, who helped me to my first professorship at the University of Applied Arts in Vienna; Jacques Herzog, Pierre de Meuron, Roger Diener and Marcel Meili, who invited me to work with them at the ETH Zurich Studio Basel; Arno Brandlhuber, who invited me to join him at A42.org at the Academy of Arts in Nuremberg; Nasrine Seraji who invited me to teach at the Academy of Fine Arts in Vienna; and Carole Schmit, who invited me to the University of Luxembourg.

I have to thank my colleagues, my staff and our students at the University of Innsbruck, where I have been given the opportunity to build up a team for architectural theory to do research and teach. Based on my experiences at the Berlage Institute and the University of Applied Arts we have build up studio work, which is dedicated to research into architectural theory. In February 2016 we will celebrate our tenth anniversary. I have to thank my assistants at the University of Innsbruck Angelika Schnell, Jan Willmann, Andreas Rumpfhuber, Mathieu Wellner, Verena Konrad, Bettina Schlorhaufer, Alexa Baumgartner, Peter Volgger, Kanokwan Trakulyingcharoen and our speakers Katharina Weinberger and Franz Xaver Sitter to make this possible. I would like to specially mention some of our tutors, notably Christian Rapp, Christoph Planer, Markus Rampl and Olaf Grawert, who have done much more than what could be expected of student assistants. The Institute for Architectural Theory and History, Dean Stefano de Martino and Rector Tilmann Märk of the University of Innsbruck have made this book possible with generous financial contributions.

I can impossibly mention all people who inspired and supported me over these twenty years, and unfortunately not always explain why that is the case. I definitely would like to mention for very different reasons Mariette van Stralen, Manuela Hötzl, Sonja Beeck, Sabine Bitter, Helmut Weber, Jeff Derksen, Theoline van Schie, Toon Prüst, Pieter-Jan Gijsberts, Gerard van Zeyl, Lex Kerssemakers, Dietmar Steiner, Florian Medicus, Gerrit Confurius,

Frédéric Migayrou, Marie-Ange Brayer, Francine Fort, Michel Jacques, Nikolaus Kuhnert, Lars Lerup, Ben van Berkel, Lars Spuybroek, Greg Lynn, Adriaan Geuze, Joep van Lieshout, Hans van Dijk and Bas Princen. I am afraid I will forget many and even if I don't I will not do justice to anyone.

This book was finished on the thirtieth of October 2015. This not only ends the process that leads to this book before it goes on sale. The 30th October happens to be the birthday of my partner Katharina Weinberger, who I love deeply. I would never have made or finished this book without her. Katharina gave me a new and different perspective in life almost ten years ago and she gave us a wonderful daughter, Lotte Lena Lootsma, in June 2015. I have dreamed of a family all of my life, but never expected it to be as wonderful as I experience it now. In an even stranger coincidence, the 30th October 2015 is also the day that Katharina and I married in Innsbruck. Of course, I dedicate this book to Katharina and Lotte Lena.

Bart Lootsma

SITUATED KNOWLEDGE

Situated knowledge

To know what one is speaking about, (...) requires that one knows who is speaking and from where: it is necessary to know that one always speaks from within a world from which comes the structure of consciousness of the one who is speaking and who, in order to know what he is saying, must know this world and this structuration at risk of otherwise remaining within an ideology.[1] Lucien Goldmann

Practice experiments

A lot of writers in the field of architecture speak from above and outside lived experiences. They lose sight of their conditional nature, take no risk in speculation, and circulate as members of a promotion campaign or form of administrative inquisition over the world paralyzing all practitioners what should be done tomorrow. When Lucien Goldman spoke his words in Paris during the turbulent days of 1968, he referred to what Karl Marx and Friedrich Engels once said in The German ideology[2] that when someone speaks, one should always ask oneself "Who is speaking and from where?" Goldman targeted people such as the philosopher Jacques Derrida and others who where stepping in the footsteps of Martin Heidegger, dealing with the world from an ivory-tower; as if life can be determined far from a consciousness determined by life itself. It is remarkable says Terry Eagleton "...that intellectual life for centuries was conducted on the tacit assumption that human beings had no genitals. Intellectuals also behaved as though men and women lacked stomachs."[3] Heidegger's rather abstract concept of *Dasein* is indeed – as Emmanuel Levinas once said a "Dasein that does not eat". In the writings of Bart Lootsma theory never speaks for itself, and neither does the lived experience; instead they inform each other in an interdependent manner. Lootsma acknowledges in many instances throughout the book that our human existence is at least as much about desire and fantasy as it is about truth and reason. "We need to understand", says Lootsma, "the influence of the new media, not only to be informed and be able to avoid traffic jams, but also to know where we are and where we want to go. They trigger our desire. They tell us not only where to buy, but also where to meet and where to kiss. They are a crucial part of public space."[4] Sociology, economy, anthropology, history, politics, philosophy, technology, art, film, music, literature, design, the city, the everyday, photography, fashion, the experience of the thing, and other fields, all inform Bart Lootsma's research what our live experience is

1   Goldmann, Lucien. *Lukács and Heidegger: Towards a New Philosophy.* London: Routledge & K. Paul, 1977.
2   Engels, Friedrich, and Karl Marx. *Basic Writings on Politics and Philosophy.* Garden City, N.Y.: Doubleday, 1959.
3   Eagleton, Terry. *After Theory.* New York: Basic Books, 2003.
4   Bart Lootsma, *The New Landscape,* p. 149 of this book.

5   Antonio Gramsci, as explained by Edward W. Said, in *Representations of the Intellectual: The 1993 Reith Lectures.* New York: Pantheon Books, 1994.

6   See Berlage Institute *Projective Theory* program as conducted by Roemer van Toorn between 2000 and 2010, *"No More Dreams?: The Passion for Reality in Recent Dutch Architecture ... and Its Limitations." Harvard Design Magazine* 21, (Autumn/Winter 2004).

about. Lootsma doesn't write about styles as we are used to from art-historians. He doesn't lock himself up in history either. The world of today and that of the future is his main concern. From within our actuality, in all its complexity, Lootsma enters the future and researches the past. From several points of view and issues he analyses how architecture and urban practices, using different categories, tactics and tools, deal with the phenomena and the opportunities of the present. The interdisciplinary weaving method of Lootsma shows that theory and practice cannot do without each other when you wish to understand the present and want to mobilize its liberating energies. Perhaps it is of no coincidence that Lootsma started as an architect, because – as Antonio Gramsci once noted – architects and other practitioners are organic intellectuals[5], they feel the obligation to organize life, they cannot permit themselves the luxury to observe the world from a quasi-neutral distance as traditional intellectuals prefer to do. Architects cannot avoid to experiment with the contemporary. Through projects they commit themselves to the present. Cannot but make their hands dirty when they transform a given reality to the better (at least that is what many hope to establish). It is these practices of experiment which Lootsma – from several different angles and with great detail situates within the large issues of modern society. The book reads both as an introduction to urbanism, how architecture, the body in space in different innovate practices functions today; what its *hidden* theories, themes and histories are; how they take part in our mutating reality.

Projective theory

Bart Lootsma is practicing what I call a projective theory[6]. He tries to mobilize theory and activates history by developing a new breed of urban and architectural knowledge that through practice experiments looks ahead. In this book many different projective practices are discussed. Instead of assailing reality with a priori positions the projective practices Lootsma describes, analyze the facts and, in the process of creation, make decisions capable of transforming a project in concrete and surprising ways. The architect waits and sees in the process of research and creation where information leads her or him. With a projective theory the distancing of critical theory is replaced by a curatorial attitude. When you practice projective theory you don't arrive at a project with a bag full of prior theory. Lootsma is not telling us what is right or wrong, but prefers to analyse what architects and planners try to do; helps them to

7   See www.agglutinations.com; *Critical Regionalism Revisited: Provisional Thoughts on the Future of Urban Design* by Kenneth Frampton, comments by Bart Lootsma and Mark Gilbert, February 2003. Site edited by Nader Vossoughian.

formulate new problems and suggest what architecture should do next facing the urgent issues and opportunities our modern society is rich of. Although Lootsma can be very critical too, he doesn't belong to a family of critics who practice pity science. There is not much talk of a loss in the essays in this book. Instead of a critique of despair – a negative critique – Lootsma looks for the opportunities in a work and tries to escape the suffocation of disenchantment. In his recent correspondence[7] with Kenneth Frampton for instance on Critical Regionalism Lootsma remarks that "It would be a pity if those serious attempts to come up with broader theories about urbanism would be put away by just considering them as sales pitches. Sales pitches that is what has become of many of the theories of the architects that do everything in the service of Architecture. Sometimes I have the feeling of listening to TV-preachers that want to convert me when I listen to them. Compared to that, I think a new generation of architects and urbanists that first want to come to a new understanding of what the city – including suburbia – has become deserves all sympathy."

With great enthusiasm and vitality Lootsma supports young and more experienced practices that develop innovative work beyond the self-congratulating effects of form. Instead of stressing the failures of a work he discovers their potential. Not the urban or architecture project in itself is celebrated in Lootsma's essays, but the broader social, economical and cultural context and processes architects enact through their interventions and research they carry out. This book is not about the autonomy of form but all about process, possible scenarios and strategies that deal with the many mutations in our urban landscape. Instead of an architecture and urbanism that escapes into the margin, Lootsma looks for strategies and practices that deal with our modernity at large. The profession of architecture and urbanism has to face the consequences of individualisation, globalisation, technology, the artificial landscape, the cyborg, the culture of mobility, the role of the new media, and be aware of what is missing.

The life of things

Rather than considering an object as a fact or a value, dividing the world in the objective powers of the thing as in the natural sciences, or only look – as in social sciences – to the object to be used as a white screen onto which society projects it ideals, Lootsma believes in a theoretical research which brings these two scientific cultures together. Research

8 Latour, Bruno. *We Have Never Been Modern.* Cambridge, MA: Harvard University Press, 1993.

9 Fraser, Marian. "Classing Queer: Politics." In *Performativity and Belonging,* edited by Vikki Bell. London: Sage Publications, 1999.

into either the *hard* or *soft* qualities of an object are naturally applied in practice, but how these two cultures function together in reality, form a complex dynamic whole, goes often unnoticed. This is remarkable to say the least because in reality we do not make a distinction into two cultures; quite the opposite, we assume hybrid and simultaneous relations all the time. For this reason, the researchers Michel Serres and Bruno Latour propose that we should cast the *soft* or *hard* object from our minds. It is better to talk of the quasi-object. The quasi-object equips us to develop a new model of knowledge that goes beyond dividing an object into two cultures. Rather than considering an object as a fact or a value, to see it simply as a (stylistic) form or social function, we must begin to grasp the facts and values as intrinsically interdependent wholes. "Quasi-objects are much more social" says anthropologist and philosopher Bruno Latour, "much more fabricated, much more collective than the *hard* parts of nature, but they are in no way the arbitrary receptacles of a full-fledged society. On the other hand they are much more real, nonhuman and objective than those shapeless screens on which society – for unknown reasons – needed to be *projected.*"[8] As Marian Fraser observed "Matter does not *exist* in and of itself, outside or beyond discourse, but is rather repeatedly produced through performativity, which brings into being or enacts that which it names."[9] It is this situated knowledge of the quasi-object Bart Lootsma is focusing upon. When we focus on a coffee cup for instance, all kinds of relations set themselves into action. We can think of the entire history of Turkish coffee making, the people who harvest the coffee beans, the manufacturing process of the cup, how the distribution and marketing influenced the design, the memories lanes and desires an Illy café can activate.

For Lootsma the real is full of circulating substance, innovation, interpretation and change. Instead of looking to form as something with a fixed and eternal meaning such as in classical architecture, Lootsma researches architecture practices that start to understand that matter is caught up in the flux of time rather than representation. In foregrounding time in urbanism and architecture Lootsma starts to deal with the encounter of perception (the program of life) and matter, that being and matter are never stable, that matter and movement are imbued with and inseparable from situated knowledge. The research Lootsma is undertaking is about how to read a work and its worldly situation. Of how a work and its discourse is about experience and not just about itself. When Lootsma analyses the work of Rem Koolhaas in

10 Lootsma, Bart. "Now Switch off the Sound and Reverse the Film: Koolhaas, Constant, and Dutch Culture in the 1960s." *Hunch* 1, 1999.
11 See www.agglutinations.com: Correspondence with Bart Lootsma. *Reflections on MVRDV, Rem Koolhaas, and Dutch urbanism,* by Nader Vossoughian.

12 Deleuze, Gilles, and Félix Guattari. *A Thousand Plateaus: Capitalism and Schizophrenia.* Minneapolis: University of Minnesota Press, 1987.
13 See www.agglutinations.com: Correspondence with Bart Lootsma. *Reflections on MVRDV, Rem Koolhaas, and Dutch urbanism,* by Nader Vossoughian.

"Now switch of the sound and reverse the film"[10] he isn't constructing yet another legend; promoting the architect as star, but situates the approach of the author within a broader context and how that informs the architects interventions.

In search of the public in a Deleuzian century

In several essays Lootsma illustrates – as always making contemporary theory comprehensible by relating it to concrete urban and architecture practices – that our modernity no longer develops mainly in instrumental, rational and linear terms, but instead takes its direction from the unintended consequences of technological revolution, globalisation, individualization and information. In a certain sense our industrial (first) modernity might be considered more ideological while our information (second) modernity today is more pragmatic. This doesn't mean the end of ideology, but somehow our modernity prefers experimentation above any grand narrative, or other teleological development; perhaps something like what Lootsma calls *Open Source Ideology*[11] is in operation instead. The classical tools and ideas of planning, urbanism, architecture and design are all no longer able to provide any answers, let alone help us to navigate in our interdependent disorderly world. As Lootsma explains we have to rethink the body, the landscape and the city now that we enter a state of total heterogeneity where the clear borders between the near and the far, the public and the private, between the city and the countryside have been blurred. Some years ago Michel Foucault remarked that the 21st century would be Deleuzian. And indeed the characterization of the rhizome by Deleuze and Guattari[12] as having neither beginning nor end, but a logic moving and proceeding from the middle, through the middle, by coming and going, while focusing on the in-between and the line instead of the point, is extremely relevant in understanding how we make sense in our life. Not only do we have to develop a new architectural and urban knowledge which can map and articulate opportunities and threats, problems and solutions, but we also should ask ourselves according to Lootsma: "Freedom – yes, but for whom? To do what?"[13]

The modernity we are facing is after all not only a success story, we are in need of a new notion of the collective, of the common good, we cannot allow corporate globalism continue to produce endless series of sameness and

14 See www.agglutinations.com: Correspondence with Bart Lootsma. *Reflections on MRVDV, Rem Koolhaas, and Dutch urbanism.* by Nader Vossoughian.

15 Deleuze, Gilles, and Michel Foucault. "Intellectuals and Power." In *Language, Counter-memory, Practice: Selected Essays and Interviews*, by Michel Foucault, edited by Donald F. Bouchard. Ithaca, New York: Cornell University, 1977.

16 See article "Something is missing", in this book p.199.

separation. Instead we should free the energies within the rhizome that are able to generate difference and presence. We have to reinvent a notion of politics in space from within practice experiments, or in the words of Lootsma: "The only thing that counts is democratic decision making that transforms ideological and philosophical questions. Politics do define the program, but not with Mao's little red book in the hand."[14] Lootsma pleas for a public sphere which is not made, but has to be created, without any prior theory that dictates what the definition of the collective should be, instead it has to be experimented upon. It is these practice experiments that Lootsma discusses in this book.

Open systems and beyond

For Deleuze and Guattari thinking in terms of circulating substance, energies, flows, desiring machines and movement was not a goal in itself, but invented to subvert and break the bourgeois processes full of order and clichés. They believed that a kind of nomadic existence that allows for spontaneous groupings and organizations of people, or with a simple definition open systems, or *multitudes*, could free us from the suffocation of normality. A similar approach can be found in the writings of Lootsma. Just as the architect Spuybroek, he is not interested in technology as a way of regulating functions and comfort. He sees it as a destabilizing force whose function is to fulfil our craving for the accidental by providing a variety of potentialities and events. An open system for all the senses could, according to Lootsma, work as an antidote to the amounts of information people are bombarded with, and travel beyond a state of almost endless disability. With the idea of the multitude in mind Lootsma maps and discusses different innovate practices that start from the conceptual idea open or endless systems in which "representation no longer exists; there is only action – theoretical action and practical action which serve as relays and forms of networks"[15]. Although Lootsma sympathizes with the open nomadic system Deleuze and others advocate he doesn't believe that a heterotopia, or rhizome, by itself can open new democratic horizons. For Lootsma[16] and Gillian Howie, Deleuze follows a too mystical romantic perspective that – although intended as a progressive route to walk – isn't able to go beyond the mechanism of control we associate with neo-liberal individualism. The culture of *sprawl* we have entered of endless sameness and separation is in need of other tools and criteria;

17 Lootsma, Bart. "What Is (really) to Be Done? MVRDV's Theoretical Concepts." In *Reading MVRDV*, by Véronique Patteeuw. Rotterdam: NAi Publishers, 2003.

18 Anderson, Perry. *In the Tracks of Historical Materialism*. London: Verso, 1983.

we cannot just live in fragmentation. Something is missing, Lootsma says; we need new forms of urban planning, organizations and institutions to develop new horizons of democracy. Now that democracy within the nation-state is under attack by corporate globalisation, those who act and struggle are no longer represented either by a group or a union that appropriates the right to stand as their conscience. Now that the Right acts big, and the Left is still engaged in a performative contradiction of continuing to dream of liberty in the face of a pessimistic scepticism about resistance and emancipation Lootsma believes that it is time to move ahead: "Particularly in the Western European tradition of the welfare state, that has somehow always carefully but successfully found a position between the totalitarianism of the communist world and the fake freedom of the capitalist world, it would be a pity if these choices would be reduced to one extreme position or the other, torn apart between a paranoid fear for ungraspable collective risks and an equally irrational belief in a metaphysics that at some point in the future promises us a natural order that will bring us the ultimate freedom. Together with politicians, it is the task of architects and planners to come up with concepts, proposals, projects and plans that enable us to make serious choices that give us an indication of, to paraphrase Lenin, what is really to be done?"[17]

Instead of a negative critic who no longer believes that any future could be realised through the logic of practice in the middle of society, or a pessimism that in the words of Perry Anderson "strafed meaning, over-ran truth, outflanked ethics and politics, and wiped out history"[18] Lootsma searches, with refined skill, for nothing but chances how creative practices through their situated knowledge within the order of things, their bodily presence and intellectual consequences have a chance to succeed in building a progressive future.

Roemer van Toorn

ARCHITECTURAL THEORY

Architectural Theory

The English word *theory* derives from the ancient Greek verb *theorein*, which means *seeing* or *observing*. The focus of architectural theory is thus the observation and interpretation of architecture and all its aspects. As is generally the case in cultural theory, the theory of architecture does not just address one selected or canonized segment of the built environment but rather general spatial practices. It does not seek to escape to hypnotic metaphysics or complex cosmologies which, taken together, can lead to catechism, to recipes for buildings. Rather, it tries to grasp the real forces shaping the environment, even in its mediocre manifestations. It analyses the conditions under which production takes place and speculates on the possible social, political and cultural effects of specific interventions.

Of course, these architectural observations and interpretations need to be communicated. Here texts can serve as an important tool. But they are not the only way to convey the perceptions of architecture. Drawings (i.e., ground plan, section and view), illustrations, films, models, lectures and dialogues can also be used for this purpose. However, one should always bear in mind that none of these media are able to communicate the direct experience, the immediacy of buildings and spatial situations.

Architectural theory is part of different social, economic, political and aesthetic discourses. It also initiates discourses and reacts to them, confirming them or seeking ways out of an unsatisfactory status quo.

Europe's great accomplishment of the 20th century was to put architecture to work for the broad masses of the population. As an intelligent organization and cultural manifestation of our society it created flats, working places, public and recreational spaces. Politicians, architects and city planners have taken on the cause of architecture by showing interest for the broad masses of the population. Even European architectural theory has contributed to this movement.

Today perhaps there are no longer the big masses. Collective interests, wishes and threats do, however, continue to exist – even if we are not always aware of them. It is thus all the more important that architects and city planners show a renewed interest in the social role of their disciplines so that they can develop new strategies for politicians to implement. It is precisely here that architectural theory could play an important pioneering role by perceiving, analyzing, interpreting, speculating and, in short, suggesting programs.

Such a critical theory of architecture does not reduce dreams to facts. Rather, it uses these facts as a foundation to formulate – following Bruno Latour – things that are essential. "The critic is not the one who discloses something but rather the one who gathers. The critic is not the one who pulls the ground from under the feet of the naïve believers, but rather the one who offers participants arenas where they can come together. The critic is not the one who arbitrarily oscillates between anti-fascism and positivism like Goya's drunken iconoclast. Rather, he is the one for whom that which is constructed is fragile and in need of care and caution."[1] Only on the basis of this understanding can architects and city planners re-conquer the future.

1   Latour, Bruno. "Why Has Critique Run out of Steam? From Matters of Fact to Matters of Concern." *Critical Inquiry* 30, no. 2 (2004): 225–48.

MORE MAASTRICHT BEAN COUNTING!

OR: WHAT MIGHT A MODERN EUROPEAN THEORY OR ARCHITECTURE LOOK LIKE?

More Maastricht bean counting!

Or: What might a modern European theory of architecture look like?

Our amalgamated wisdom can be easily caricatured: according to Derrida we cannot be 'whole', according to Baudrillard we cannot be 'real', according to Virilio we cannot be 'there'. Rem Koolhaas[1]

Samuel Beckett said that if at first you don't succeed "Fail, fail again, fail better". The genius of Europe is that it carries on trying. Mark Leonard[2]

The great European achievement of the 20th century was that architecture – as the intelligent organization and cultural expression of our society, as living, working, public and leisure spaces – came to benefit the masses. For this to be possible, politicians, architects and urban planners had to take an interest in the lives of these ordinary people. European architectural theory, too, was largely committed to this effort. Perhaps the masses as such no longer exist today. But this doesn't mean that collective interests, collective wishes or collective threats have disappeared. In fact, it is now more important than ever for architects and urban planners to take a greater interest in the social role of their discipline, so that they are able to develop new strategies to offer to policy-makers.

What might constitute a European theory of architecture in this context? Could it once again play a role in formulating new collective interests? Would it be different from the architectural theory of other countries or of other continents? And if so, how? Are there perhaps certain traditions that European architectural theory would want to perpetuate or break away from? Are there specific values it would want to express, objectives it would want to follow? What might it have to offer us? And is it not strange that we should be concerned about this here and now, in our globalized world, of all places? When we say *European*, do we perhaps actually mean something different, something much more general, something we cannot find the words for?

I don't know whether I can answer all these questions here, but I do have a few specific reasons why we should be thinking about them. Two of my reasons are related to attitudes to the Zeitgeist. The first is the attempt by some of our American colleagues to monopolize architectural theory

1   Koolhaas, Rem. "What Ever Happened To Urbanism?" In *S, M, L, XL*, by Rem Koolhaas and Bruce Mau, edited by Jennifer Sigler. Rotterdam: 010 Publishers, 1995.
2   Leonard, Mark. *Why Europe Will Run the 21st Century*. New York: Public Affairs, 2005.

3 Boeri, Stefano. "Notes for a Research Program." In *Mutations*, by Rem Koolhaas, Stefano Boeri, Sanford Kwinter, Nadia Tazi, and Hans Ulrich. Obrist. Barcelona: ACTAR, 2000.

4 Miessen, Markus. *The Violence of Participation*. Berlin; New York: Sternberg Press, 2007.

5 Krier, Rob. *Stadtraum in Theorie Und Praxis:*. Stuttgart: Krämer, 1975.

as an all but exclusively American phenomenon. In their view, architectural theory is a critical position that turns against the Zeitgeist, withdraws from the world and consoles itself with philosophy. My second reason is the current collective obstinacy of European theorists, undoubtedly inspired by Rem Koolhaas, to concern themselves more with architecture and urban planning in China or in the Gulf States than in Europe. The idea behind this is obvious: nowhere can the Zeitgeist be felt more clearly than in places with high volumes of construction and/or where the most extreme forms are being created. This one-sided interest in the non-European context means, however, that virtually no instruments are left for the assessment of European cities. At the moment it appears that only questions and research programs remain. Is the European city more than its past? Is it true, as Stefano Boeri claimed in Mutations (2001), that "the emergence over the last few years of a process of political unification in Europe and the debate over the best forms of *integration* appear to have heightened uncertainty about the nature of the European territory"?[3] Is Europe, in the words of Markus Miessen in The Violence of Participation (2007), nothing more than "a construct in need of constant renegotiation"?[4]

History

In recent years the adjective *European*, as used in connection with architecture and urban planning, has taken on a rather conservative, even reactionary tone in the context of the "reconstruction of the European city". This reconstruction is generally taken to mean a return to the idealized forms of pre-Modern or even medieval urban development. To a certain extent interest in historical examples is perhaps understandable in the context of a type of protracted reconstruction of the (mostly German) cities destroyed in the Second World War, as, for example, Berlin. However, the movement to reconstruct the European city goes much further than this, as it also strives to reverse architectural and urban-planning interventions of the post-war years. For an example of this one still thinks of the reconstruction of downtown Stuttgart as proposed by Rob Krier in his book Stadtraum in Theorie und Praxis (1975).[5] Here he sometimes proposed not genuine reconstruction, but rather the construction of structures and images that had never existed before, as is seen in the majority of Krier's and Kohl's or Hans Kolhoff's proposals. The *typicality* given to historical examples in this context fully ignores the fact that historical inner cities make up only a

6 Stolz, Matthias. "Historische Altstädte in Deutschland." *Die Zeit*, November 20, 2008, 48.

minute portion of our built environment. A list of 300 historically important and well-preserved old town centres in Germany was recently drawn up by group of German state curators of historic monuments commissioned by <u>Die Zeit</u> newspaper. "The result: western Saxony, Thuringia, northern Hesse, Franconia and Swabia have a wealth of old town centres, while the extreme west and Lower Saxony have very few. The geographic centre of Germany, it would seem, is also its original core region. Towns along the western edge of the country and in the north are simply too young, or their old towns were destroyed in World War II – or indeed in the early post-war period. The mania for demolition was extreme, as if it were a way to get rid of history. In the GDR it was less prevalent, and here the majority of structures survived. But had the GDR existed for much longer than forty years the walls would have fallen anyway, if not through the use of dynamite then of their own accord."[6]

A rapid calculation for the five largest or most important Austrian cities – Vienna, Graz, Linz, Salzburg and Innsbruck – shows us that historic city centres normally do not make up more than one or two percent of the city's territory, with Salzburg and its maximum of 3.3% being rather an exception to the rule. The situation is probably quite similar in Germany: German cities mostly date from after World War II. It is therefore more than justified to wonder whether the reason many people find historic town centres attractive is their *rarity value* rather than their absolute, formal, social, political and aesthetic typicality. In spite of a long tradition of deriving architecture theory from historical examples, and even though one sees the tendency to build interpretations of historic European cities as real projects inspired by *lifestyle* issues – something which, with New Urbanism for instance, has been globally successful up to a certain point – none of this constitutes a particularly valid argument for architectural theory to be based exclusively on an interpretation of historic town centres. The far larger part of our built environment is determined by other principles.

A city's cultural capital

In 2008 Katharina Weinberger and I undertook the <u>Linz Status quo</u> project for <u>Linz '09 European Capital of Culture</u>. Here it became painfully clear that today's architecture theorists simply don't have the ideas, references or methods to deal with a relatively normal European city. As cultural capital, <u>Linz '09</u> offers a broad range of activities in all art forms: from music, dance and theatre through to visual arts,

7   Bourdieu, Pierre. "The Forms of Capital." In *Handbook of Theory and Research for the Sociology of Education*, by John G. Richardson. New York: Greenwood Press, 1986.

film and architecture. But being European Capital of Culture means more than producing a sparkling display of more or less easily-digestible events. To be selected as Europe's cultural capital, a city also needs to develop proposals for more sustainable cultural development, for increased social cohesion and tourism, and in particular for programs to protect the city's architectural heritage and develop urban planning strategies.

As used in <u>Linz Status quo</u>, the expression <u>cultural capital</u> has a double meaning. Of course it primarily means that Linz, together with Vilna, will be the cultural capital of Europe for 2009. But the second meaning refers to Linz's actual cultural capital. For sociologist Pierre Bourdieu, who coined the concept, cultural capital refers to all material goods and all forms of knowledge, education and skills that facilitate people's access to status and power. There are three forms of cultural capital. In its institutionalized state, cultural capital is acknowledged through institutions which confer academic credentials and titles. The objectified condition refers to objects that can be owned and sold, for instance instruments, books or works of art. And in its embodied form, cultural capital is inherent to each one of us, within our individual hereditary or acquired characteristics.[7]

What might the cultural capital of a city be? If Bourdieu's theory is applied to Linz, being selected as capital of culture is clearly in itself a form of institutionalized recognition. The city has a great number of cultural landmarks – museums, theatres, concert halls, universities – representing the objectified condition of its cultural capital. But the most elusive factor is the city's embodied cultural capital. How can this asset be determined and described? How valuable is such capital? And how can it be expanded?

We considered that architectural theorists could use these questions as excellent springboards to delve into a number of fundamental issues. Theory means observation, analysis and interpretation of different realities. Theory, in this case, does not try to hide behind hypnotic metaphysics or complex cosmologies for which one must seek the proof in some proverbially extraordinary buildings. Instead architectural theory explores the production of architecture. It analyzes the conditions under which this production takes place, and it makes assumptions about the possible social, political and cultural consequences of specific interventions. It tries to understand the real, actual forces that shape our world, however unimpressive these may be.

Together with the Vienna Academy of Fine Arts, we began with a research project analyzing the present condition of Linz and its surrounding region. The results of our analysis, together with other contributions by Linz-based experts, were presented in book form to three architectural critics of international renown whom we had invited to participate in the project – Shumon Basar (London), Roemer van Toorn (Amsterdam), and Angelika Schnell (Berlin). These guest critics wrote essays about Linz that were then published in the book Linz Texas by Angelika Fitz and Martin Heller as well as in the web-based journal Architekturtheorie.eu and as a series in Architektur und Bau Forum. And finally, the authors presented their essays at a public symposium where they were commented on by co-speakers, key personalities from the Linz and Upper Austrian cultural world, architects, urban planners and politicians.[8]

Shumon Basar, Angelika Schnell and Roemer van Toorn represent a direction in architecture criticism that no longer concerns itself exclusively with architectural objects, but instead with a broad spectrum of spatial practices, reflecting more and more on cities. Shumon Basar is co-editor and author of several books on urban and regional planning practices in the Middle East – for instance Did Someone Say Participate? or With/Without and Cities From Zero.[9]

Angelika Schnell had just published the text Phantoms of Rotterdam within the scope of a similar project.[10] And Roemer van Toorn is a tireless traveler, critic and photographer, a man who has indeed seen the world.

Our hope was that Linz Status quo might trigger a rapprochement between architecture theory and architecture criticism on the one hand and urban planning and political trends on the other, a kind of inventory of weaknesses and strengths, problems and opportunities – something that could be useful in the next phase of the project and help formulate new programs for the city. In actual fact, this rapprochement never took place. The critics strayed off into comparisons with other cities (Van Toorn, Schnell) or honestly admitted their inability to ask the right questions in a city that, unlike so many other cities in the world, has hardly any problems at all, a city that is downright successful (Basar). The politicians and prominent Linz architects and urban

8   Schnell, Angelika. "Dejà Vu."; Shumon Basar, "Wo liegt das Problem? Das ist das Problem."; "Für ein anderes Stadtspektakel." In Linz Texas: Eine Stadt Mit Beziehungen, by Angelika Fitz and Martin Heller. Wien: Springer, 2008.

9   Miessen, Markus, and Shumon Basar. Did Someone Say Participate?. Cambridge, MA: MIT Press, 2006.; Basar, Shumon. Cities from Zero. London: Architectural Association, 2007.; Basar, Shumon, Antonia Carver, and Markus Miessen. With/without: Spatial Products, Practices & Politics in the Middle East. New York: Bidoun, 2007.

10   Schnell, Angelika. "The Phantoms of Rotterdam." In Rotterdam Herzien: Dertig Jaar Architectuur, 1977–2007, edited by Wijnand Galema, Piet Vollaard, and Sjoerd Cusveller. Rotterdam: 010 Publishers, 2007.

11 cf. Gstöttner, Erhard. "Linz Ist Wie Singapur Und Mannheim." Oberösterreichische Nachrichten, June 12, 2008.

12 Jarzombek, Mark. "The State of Theory." In Architektur & Theorie – Produktion Und Reflexion: Architecture & Theory – Production and Reflection, edited by Luise King, 262–73. Hamburg: Junius, 2009.

planners were either offended by the comparisons (Van Toorn: <u>Linz is Singapore without the death penalty</u>) or found them meaningless. The discrepancy between a searching theory and successful everyday policies was enormous.[11]

American theory

If we compare these uncertainties with American theory, we can say without the shadow of a doubt that American theorists have – or rather: theorists "teaching at American Ivy League universities" have – in the past twenty-five years, dominated the debate. With unfathomable casualness, one philosopher is replaced by the next even faster than the *isms* can tumble over each other. I could hardly formulate it better than Mark Jarzombek in the foreword to his essay on <u>The State of Theory</u>: "In the 1970s, architects were reading Adorno, Wittgenstein, Benjamin, Derrida, Heidegger, and Barthes, creating a movement that has become known, somewhat simplistically, as *theory* but that when taken in its broadest sense aimed to critique Postmodernism's loose attachments to historicism and pop culture. The translation of the work of philosophy into architectural discourse took place primarily in England and the US rather than in Europe. The reasons for this are numerous and range from a general dissatisfaction with the profession to the creation of new graduate-level masters programs. Another factor was the small size of schools such as the AA in London, and – in North America – Yale, MIT, McGill, and Columbia, which allowed for a pedagogy that was more flexible and experimental than was possible in the large, government-sponsored architectural schools in Europe. The US publication boom of the 1980s also played a role in that it helped theory gain access to a wide readership."[12]

Like boxers defending their titles and overeager to demonstrate their superiority, our ivy-league theorists have been challenging architects and theorists around the world in polemics and debates – for instance at the <u>ANY</u> conferences – and taking home one simple victory after the other.
For it must be admitted that American architecture theory offers methods; not only productive methods of analysis and criticism, but also methods that could be applied to the organization of design processes. And though American theory may perhaps offer no consensus, it is characterized by clearly defined discourse, discourse that is indeed so clearly defined that it fully excludes any other. And all of this only a few decades after Peter Eisenman, the godfather of American architecture theory, decided to continue his studies

13 Eisenman, Peter. "Afterword." In *The Formal Basis of Modern Architecture*, by Peter Eisenman. Baden, Switzerland: Lars Müller, 2006.

14 Rowe, Colin. "Introduction." In *Five Architects: Eisenman, Graves, Gwathmey, Hejduk, Meier*, edited by Arthur Drexler, by Colin Rowe, Kenneth Frampton, Philip Johnson, and Arthur Drexler. New York: Oxford University Press, 1975.

in Europe because a British fellow student had told him that he had no idea of how to understand the theoretical and ideological foundations of modern architecture. So Eisenman went to Cambridge, studied with Colin Rowe, and wrote a doctoral thesis on what he saw as the Formal Basis of Modern Architecture.[13] This dissertation is still a fascinating and fundamental book containing whole series of formal analyses of buildings belonging to the canon of the Modern Movement. It is, however, completely blind to anything but the formal aspects of architecture, above all to any aspect relating to social housing and urban planning, for instance demographic, political, cultural or economic factors. Every one of the analyses deals exclusively with freestanding buildings and their internal coherence.

In an epilogue to The Formal Basis of Modern Architecture included in the 2006 Lars Müller facsimile edition, Eisenman positions the book carefully as a response to Christopher Alexander's Notes on the Synthesis of Form – published in 1964, also in Cambridge – and as an attempt to move away from Colin Rowe's formal ideas towards a more linguistic discourse. This *linguistic turn* makes it possible – or perhaps even imperative – for more and more aspects of architecture to be ignored as though they were forms of a voiceless metaphysics. From this moment on, the deeper syntactic structure of the language of architecture *discovered* by Eisenman becomes the reality of architecture. Eisenman's first major theoretical work can therefore be seen as a move in an existing discourse that is, however, only implicitly present in the book itself. Today, Jarzombek still sees *theory* as a *movement* within the dynamic, constantly changing American architecture debate. Within this process in the United States one *pars* of theory has imperceptibly developed into the *totum*, the whole.

But it is not only demographic, political, cultural and economic factors that have slipped (or been pushed) from the focus of our attention: the entire history of theoretical tracts and discourses since Vitruvius has also been pushed aside. Instead, American theory has consciously been encapsulating itself into a position that is critical of every-thing going on in the outside world, so that it can survive only at Ivy League universities. At the latest in Colin Rowe's foreword to the 1972 Five Architects catalogue, it definitively turns its back on the dictatorship of the Zeitgeist, and thus on the outside world as a whole.[14] Or, in the words of Manfredo Tafuri in 1974: "The *disenchanted avant-garde*, completely absorbed in exploring from the comfort of its charming boudoirs the profundities of the philosophy of the unexpected writes down, over and over again, its own reactions under the influence of drugs prudently administered. Its use of hashish is certainly a conscious one: but it makes of this *consciousness* a barrier, a defense. Of the *perfidious enchantment* of the products that come out of the laboratories of the imaginary it is good to be distrustful. With a smile, we have to catalogue them in the imaginary museum of the bad conscience of our *small age*, to be used as rearview mirrors by whoever recognizes himself to be caught in the midst of a crisis that obliges him to remain stuck in the minefield of the *evil present*."[15]

The city has hardly played a role at all in the American debate since <u>Learning from Las Vegas</u> – as otherwise it would have been about the city in that dirty world out there. Only recently does the situation seem gradually to have changed under the influence of Rem Koolhaas and his <u>Harvard Project on the City</u> as well as in the collaborative work of AMO, <u>Archis</u>, <u>Volume</u> and Columbia's <u>C-Lab</u>.

La Trahison des Clercs or Dirty Hands?

Rem Koolhaas – in the eyes of American theorists the only European architect and theorist worthy of mention – is even berated by Jarzombek for marketing the avant-garde as a consumer item.[16] Americans seem to believe that Europeans have nothing more than this to offer. In 1999 Sanford Kwinter published an essay entitled <u>La Trahison des Clercs (and other Travesties of the Modern)</u>. The title refers to an eponymous book published in 1927 by Julien Benda in which the author accuses certain intellectuals of having lost their independence by having allowed themselves to become too closely involved with the government, the state or political parties. Kwinter's attack is directed at a generation of (for the most part) Dutch architects who had come to fame in the nineties and who, in Kwinter's view, had been increasingly confusing design and theory. He accused the group of producing nothing but offshoots of Rem Koolhaas' work and of replacing the qualitative research presented in <u>Delirious New York</u> (Koolhaas' retroactive manifest written for the most part at Peter Eisenman's <u>Institute for Architecture and Urban Studies</u>) by a quantitative research which Kwinter, in a reminder of the 1992 Maastricht EU Treaty, then dismissed as <u>Maastricht Bean Counting</u>.[17] To refresh the reader's memory: the Maastricht Treaty is the agreement that created the European Union (EU)

15 Tafuri, Manfredo. "L'Architecture Dans Le Boudoir: The Language of Criticism and the Criticism of Language." In *Architecture Theory since 1968*, edited by K. Michael. Hays. Cambridge, MA: MIT Press, 1998.

16 Mark Jarzombek, op. cit.
17 Kwinter, Sanford. "La Trahison Des Clercs (and Other Travesties of the Modern)." In *Far from Equilibrium: Essays on Technology and Design Culture*, by Sanford Kwinter, edited by Cynthia C. Davidson and Michael Kubo. Barcelona: Actar D, 2008.

18 Lootsma, Bart, and Mariëtte van Stralen. *Research for Research*. Rotterdam: Berlage Institute, 2001.

19 Soja, Edward W. *Postmodern Geographies: The Reassertion of Space in Critical Social Theory*. London: Verso, 1989.
20 Hacking, Ian. *The Taming of Chance*. Cambridge: Cambridge University Press, 1990.

as a supranational federation of the European Communities with the intention of achieving a common external and security policy and cooperation in the area of justice and interior affairs.

Now here this blind spot becomes more and more of a problem, irrespective of whether some of these architects had not actually contributed significantly to the results or methods of the Koolhaas offices OMA and AMO (as opposed to having been employees working for one unique Genius) before founding their own firms. Quantitative methods are the most important constant factor in 20th-century architecture and urban planning. Apart from a few villas and some religious and public buildings, the most important designs, buildings and urban projects realized in the 20th century are unimaginable without quantitative preparatory work. Worthy of mention in this context are Otto Neurath's work for the settlers' movement and for the Red Vienna of the 1920s, Le Corbusier's Ville Contemporaine designed for three million inhabitants, Hilberseimer's Großstadtarchitektur and later his Decentralized City, Ernst May's Das Neue Frankfurt as well as Van Eesteren and Van Lohuizen's Amsterdam (AUP). The list could go on.[18] All of these – projects involved statistics being interpreted, extrapolated and, above all, spatialized, in other words physically realized in architecture and urban planning.

This blind spot is perhaps not quite as surprising from the point of view of an architect or architectural theorist. More surprising, however, is that a Marxist social scientist and regional planner like Edward Soja has a similar blind spot for European theory when, in Postmodern Geographies, he negates the entire tradition of human geography which is and was the foundation and driving force behind the production of social and subsidized housing, urban development and land-use planning in all European communist, socialist and welfare states: the tradition of the *survey*.[19] As Ian Hacking states in his book The Taming of Chance, statistics are not only essential to any form of state bureaucracy, they are the success story of the twentieth century. Even Karl Marx would be unthinkable without official statistics. "One can ask: who had more effect on class consciousness, Marx or the authors of the official reports which created the classification in which people came to recognize themselves."[20] Soja's late-Marxist Postmodern Geographies is therefore not so much about space reasserting itself in *critical social theory* – as suggested by the subtitle of the book – but rather about a paradigm shift with regard to the role of space in theory: from a programmatic and pro-active to a critical and retro-active role. Soja never intends it to have an actual planning role.

This generation of architects criticized by Kwinter was in actual fact successful in the sense that it – in contrast to those American colleagues – also managed to build great numbers of buildings in a relatively short time. We should ask ourselves whether this should be interpreted as a Benda-style *Trahison des Clercs*, or as evidence of *dirty hands* à la Sartre. Conversely we see in Adriaan Geuze and West 8's projects (In Holland staat een Huis, for instance), or in the work of MVRDV, attempts to influence public opinion, politics and the corporate world with quantitative and qualitative methods and to prevent fatal decisions – with actualized forms of 1920s methods. But MVRDV's datascapes are more than visual representations of statistical data. Statistics have long since been implemented in laws and standards that determine our behavior. Datascapes are visualizations of the direct or indirect consequences of what sociologist Anthony Giddens calls *expert systems* and *abstract systems*.

Contemporary society is defined by many such abstract systems – as is our built environment. To quote MVRDV: "Because of tax differences, the borders between Belgium and the Netherlands are occupied with vast numbers of villas generating a linear town along the frontier. In Holland market demands have precipitated a *slick* of houses-with-a-small-garden. Political constraints in Hong Kong generate *piles* of dwellings around its boundaries. The popularity of white brick in Friesland causes a *white cancer* of housing estates alongside all the villages. In its desire for a nineteenth-century identity, Berlin forces its new buildings into tight envelopes. This pushes larger programs underground, turning the streets into mere components in the midst of vast programs. Monumental regulations in Amsterdam limit the demand for modern programs, generating *mountains of programs* invisible from the street behind the medieval facades. Throughout the Ruhr, demands of accessibility create virtually enclosed types of infrastructure, precipitating a string of linear towns. In La Défense in Paris, to avoid the high-rise regulations, massive programs have manifested themselves as ziggurats with 18-meter high accessible *steps* so that all offices can be entered by the maximum length of the fire ladders. Psychological issues, anti-disaster patterns, lighting regulations, acoustic treatments. All these manifestations can be seen as *scapes* of the data behind it."[21] In contemporary society these systems are the equivalent of traditional authority. They are bureaucratic systems where confidence in the system is based on assumed expertise in a specific field.[22] The status of a person who is in a position of responsibility in one system says nothing about this person's status in another system. Moreover, even the objectivity of information in the various systems is open to debate. Particular interest groups can call in their own experts to question information proposed by others. The implementation of laws and regulations depends on their interpretation. In addition, a secondary consequence is seen in collective attempts to circumvent laws that have spatial consequences. Indeed, in contrast to Michel Foucault's idea of *biopolitics* or Giorgio Agamben's Homo Sacer: society is so complex, and the laws are so full of contradictions, that total control and the disciplinary measures this entails cannot be achieved.[23]

Koolhaas' Europe

It is interesting to note that it is precisely Rem Koolhaas who, together with his offices OMA and AMO, recently produced an impassioned plea for quantitative methods in a project that well and truly celebrates Europe. The Image of Europe is first of all a proposal for a new striped flag composed of the colors of all the flags of all the EU members. Quite a colorful thing. Whenever the EU is expanded, colors could be added without anyone necessarily noticing right away. The idea generated much response. In a highly sarcastic commentary, science-fiction author Bruce Stirling tried to imagine an *Iwo Jima*-like scene showing how the flag might give young European soldiers on the battlefield dignity in their final moments: "So here I am, dying in battle. My fellow Europeans run by to avenge me, and they're waving this enormous, psychedelic bar-code. This great vivid flapping thing with about a hundred vertical stripes. This huge flashy emblem that is all things, to all people, at all times, all at once. That incredible flag! I think I would at least pause for one second in my final agony and think: Damn! Just look at that thing! Maybe it's worth it!"[24] But there is, after all, no such thing as a European army, and none is likely to be created soon, in spite of proposals by Jeffrey Rifkin, another American and Europe fan.[25] Koolhaas finds this type of

21 MVRDV, *Datascapes*, unpublished manuscript.
22 Giddens, Anthony. "Living in a Post-Traditional Society." In *Reflexive Modernization: Politics, Tradition and Aesthetics in the Modern Social Order*, by Ulrich Beck, Anthony Giddens, and Scott Lash. Cambridge (UK): Polity, 1994.
23 Foucault, Michel. "Die Geburt der Biopolitik/The Birth of Biopolitics." In *Analytik der Macht*, by Michel Foucault, Daniel Defert, François Ewald, and Thomas Lemke. Frankfurt Am Main: Suhrkamp, 2005.

24 Sterling, Bruce. "A Talk at the Berlage Institute." *Hunch* 5, 2002.
25 Rifkin, Jeremy. *The European Dream*. New York: Jeremy P. Tarcher/Penguin, 2004.

26 When I just remember how Rem Kollhaas reacted to my book SuperDutch: 'Imagine how we would puke if there were a book called SuperGermans; laugh at SuperBelgians, snicker at SuperFrench, complain about SuperAmericans' (Rem Koolhaas with Herman Hertzberger, "Rem, Do You Know What This Is?" *Hunch* 3, 2001.) Without effort, one could add: 'be confused about Mühelos SuperEuropeans'.

27 Liebs, Holger. "Rem Koolhaas über Propaganda." *Süddeutsche Zeitung* (Munich), October 9–10, 2004, Wochenende ed., Das Interview sec.

28 Koolhaas, Rem. "The Image of Europe." In *AMO History of Europe and The European Union.* Vol. 1. 2005.

traditional nationalism alien and repulsive.[26] His Europe is not a territory with solid borders to be defended by force of arms or even expanded: it is, instead, a construct that has found a way of achieving a permanent peace after three thousand years of multifarious wars, a peace that has now held for sixty years. Criticism that the flag is *boring* and *of no consequence* doesn't bother him: "At the same time, they said that the old flag with the stars was much nicer. The Brits, of all people, suddenly discovered their love for traditional EU symbols."[27]

The design could of course be different. For Koolhaas it is only important that it be able to compete with the American ability to handle symbols. After all, it is hardly surprising that most of the logos AMO has produced for Europe are ironic references to American models. This, however, immediately gives them a self-mocking touch too. At the AMO exhibition in the Munich Haus der Kunst[28] there were machines where visitors could buy passport covers decorated with the flag. Marked with *Made in China*. Not so long ago this would have been blasphemy, but these days it simply reflects the reality that even euro banknotes are now printed in China.

The exhibition was in general full of irony. True, the panoramas of European history, with their important buildings and protagonists, had a monumental effect, but they were too full of commentaries and manipulations to be perceived as having genuine epic character. The panoramas were produced as digital prints of Photoshop files. But where Photoshop or any other modern digital technologies make smooth, flowing transitions between photos possible, the OMA rendition nevertheless remained primitive, so as to produce the effect of a collage by a laid-back artist from the late-seventies punk era. Such collages were often used to ironize dignitaries like the British queen, and it is difficult not to interpret them that way here, too. The pinnacle of the irony was that some of the prints were framed in gold, giving the entire exhibition the flavor of a simulacrum of similarly pompous 19th-century historical painting intended to glorify the merits of a nation. Calvinists should simply not design images.

29 Leonard, Mark. "The Project for a New European Century." The Globalist. May 27, 2005. Accessed April 18, 2016. http://www.theglobalist.com/the-project-for-a-new-european-century/.

30 See 2.
31 See 27.
32 Leonard, Mark. "Combine and Conquer." In "Koolworld." Special issue, Wired 11, No. 06, June 2001.

Empire

Koolhaas' Europe is essentially something different: something invisible, and as in so many cases, the converse of something else. "Instead of accepting its complex history as an alibi to excuse more turmoil and tragedy, it (Europe) decided to reverse History. After World War II, visionary politicians created a new structure with new codes of behavior for the entire continent in a series of highly improvised steps and arrangements. Because the operation was so radical, it could only take place by stealth; in the initial stages of the European Union's existence, its ulterior motives could never be openly stated. [...] The image of Europe celebrates an end to its inhibited iconography, its coming out." Thus writes Koolhaas in the foreword to AMO's History of Europe and the European Union; he then adds, somewhat ironically: "From now on the EU will be bold, explicit, popular (...)"[29] Of course things cannot, and probably should not be so simple. In actual fact, Koolhaas would probably have preferred to find something like a hologram of the Eiffel Tower standing on its head that should have adorned the international exhibition in Paris.

Political scientist Mark Leonard, head of the London-based Foreign Policy Centre and main adviser for The Image of Europe, writes: "Europe is open-ended, vague, an unidentified political object with no final shape, no clear final borders and no real definition of what it is as a political creature. [...] In many ways this is still Europe's most attractive feature."[30] In his book Why Europe Will Run the 21st Century, Leonard argues that "By keeping a low profile at home and working through international structures, Europe has managed to spread its wings without attracting much hostility. [...] The EU's secret weapon is the law. Military power allows you to change the regime in Afghanistan or Iraq, but the EU is changing all of Polish society, from its economic policies to its property laws to its treatment of minorities. Each country that joins the EU must absorb 80,000 pages of new laws on everything from gay rights to food safety."[31] This acquis communautaire is precisely what AMO has collected for The Image of Europe and placed – in a four-and-a-half-meter-thick (or long) book – at the centre of the exhibition. "Anyone can look", says Koolhaas. "The centre of power is very visible here."[32]

On the topic of the EU's political power, Mark Leonard convincingly describes the effects of the acquis communautaire on the many other countries assuming this

33 Hardt, Michael, and Antonio Negri. *Empire.* Cambridge, MA: Harvard University Press, 2000.

34 Hardt, Michael. "Second Empire, The 18th Brumaire of George W. Bush." In *Linz Texas: Eine Stadt Mit Beziehungen,* 2008.

35 Idem.

body of law. In an article published in Wired, he compares the functioning of the EU with the success of a global network organization such as Visa. "The emergence of the European model is a paradigm-changing event – it is not about a particular country or region going up or down for a few years. The EU already covers 450 million citizens, but beyond them there are another 1.5 billion people in about 80 countries umbilically linked to the EU through trade, finance, foreign investment and aid. This is the Eurosphere – Europe's growing zone of influence. Through continued enlargement and the EU's new neighborhood policy, nearly a third of the world has come under the influence of a zone of peace, prosperity and democracy."[33] Taken from this point of view, the *acquis communautaire* would be the software of a peaceful alternative to the late-capitalist global empire analyzed by Antonio Negri and Michael Hardt.[34] Koolhaas also visited Negri, and Michael Hardt is one of Content's authors[35]. Negri and Hardt, too, indicate a utopia which lies beyond Empire and is only realizable through Empire. Thus, Empire would be an inevitable or even necessary stopover on the way towards the new communism. Along with Spinoza, Negri and Hardt believe that nature as an amorphous force will keep conquering prevalent political systems. They just don't talk about how this transformation is going to take place. The Acquis Communautaire could then maybe be the Open Source, Open Ended Software that furthers this process like a virus.[35]

Maastricht bean counting

The great European achievement of the 20th century was that architecture – as the intelligent organization and cultural expression of our society – came to benefit the masses. For this to be possible, architects and urban planners had to take an interest in the lives of these ordinary people. Perhaps the masses as such no longer exist today. This makes it more important than ever for architects and urban planners to take a greater interest in society, so that they are able to develop new strategies, and offer these to policymakers for implementation. By far the greater part of our built environment today consists of buildings that are no more than fifty or one hundred years old. One of the primary goals of our architects and urban planners should be to understand this greater part of our built environment. Just as the restrictions and freedoms of our society are determined on many levels by laws, norms, regulations and *policies* (with all their contradictions and interpretations),

36 Latour, Bruno. *Elend der Kritik: vom Krieg um Fakten zu Dingen von Belang.* Zürich: Diaphanes, 2007. 55.

so the same can be said of architecture and urban planning. How do these laws and regulations influence our culture, and how can our culture, conversely, shape them? If today we want to understand architecture and urban planning, we will have to deal with their actual and inherent laws and patterns.

A form of architectural criticism based on such a theory does not reduce dreams to facts. Instead, to speak with Bruno Latour, it formulates important concepts on the basis of these facts: "The critic is not the one who uncovers, he is the one who assembles. The critic is not the one who cuts the ground under the feet of naive believers; he is the one who offers partakers arenas where they can gather. The critic is not the one who wavers arbitrarily between anti-fetishism and positivism, like Goya's drunken iconoclast: he is the one for whom constructed structures are fragile and in need of care and caution."[36] It is only by understanding this that architects and urban planners can reconquer the future.

BODY & GLOBE

DWELLING IN AN AGE OF RADICAL MOBILITY

Body & Globe

Dwelling in an age of radical mobility

"Man in Space" announced the headline of the newspaper Dimanche on the 27 of November 1960. That must have attracted its share of attention at the time. The subtitle read that an artist had leaped into the void. What we see in the picture is a man in an ordinary business suit that is leaving the window of an ordinary suburban Parisian house in an upward move, as if he were Superman, in such a hurry to save the world that he had even forgotten to change clothes. In other photographs we see the same man, the artist Yves Klein, against a more vague background and in a pose that suggested that he was rather falling than levitating. Of course, the newspaper was a fake, a clever imitation of the Journal de Dimanche, the Sunday edition of the Parisian daily France Soir. But this will certainly have escaped many Parisians that were still wiping the sleep out of their eyes.

In 1965, Friedrich Kiesler displayed a group of sculptures entitled US, YOU, ME, which he had just finished, in the Museum of Art of the University of Iowa. It was one of his last works and I am not so sure if I find it one of his best. But, with the text that accompanies it, it almost works like a testament. Among the many different figures, which are dominated by a big ring with a gong inside, two are taller. According to Kiesler's description, "One is an image of young David, and, at the other end, is the flying figure of a man escaping into outer space."[1]

Whatever one may think of them, both works refer – in a very critical way, as we will see later – to the first manned spaceflights that were realized in the early sixties. Klein made his jump just before the first manned spaceflight; Kiesler incorporated his figure escaping into outer space just after that. But apart from their criticism, both works, read in relation to the rest of the oeuvres of the artists/architects, give us a clue about the impact spaceflights would have on the way we see the world – or better: how we see the earth and how we see ourselves – and on our conception of dwelling. This impact is reflected already in an early stage in the arts and in architecture, but it continues today, even if we are not always aware of it and spaceflights are no longer front-page news. Spaceflights had an impact on the way we see the body, but also on the place our body takes in a larger whole. This drastically changed the concept of architecture. It became radically footloose and lost the

1   Kiesler, Frederick. "US, YOU, ME." In *Frederick J. Kiesler: Selected Writings*, edited by Siegfried Gohr. Stuttgart: Gerd Hatje, 1996.

aspect of marking the ground, focusing more on the physical aspects of providing shelter or even more: providing bodily comfort and connections to infrastructure. Both the positions of Kiesler and Klein can be used to paint a possible alternative history of recent architecture.

Mirror-stage

The first spaceflights could be interpreted as a kind of mirror for the world – literally, if we see how satellites bounce radio waves back and especially when we realize that spaceflights made it possible for the first time to see the earth as a whole. The Global Positioning System with its 24 geostationary satellites makes it possible to localize every place on earth instantly.

For Jacques Lacan, the mirror stage is a crucial phase in the psychological development of a child. It is a phase that occurs between the first 6 and 24 months of its existence, in which it recognizes itself for the first time in its mirrored image and identifies itself with it, to such an extent even that when one would call its name, it would look at the mirror instead of reacting from inside. Before the mirror stage, the child can only see and feel parts of its body. It prefers the mirrored image because it gives a total image. In retrospect the body as it was experienced before the mirror stage appears as a fragmented body, a *corps morcelé*. The mirror image is the foundation for an identity, because it is also an identification with something that is *not* the child. Of course it is not the Other either, but the identical Other. The mirror-stage marks the initiation in the imaginary order, which is connected to the image. Around the same time the child is introduced in the symbolical order that is language. It becomes a name that it identifies with, and it discovers that everyone is different, just as well as it gets confronted with the taboos and rules of society.[2]

If spaceflights changed our perception of the world, they certainly changed the perception and conception of the body as well, radically, but strangely enough almost in the opposite way than in the mirror stage. Seen from space, the body is not even perceptible, it is less than an ant. But in order to be able to undertake spaceflights, the body needed special adaptations, training, and prostheses in order to survive. The individual body became a cyborg, a cybernetic organism, a human being who has certain processes aided, controlled or replaced by mechanical, pharmaceutical or electronic devices. More than ever, the body became

2   Lacan, Jacques. "The Mirror Stage as Formative of the Function of the I." In *Écrits: A Selection*, by Jacques Lacan. New York: Norton, 1977. See also: Mooij, Antoine. *Taal En Verlangen: Lacans Theorie Van De Psychoanalyse.* Meppel: Boom, 1975.

something that is under the influence of external forces
and that adapts itself to them with technological means,
a desire machine. Strangely enough, from the moment
that we were able to perceive and think the earth as a whole,
in a reversal movement, because of the spaceflights,
the body became a *corps morcelé* again and the matter
of identity became even more problematic than ever before.
Identity became makeable, depending on the will and the
passion, something that individuals themselves must
produce, cobble, and stage together in an experimental way.

Lost in Space

The Dimanche with the notorious article on Klein's jump
in it appeared little more than three years after the flight of
the Sputnik on October 4, 1957, the first satellite in space,
and the Sputnik-2, on November 3, 1957, with the cute
little doggy Laïka aboard. It had died for lack of oxygen after
a week and later burned in its thermally badly insulated
capsule on April 14, 1958 when returning into the earth's
atmosphere. The photographs that we know depict a similar
dog, but not Laïka. Ever since, the United States and
the Soviet Union had been caught in a rat race to bring
the first man in space – and to bring him back alive,
whenever possible. This battle actually reached a first climax
in September and October 1960, when there were rumors
that the Soviets were short before a manned flight.
The excitement was caused by the flight of Sputnik-5. It had
a complete zoo aboard – two doggies this time, Belka
and Strelka, two rats, four mice and furthermore ordinary
flies, plants, etcetera – and it returned to earth, although it is
unclear whether the animals survived. But even before, in
August of that year, satellite spotting had become quite
popular after the launch of the first American communication
satellite Echo-1, which was clearly visible in the sky. Satellite
spotting would become even so popular that newspapers
would print the schedules of the satellite passages like
the radio program. It was a time that everything seemed
possible. Man had just proven able to split atoms and now he
was already conquering the cosmos. Several years later,
in 1968, Charles and Ray Eames were able to express this
feeling and the joy it produced in their film Powers of Ten, in
which we make an imaginary travel from the edge of the
universe to an atom in the hand of a sleeping man. Science
and technology had no limits. It must have been an experience
like watching fireworks. It would take until April 12, 1961
however until the first successful manned flight was realized,
in the Russian Wostok-1, with Youri Gagarin aboard.

3   Mraveinik, Piotr. "Episodes in a Life Devoted to Space." In *Sputnik: Catalogue of the Exhibition with the Same Name.* Madrid: Fundación Arte Y Tecnología, 1997. Of course, this book is too beautiful to be true, but for the sake.

If we are saying that "*man*" was able to do all this, we have to observe that it was most of all a collective effort, or better: an effort of collectives, like the Russian RNII and NASA. Of course, we remember the names of some heroes that were involved, notably the first dogs, rats, monkeys, and men in space, but the conquest for space has cost the lives of many anonymous victims. Only in recent years some of them are memorized, like in the Astronauts Memorial on Cape Canaveral, which was built after a design by Holt Hinshaw Pfau Jones in 1990. It consists of a plane of black granite, that mirrors the sky and in which the names of the astronauts are cut out. A mirror that reflects the rays of the sun or, at night, by lamps, lights them from behind.

But probably many of the Russian cosmonauts that have died, disappeared literally, as if they had never existed. Like Ivan Fiodorovich Istochnikov, who left on a twin-flight with the Soyuz-2 and Soyuz-3 in 1968. His story is probably an invention, a fake. But who cares when we refer to a subject that was surrounded by the utmost secrecy, in a time when espionage and counter intelligence made almost all facts questionable and photographs were carefully retouched?[3] Remember what happened to Laïka. Remember <u>Dimanche</u>. For this essay it makes no difference at all.

Anyway, on his flight, the dog Kloka, with whom he was supposed to make a space stroll, accompanied Ivan Fiodorovich Istochnikov. The two Soyuz's were supposed to dock together, but failed and lost contact. The following day when they found each other once again, Istochnikov had disappeared and his module bore the marks of an impact with a meteorite. In fact, it is not clear what had really happened and the mystery provoked a whole series of conjunctures. But the Soviet authorities were clear about not wanting to admit another new fiasco and they designed a Machiavellian explanation: they announced that the Soyuz-2 had been an automatic, unmanned flight. For the official record Ivan Istochnikov died from an illness a couple of months later. To contradict voices his family was confined, his colleagues were blackmailed, the archives were doctored and photographs retouched.[4] His widow was sent to a <u>sharaga</u>, a special kind of gulag or prison for intellectuals. On her question what would happen if she would say anything, the Ministry of Defense answered her that they were concerned about her anti-communist background and anti-patriotic attitude: "What is the honor of one man,

4   Ibid.

compared to the shame of an entire country? (...) We would be very sorry if you, or one of your friends, were to have an unfortunate accident. (...), don't oblige us to send you to the Lubianka (the KGB, B. L.)."[5]

Astronauts were in the beginning no more than test dummies, literally strapped into straight jackets and space suits in which they could hardly move. These devices offer everything, like a womb: protection, comfort, oxygen, water, food, communication, and devices to allow for defecation. But they also restrict the freedom of the astronauts. If they could actually move, the capsules were so small that it would hardly have made any sense. Tom Wolfe tells in his book The Right Stuff that the most famous American test pilots, like Chuck Yeager, actually refused to take part in the American space program, because there was nothing they could do, nothing that a monkey couldn't do anyway.[6] The Americans demanded at least a small window in the capsule, so that they could look out, explosive bolts in the door, so that they could open it themselves, and something with which they could steer, for example to control the position of the capsule when it would return into the atmosphere. These were installed, but the steering device appeared to make no difference at all. It was more the idea.

Propagandistic issues aside, for NASA the ideal astronaut would be a cyborg. It would become a little more interesting when the astronauts would make strolls outside of the capsule. The first spaceflights were more *experiences* than *actions*. No one really knew what was out there and how the human body would react to zero gravity and the enormous G forces during take-off and landing. John Glenn, one of the first Americans to make a spaceflight in 1962, wrote that he could actually adapt himself to weightlessness quite quickly, and that it was an agreeable experience. The pulse and blood pressure of the first astronauts were not exceptionally high or even quite normal, even during take-off and landing. Nevertheless, astronauts are subjected to heavy physical tests and exercise programs before they can actually join a flight. We know that they exercise in centrifuges and under water. In recent years also dance practice has become a regular training method, because it gives the astronauts a better awareness and control over their body. More than the rational identification process by means of the mirror that is outside of the body, the training of proprioception became crucial again.

5 Ibid.
6 Wolfe, Tom. The Right Stuff. New York: Farrar, Straus, and Giroux, 1979.

7   See Restany, Pierre. *Yves Klein.* New York: H. N. Abrams, 1982.; Wember, Paul. *Yves Klein.* Cologne: Du-Mont Schauberg, 1972.; Klein, Yves. "My Position in the Battle between Line and Color." *ZERO*, no. 1 (1973): 10–11.

8   McEvilley, Thomas. "Yves Klein, Messenger of the Age of Space." *Artforum* 20 (January 1982); Wember, see note 5, Restany, see note 5.

Levitation

If we look back now on Yves Klein's leap and his claim to be the first man in space it becomes clearer what he was after. Klein's work is often viewed as an attempt to reconcile life with art, resembling in this respect much art of the fifties and early sixties – art that entailed an abandonment of higher realms in favor of the everyday. On consideration however, this view is quite untrue, or the statement entails at the very least an ambiguity. While Klein cooperated with the Nouveaux Réalistes and was a close friend of theirs, he was not one of them – not, at least if we are to view Nouveau Réalisme as a French variant of Pop Art, a movement that specialized in appropriating banal subjects from the consumer society and bringing them into an art context. Klein's aim however was to use art as a way of bringing people into contact with a higher form of life. Life, as Klein saw it, was not at all something that mankind owned, but in the first instance something that belonged to a higher order. It was possible to gain possession of Life, however, by developing what he termed "Cosmic Sensitivity."[7]

Klein's ideas were based to a considerable extent on the ideas of Max Heindel on theosophical cosmology. Klein was a member of the Rosicrucian Brotherhood for six years between 1948 and 1954, and studied and practiced their teachings as formulated by Heindel. Human evolution, according to Heindel, is approaching the end of the age of form and solid matter, and soon will reimmerse itself in an age of Space/Spirit/Life that will restore the condition of Eden.[8]

Klein's monochrome paintings are intended, through pure color, to absorb and transport the spectator who thereby gains intimation, albeit momentary, of total mental and physical freedom. Klein did not restrict himself to paintings as his means of offering an intimation of higher things, but pondered at many different levels about techniques for achieving greater Cosmic Sensitivity in everyday life. The word "techniques" is meant literally here. It sometimes looks as though Klein, in his impatient longing, set technical progress on a par with spiritual transcendence. In this light it was no more than logical that, in the late fifties, he should turn his hand to architecture as offering a more comprehensive spatial experience. Together with architect Werner Ruhnau, he developed plans for an "air architecture." The concepts entailed the climatic conditioning of large parts of the earth's surface, use being made of the elementary energies of air, water and fire. The plans of Klein and Ruhnau can be seen as an expression of a longing for an immaterial architecture that would not only offer absolute comfort but would also bring its inhabitants to a higher state of consciousness. Klein saw air architecture as a potential way of using technology to create a paradise on earth, an Eden, where mankind could walk naked: The technical and scientific conclusion of our civilization lies buried in the bowels of the earth and assures comfort by the absolute control of the climate at the surface of all the continent.[9]

The simplest principle of air architecture entailed a roof of air fed by bellows. This would create a zone that would protect against rain, dust, and electrical phenomena, while still being transparent to ultraviolet and infrared radiation and thus allowing the warmth and light of the sun to penetrate. A subterranean air conditioning system was proposed to regulate the temperature of the earth. In executing their plans, the architects would make the most of the given natural circumstances. In a valley, for instance, it ought to be possible to use a stream of air to cover off the entire space between the two slopes. The space of the individual person would be conditioned by compressed air. In this area, Klein devised among other things an "air bed", a mattress of compressed air on which one could lie and relax. The flow of air would also continually massage the body.

Air architecture, it was proposed, would instigate Planetary Sensitivity, the eventual goal being Universal Levitation: "Man's will can finally regulate life at the level of constant 'wonders'. The free man has reached a point where he can even levitate!" Thus we will become aerial man, we will experience the force of attraction upward, toward space, toward nowhere and everywhere at the same time; the force of earthly attraction thus mastered, we will literally levitate in total psychical and spiritual freedom.[10]

Seen in this light, Klein's action was the complete opposite of what was happening in the technological conquest of space. As he wrote in <u>Dimanche</u>: "Today anyone who paints space must actually go into space to paint, but he must go there without any faking, and neither in an aeroplane, a parachute nor a rocket. He must go there by his own means, by an autonomous, individual force; in a word, he must be capable of levitating."[11]

Klein's preoccupation with levitation continued through the last years of his life. "He kept practicing breathing exercises

9   Restany, Pierre, see note 7.

10 Ibid.
11 Yves Klein, "Un homme dans l'espace", *Dimanche*, November 27, 1960., as quoted in: Stich, Sidra. *Yves Klein.* Stuttgart: Cantz, 1994.

and never abandoned the idea of body elevation in a public space. As a result of his development of the leap into the void (and in strange contradiction to his claim that there should be no faking, B. L.), he became enamored with the possibilities of photomontage imagery and other manifestations of space travel."[12] One of these photomontages shows Klein sitting on the floor, contemplating the apparent levitation of the globe in his work "Le globe terrestre bleu." Other works, the "Blue planetary reliefs" from 1961 show a kind of landscapes as seen from outer space. Both in the way he used his own body and investigated that in works of art as well in these planetary reliefs and globe, Klein captured an awareness of a new perception of the body and earth as it was triggered by space travel. This specific awareness preceded many works that were to come, be it without the cosmological implications Klein attached to them. The body itself became the focal point and as such became a tool to question, criticize, and transgress architecture from within, whereas the contemplation of the earth from outer space gave another meaning to place, as it became part of a larger whole.

The Endless House

When Friedrich Kiesler produced his group of sculptures US, YOU, ME in 1965, and singled out the "flying figure of a man escaping into outer space," the first manned spaceflights had already taken place and the rat race for the conquest of space between the USA and the USSR was at its climax. In his explanation of the project, Kiesler was very clear about the criticism he wanted to express with it. "The root of the composition is a deep feeling of mine that most people in the western world are immensely active, primarily with the purpose of accumulating tangible wealth, and see in possessions the varied securities of life. This large composition of sculptures shows people rushing about, singularly or in groups, most of them without torso and head, only with their feet dashing about. They go to offices, they rush to lunch, they hurry back, and, in rush hour you can see the scramble and tumble of the masses on the streets, in the subways, in the buses, jammed, into their cars, only to repeat, day after day, year after year, life after life, the same mad hustle and bustle to earn money; property, houses, cars, investments, to secure their survival in case of economic crashes. Nothing is done in depth because they cannot catch depth like a billfold, and deposit it in their bank accounts. They don't realize that every human being is an island born to itself and is its sole keeper. He is both the creator and the

12 See note 11, Stich, Yves Klein.

gardener of that ever-blooming flower island, glowing in the darkness of his inside."[13] And then, in a sentence that almost ridicules the conquest of space and the moon, he exclaims "Yes! The human body is the most extraordinary universe. It is the summa summarum of the planets. How poverty stricken, by comparison with the human being, is our Earth, without a will of her own, subject to innumerable influences, from hard rocks to invisible forces, living in all its details, from birth to death, from death to birth, and the intervals are called life."[14]

So, also Kiesler falls back on the body. But for him the body was more than just an isolated entity. It was part of and symbol for what he called the *Endless*. "All ends meet in the 'Endless' as they meet in life. Life's rhythms are cyclical. All ends of living meet during twenty-four hours, during a week, a lifetime. They touch each other with the kiss of Time. They shake hands, stay, say goodbye, return through the same or other doors, come and go through multi-links, secretive or obvious, or through the whims of memory."[15] Therefore he designed the Endless House that is "endless like the human body – there is no beginning and no end to it. The 'Endless' is rather sensuous, more like the female body in contrast to the sharp-angled male body."[16] The Endless House looks like something that has grown organically, a continuous space from which nevertheless individual, smaller spaces can be secluded. According to Kiesler, nature creates bodies, but art creates life, that the inhabitants have to reinvent constantly. Therefore the Endless House is a space in which nothing is taken for granted. There is no clear distinction between floors, walls and ceilings. Mechanical devices are events and must constitute the inspiration for a specific ritual. It is, in Kiesler's words, "the last refuge for man as man."[17]

Capsules, suits, and megastructures

Space capsules and space suits are the most elementary architecture one could imagine. The functions of a space capsule or space suit are exactly the same as those of architecture: offering comfort and protection in a hostile environment and a connection to an infrastructure of water, gas, sewers, communication, and transport. There is only one difference: the astronaut carries the capsule and the suit with him like a snail, or better: a shell. He moves in and with his house and is completely dependent of technology. He is not bound to a place, but is the center of the universe. Maybe the most difficult aspect for the first astronauts was

13 See note 1.
14 Idem.
15 Kiesler, Frederick. "The Endless House: A Man-Built Cosmos." In *Frederick J. Kiesler: Selected Writings*, 1996.
16 See note 1.
Idem.
17 Idem.

18 Arena, Michael, and Piotr Muravenik. "Beregovoi's Report." In *Sputnik:*, 1997. See note 3.

19 Cook, Peter. *Archigram*. Basel: Birkhäuser, 1991.

20 Cook, Peter. "Archigram." Lecture, the New Babylon Symposium, TU Delft, January 26, 2000.

21 Asendorf, Christoph. *Super Constellation – Flugzeug Und Raumevolution.* Vienna: Springer, 1997.

22 Schöllhammer, Georg. "The Bolted Gesture." In *Pichler: Prototypen/prototypes 1966–69,* edited by Sabine Breitwieser. Vienna: Generali Foundation, 1998.

the loneliness up there, and many of them tried to smuggle aboard at least some small insects or objects to keep them company. If we may believe it, our friend Ivan Fiodorovich took, apart from Kloka and a small foldable chess-set, a vodka-bottle with him, that he would throw in space with an SOS message if anything went wrong. Russian instructors would tell their trainees in all seriousness to do so in such cases, and then patiently wait for rescue.[18]

Of course, the space capsule and the suit fascinated architects from the start. In the nineteen sixties, capsules appeared in architectural proposals everywhere. They became the individual unit and urbanism would be the almost endless addition of it, providing infrastructures where they could temporarily settle. But the ways in which these capsules were reflected upon were very different.

The British Archigram group was the most explicit about this. "From whatever side one may look at it: the space capsule was our source of inspiration," they wrote in retrospect.[19] But it was not just the space capsule they were interested in, not the scientific precision. It was also a place for new rituals and most recently, Peter Cook characterized the work as "Kiesler meets the space capsule."[20] Archigram recognized the space capsule as something radically different from anything that preceded it and offering a much greater performance. Their architectural answers were the Capsule Homes, designed by Warren Chalk in 1964. It was a completely new concept of dwelling in the form of a capsule with the same over-functionality and sophistication as a space capsule. The parts would be tailor-made, industrially produced, reflecting the level of contemporary technology and easily exchangeable when the desires of the inhabitants would change.

Archigram focused on capsules in relation to comfort, mobility and infrastructures, such as Plug-in City. In an apology to Le Corbusier, they called the house a device that one carries around, and the city a machine to plug it into.[21] Many of their proposals kept the middle between camping and space travel, like Michael Webb's Cushicle and Suitaloon, devices that kept the middle between a tent and a space suit from 1966 and 1968. And already in 1965 Reyner Banham and François Dallegret drew their Un-House, a kind of balloon with a television and a stereo set in the middle in which they depicted themselves naked "thus unconsciously illustrating McLuhan's statement that in the television age we have all mankind as our skin."[22]

23 Banham, Reyner. "Triumph of Software." In *Design by Choice*, by Reyner Banham, edited by Penny Sparke. London: Academy Editions, 1981.

24 McLuhan, Marshall. *Understanding Media: The Extensions of Man*. New York: McGraw-Hill, 1964.
25 See note 15.

In Archigram's optimistic view, technology opened the doors to a future dedicated to pleasure and comfort. Technology was for them the *Excessive Machine* in the science fiction movie Barbarella: a machine which tries to kill Barbarella with pleasure, but impotently blows its fuses instead, thus giving her opponent O'Shea the opportunity to say the, according to Reyner Banham, best line in the script: "Have you no shame?" This "triumph of software," as Banham called Barbarella's heroic shamelessness, gave Archigram a free ticket to speculate about all the positive possibilities technology has to offer.[23]

Mind Expanders

In Austria, architects seemed to be much more interested in the corporeal and psychological effects and consequences of the capsule and the suit. Hans Hollein and Walter Pichler, Haus-Rucker-Co and Coop Himmelblau knew about Kiesler – a former fellow countryman – from first hand and many of them even visited him in New York by the end of the fifties or in the early sixties when he was working on the Endless House. A lot of their earliest work is formally clearly inspired on it. But apart from Kiesler, they were very much inspired by Marshall McLuhan, Timothy Leary, Wilhelm Reich, and the French existentialist philosophers as well. McLuhan sees in Understanding Media art as an ideal antidote to the amounts of information that people are bombarded with. Or rather: he hoped that a certain kind of artistic multimedia environments could immunize the people against the increasingly aggressive way they were taken under fire by their *extended faculties*. The artist could show us, like a boxer, "how to ride with the punch instead of taking it on the chin."[24] It was a strategy comparable to the way astronauts were trained for their spaceflights. Very different from Archigram, whose proposals never left the drawing board, they realized many of their proposals in the form of temporary installations and working prototypes.

Crucial here was the role of Hans Hollein and notably Walter Pichler. Just like Archigram, Hollein and Pichler, in their first exhibition Architektur in 1963 in Vienna, incorporated a visual panorama of rockets, fashions, architectural history, and technology, but they drew very different conclusions from them. They drew and modeled cultic subterranean cities, monumental city centers, and buildings for communicational purposes with an almost gloomy and overtly repressive and totalitarian atmosphere that was even more emphasized in their texts.[25] When staying in

New York in 1964, Pichler would work as a graphic designer for the MOMA, in which capacity he would make a children's book in which pictures of technological devices from National Geographic and Scientific American were placed in visual relation to historic architecture and cult objects.[26]

Much more interesting maybe were the 8 Prototypes Pichler developed a couple of years later and that were exhibited in the Galerie nächst St. Stephan in 1967. Apart from cultic objects with a strong sexual overtone, furniture, and drawings for suits, he presented the Großer Raum (Large Room), a balloon reminding of Banham and Dallegret's Un-House, but in which the multimedia equipment was replaced by a more mysterious shrine, the Kleiner Raum (Small Room), and the Fernsehhelm (Tragbares Wohnzimmer) (TV Helmet [Portable Living Room]). The latter two were meticulously made prototypes for apparatuses that were clearly thought for mass production. The Small Room was a kind of helmet that changed the head of the bearer in something that looked like a radio in the most modern design, consisting of two intersecting balls. By means of a built-in microphone one's speech was amplified by an external speaker system. Small holes, as where normally a loudspeaker would be hidden, made it possible to see the surroundings without being seen oneself. The TV Helmet was the exact opposite of this. Here the bearer was completely isolated from his surroundings, his only view being a small TV screen. The longitudinal shape of the design gave it a precise direction that produced associations with Marcuse's One-Dimensional Man.

The writer Oswald Wiener dedicated a special appendix to Pichler's installations and drawings – notably for the Intensivbox from 1967 – in his book Die Verbesserung von Mitteleuropa from 1969. Here he expanded Pichler's fantasies to an apparatus that would liberate consciousness from its organic and psychological base within the human body: "It offers the chance of the century: the liberation of philosophy by technology. Its purpose is to substitute the world by taking control of the 'found environment' which has, so far, proved utterly inadequate as a transmitter and receiver of vitally important messages (food and entertainment) and by responding more fully to individual needs than the now outmoded 'universal' environment generally referred to as the natural environment has hitherto succeeded in doing. (...) The bio-adapter now controls the physical and mental states of its 'cargo' right down to the very last detail. In other words, it has taken the place of

27 Wiener, Oswald. *Die Verbesserung von Mitteleuropa, Roman.* Reinbek Bei Hamburg: Rowohlt, 1969.

28 Virilio, Paul. *L'inertie polaire.* Paris: Christian Bourgois, 1990.
29 Asendorf, Christoph. See note 21; Wolfe, Tom. See note 6.

the state and can now move on to the expansion (improvement) of the bio-module's consciousness. The bio-adapter requires only a minimum of anesthetic, as it can connect all afferents to its own stimulant transformer: for example, while a leg of the bio-module is being amputated, it may be enjoying a refreshing walk through delightful Hungarian scenery. The adapter simulates the complex interaction of afferent nerves with kinesthetic and proprioceptive fibers and a glance at his legs merely tells the bio-module that his pleasure in movement is stimulating his limbs. The process is assisted by the superior processing speed of the adapter electronics, for the adapter is able to recognize errors by means of centrally located control sensors and revoke them before they reach the consciousness of the bio-module. (...) Consciousness, this cuckoo's egg of nature, thus represses nature itself. whereas previously the forms of sensory perception were simply products of the conditioned reflexes of a superior order of experiment, ghosts of the human sense of chance (...), high quality products of the social process, monstrous prodigies of language, now consciousness rests, immortal, within itself and creates transient objects from its own depths."[27]

Here, the consequences of taking the mentality of space travel seriously and projecting them onto architecture were taken to their limits. The image that comes up reminds one of the outline of human development Paul Virilio would give more than twenty years later in his L'inertie polaire, where he envisages man as an inert disabled in a perfect cockpit.[28]

Interesting in Wiener's description is the aspect of simulation. Space travel produced a boom in simulation technology. Most of the reality of space travel was experienced second hand of course and not only that, but as Tom Wolfe put it, the most important result of it was that it opened up to an era of preconceived experiences. It seems that Alan Shepard, during his first Mercury Flight, experienced nothing new after all the simulations he went through and was even a bit disappointed: reality did not feel realistic.[29]

The chief designer responsible for the development of the NASA simulation program, Joseph LaRussa, had the official task to make the most perfect visual simulations of the real flights. In doing that, NASA realized a project, as far as it was possible, that had occupied artists from the Renaissance up to Modernism, writes Christoph Asendorf:

"The simulator has achieved the image maker's long, long dream of creating a three-dimensional window into space, a window through which the illusion approximates reality."[30] According to Asendorf, this put the physiological simulators in the shadow – but that is not completely true. Notably the other Austrian groups, Haus-Rucker-Co and Coop Himmelblau, were in the first place interested in the completely psycho-physiological aspects and implications of a new, completely artificial technological architecture. Haus-Rucker-Co's Mind Expander (1967), Gelbes Herz (1967/68), the Viewatomizer and the Environment Transformers (1968) used helmets, spectacles, light, sound, and pulsating multicolored transparent membranes to create joyful psychedelic experiences – the early installations of Coop Himmelblau like Villa Rosa (1968) did something similar.

The Global Scale

The Italian Groups Archizoom and Superstudio were much more interested in the relationship of building on a global scale versus the individual with his personal equipment, as it was most clearly expressed in Archizoom's No-stop City from 1970: a kind of giant acclimatized parking garages in which the inhabitants would move around their mobile furniture and equipment. In The Hot House Andrea Branzi states that "in opposition to the purely formal utopia's of the Archigrams and the Japanese Metabolists, which clung to the old idea of a Machine Civilizati – on by proposing a mechanical architecture and metropolis, the Italian groups conceived of a critical utopia, in so far as their use of a utopian system was purely cognitive and represented a level of clarity beyond that of reality itself. This was an instrumental, scientific utopia, one that did not put forward a different world from the present one, but rather presented the existing one at a more advanced level of cognition."[31] This was notably the case in Superstudio's The Twelve Ideal Cities from 1971. In the first city of that cycle, the City 2000t, people would live in cells with all possible infrastructure. A computer would balance all the individual needs and desires in a perfect way. The inhabitants could revolt three times against the system, before the ceiling would come down with a weight of 2000 tons, to clear the cell for a new inhabitant. Even though most of their work is much more based on an extrapolation of the tendencies they saw in building technology, notably the global view, as most explicitly expressed in Superstudio's Monumento Continuo, a grid encompassing the whole world, must have been inspired by the view from outer space.

30 See note 21.

31 Branzi, Andrea. The Hot House: Italian New Wave Design. London: Thames and Hudson, 1984.

Spaces of performances

In his leap into the void, Yves Klein was one of the first artists to use his own body in a work of art. Before using his own body, he had already used women that he smeared with paint to produce paintings in the context of a ritual. Of course, as we realize today, body art has a longer and much broader history starting at least with Marcel Duchamp and maybe even going back on the first presentation of Manet's Olympia, with two bodyguards standing next to it. Independent from Klein, by the end of the nineteen fifties, in painting, and notably in abstract expressionist painting, the corporeal gesture had won importance to such a degree that this gesture became the crucial aspect of the work. As a consequence, painters like Karel Appel and the Austrian Hermann Nitsch had themselves filmed while they were working. Arnulf Rainer had himself photographed while he pulled faces in order to find a different mode of non-verbal communication that he thought was lost in the process of civilization. In the United States, Allan Kaprow began to make live art that he called happenings, while others like Robert Morris produced a specific kind of sculpture in which he explored the relation between architectural objects and his body. For the purpose of this article, which tries to investigate the new relationship between the body and a larger whole – the earth as a whole, or even the cosmos – I am however mainly interested in a specific reading of the history of body and performance art, that is in what this increased interest in the body did or might have meant to architecture and urbanism.

In the course of the nineteen sixties, performance art was established as a new art form. All aspects of the body were investigated: from the body as a body to matters of personal history, gender, rituals, the relation to architecture, the relation to other bodies, and so on. It seemed as if in a period in history in which, by the influence of technology, the body was almost reduced to an anonymous dummy, artists rediscovered it as the basis of existence and they started measuring the world by means of it. Artists seemed to go back to the phase before the aliena-ting, estranging mirror stage and started to find a new coherence in the world starting from there. The body became a space in itself, it moved in space, extended in space, conflicted with space, it loaded space with meaning and energy. In other words: it created space by itself.

This creation of space by the body often conflicted with architecture, as in the performances of Charlemagne Palestine and notably Ulay and Abramovic. In Expansion in Space, a performance carried out at the Documenta 6 in Kassel in June 1977, Abramovic and Ulay installed two mobile columns between the existing stationary ones. By hitting the columns with their nude bodies, they moved them to the side, opening the space. In another performance, Imponderabilia from 1977, they produced a psychological barrier by standing nude in the entrance to an exhibition in Bologna, forcing the public to move between them. Vito Acconci "loaded" spaces with his physical presence, confronting the audience with his physical aggression, or with his sex, as in the notorious Seedbed from 1972, where he would lie hidden under the floor and masturbate when visitors came in while talking to them. In the course of time, some of these performance artists started developing architectural concepts as well, as for example Vito Acconci and Hermann Nitsch. The latter made series of drawings for his Orgien Mysterien Theater: a kind of subterranean bowels and intestines in which his slaughter parties should take place.

In the late nineteen seventies, it was notably architect Bernard Tschumi who recognized the transgressive architectural consequences of performance art and explored them in a series of texts, installations and Advertisements for Architecture, culminating in a theory about architecture as an *event space*. The text of his most famous advertisement reads: "To really appreciate architecture, you may even need to commit a murder. Architecture is defined by the actions it witnesses as much as by the enclosure of its walls. Murder in the Street differs from Murder in the Cathedral in the same way as love in the street differs from the Street of Love. Radically."[32] This shows that architects became more and more aware of the tension between their architectural proposals and the life that would take place within them, between the organizing and disciplining power of architecture and the desire of people to organize their own activities and live their own life in freedom. Of course, Michel Foucault's reading of architecture as in his Surveiller et Punir played an important role in this process as well.[33] At first, inspired by Jacques Derrida, architects tried to modestly produce a kind of free zones, in between spaces and heterotopias as margins within the system.[34]

32 Tschumi, Bernard. *Architecture and Disjunction.* Cambridge, MA: MIT Press, 1994.
33 Foucault, Michel. *Surveiller et punir: Naissance de la prison.* Paris: Gallimard, 1975.
34 Derrida, Jacques. "Maintenant, Point de folie – Maintenant L'architecture." *Forum* 32, no. 2 (May 1988).

Body, Technology, and Landscape

35 See also Lynn, Greg, ed. "Folding in Architecture."
Architectural Design Profile, no. 102 (1993).

In recent years there are many attempts to reconcile the body with the vast scale of the landscape in a different way. The reading of the smooth and the striated space as in the work of Gilles Deleuze and Félix Guattari, and later on Deleuze's thoughts on the fold inspired architects to develop an architecture and an urbanism that try to get rid of forms of striation as much as possible and that are more based on an endless folding of the landscape to allow for a kind of nomadic existence that allows for spontaneous and changing groupings of people.[35]

Within the framework of this article it is the work of Raoul Bunschoten that offers the most striking example. For his installation Soul's Cycle for the manifestation Architecture and Imagination, that took place in the Fort Asperen in 1989, Bunschoten made a series of large balls with wrinkled surfaces, which were installed in the circular corridor of the fortress, thus suggesting a kind of a planetary system. In the beautiful black and white photographs that were made by his wife, the photographer Hélène Binet, the planetary aspect of these balls was even more emphasized. The details she photographed looked like the first photographs that were taken from the moon during spaceflights – even the soft pale light seemed to be there. In his project The Skin of the Earth from 1990, Bunschoten took this one step further and investi-gated just fragments of this folded surface for architectural potential, implying that they would allow for dwelling themselves. In his recent work, Bunschoten takes that literally: studying the surface of the earth, by investigating cities and regions on a very large scale and mapping the processes at work there, using both aerial and satellite photographs and more situationist methods of investigation into the behavior of small groups of people. The forces that regulate these processes are discovered by extensive fieldwork in the area and drawn onto the larger maps. The final drawings of these projects resemble satellite photographs again, but then with specific hints of processes changing the landscape.

Whereas Bunschoten seems to be mainly interested in the very large scale of the skin of the earth, many contemporary architects are more interested in creating just the folds to produce more specific architectural forms on a smaller scale. Examples are to be found in the work of such different architects as OMA, MVRDV, Ben van Berkel, NOX, and Greg Lynn.

The first two offices are mainly interested in creating
a minimal, open architecture that allows for spontaneous
groupings and organizations of people and are therefore in a similar way as Bernard Tschumi interested in
performances and film. Rem Koolhaas for example sees his
buildings as a kind of film studios in which temporary
sets can be built up for specific programs and MVRDV refer
notably to Abramovic and Ulay. Greg Lynn however is
still interested in the bodily analogies of architectural form
in a similar way as Kiesler was: as a representation of
the endless. The same is true for NOX, but they most
consciously take the folding of the landscape as a means to
overcome the threatening inertia that, according to Virilio,
is caused by the developments in technology and the media.
In that respect, their work comes closest to the intentions
Kiesler had when he built the Endless House. In NOX's
H2O Pavilion in Zeeland, an exhibition pavilion dedicated to
water, the interior is an undulating landscape, animated
with all kinds of interactive technology, in which the visitors
are forced to climb up and down in order not so much
to be disorientated, but to be activated and experience their
bodies in relation to the surroundings. Also in the V2 Medialab
in Rotterdam the floor is a kind of relief on which even
special adjustable chairs are necessary to be able to sit
stable and work – for a while. In these highly technological
environments, in which the borders between the physical
and the virtual, the floor and the ceiling, the construction and
the machine, the interior and the surroundings are constantly
blurred, we are reminded over and again of it that our
body is the only thing we can rely on. According to NOX's
Lars Spuybroek we have to train its proprioception
constantly to overcome the danger of a technology that
seems to be instrumental but finally is only after it to comfort
and pamper us, to put us asleep, to bring us in a state
of polar inertia. The only thing we can dwell in and upon is
our body.

NOW SWITCH OFF THE SOUND AND REVERSE THE FILM

KOOLHAAS, CONSTANT AND DUTCH CULTURE IN THE 1960S

Now switch off the sound and reverse the film

Koolhaas, Constant and Dutch culture in the 1960s

To each bastard, a genealogical tree.[1]
Rem Koolhaas

En Indonesie, nous habitions les écuries d'une très grande maison, entourée par un mur. Et, de l'autre côté du mur, il y était un lavoir avec une série de bassins très longs et parallèles. Il y avait là de très belles femmes qui lavaient les draps de façon très lente, très érotique... A un moment une sonnerie a reteni; c'était l'heure du déjeuner, les femmes sont parties. Des hommes sont arrivés, ils se sont déshabillés, ont pissé dans l'eau et ont commencé à nager entre les draps. C'était une grande expérience...[2]
Rem Koolhaas

It is an intriguing photograph in itself. On the far left, we see the artist/architect Constant Nieuwenhuys in his atelier in Amsterdam. He points towards a complex construction in the background. Two figures stand next to him, but the ink on the pink paper has faded to the point that they are nearly unrecognizable. The image originally accompanied an interview with Constant published in a 1966 issue of the Haagse Post, a leading Dutch weekly magazine, on the occasion of the presentation of his work in the Dutch pavilion at the Venice Biennale.[3] The interviewers are art critic Betty van Garrel and – on the far right of the picture, 22 years old and with a Beatles-hairdo – Rem Koolhaas. At first, it may not seem strange to see Koolhaas pictured with Constant; given Koolhaas's place in the architectural world today, it seems logical that he would have been attentive to Constant's work in the sixties. But at the time, Koolhaas was a journalist for the Haagse Post; nothing indicated that he was particularly interested in architecture. According to his former colleagues, he was mainly occupied filling the magazine's gossip page called "People, Animals and Things", in which capacity he "excelled in making up the most improbable details."[4] His other, more important job, was the definitive layout of the magazine, which was printed like a newspaper – with lead type. He worked in the composing room at the printing office of the daily newspaper De Telegraaf.[5]

1 Koolhaas, Rem. "The Terrifying Beauty of the Twentieth Century." In *S, M, L, XL*, by Rem Koolhaas and Bruce Mau, Rotterdam: 010 Publishers, 1995.
2 Noviant, Patrice, and Bruno Vayssière. "Interview with Rem Koolhaas." *AMC*, December 1984.
3 Koolhaas, Rem, and Betty Van Garrel. "De stad van de toekomst. HP-gesprek met Constant over New Babylon." *Haagse Post*, August 6, 1966, 14–15.
4 Koolhaas, Rem. "Cherry Duyns als geciteerd door Annejet van der zijl." *HP/De Tijd*, Oct. 23, 1992, 30–41.
5 In a conversation with the author, Rem Koolhaas described this experience as important for his career as an architect, as he had to deal very quickly with the material different composers would bring to a table. Decisions for one page would have direct consequences for another.

But Koolhaas was also responsible for a series of larger articles and interviews on subjects ranging from the most kitschy displays of Dutch schlager-culture (the Song Festival in Knokke); to literature, film, and motorsports (the 24 Hours of Le Mans); to politics (the PROVO movement) to sex. He wrote only two articles on architecture: one on Le Corbusier and another on H. Th. Wijdeveld. The interview with Constant thus seems to have been a rare exception. What would have provoked Koolhaas's interest in Constant at the time? What is its importance today?

In recent years, academics in Europe, and particularly in the United States, have taken a renewed interest in the Situationists, the group of activists that radicalized cultural and political criticism between 1957 and 1972. As a result, several fundamental Situationist texts such as Guy Debord's The Society of the Spectacle and Raoul Vaneigem's The Revolution of Everyday Life have recently been translated into English or reprinted. Recently, the contribution of Constant Nieuwenhuys, another former-situationist, has also been made available in Mark Wigley's Constant's New Babylon: The Hyper-Architecture of Desire, published on the occasion of a major exhibition on the project at the Witte de With center for contemporary art in Rotterdam.[6]

Not surprisingly, several critics have begun to speculate on the possible influence of situationist thought on Rem Koolhaas.[7] But they remain puzzled that Koolhaas's thinking refrains from the radical criticism of the "spectacle" and of capitalism that is so central to situationism, or at least that he presents this criticism in a different way, for instance by coining the term Junkspace (TM) to describe the "artificial labyrinthine, kitschy ambiences that fester inside modernist containers like airports and shopping malls, to accommodate shops, bars, restaurants, casino's …"[8] Indeed, the article in the Haagse Post proves that Koolhaas was aware of Constant's ideas in the sixties, but it doesn't openly reveal what he thought of them. Since Constant has become canonized, no one seems to consider any more that Koolhaas could have been influenced by Constant in a negative or more ambivalent way, or that this influence might have been colored by or mixed with others.

Koolhaas himself provides these critics with few clues as to his possible links with the Situationists

6   i.a. Debord, Guy. The Society of the Spectacle. New York: Zone Books, 1994; Vaneigem, Raoul. The Revolution of Everyday Life. Welcombe: Rebel Press, 1994; Wigley, Mark. Constant's New Babylon: The Hyper-architecture of Desire. Rotterdam: Witte De With, 1998.

7   Mark Wigley, see note 6; Kwinter, Sandford. "question after a lecture of Rem Koolhaas", Architectural Association, London, January 26, 1999; Van den Heuvel, Dirk. "Occupation of Desires, Concerning the Sudden topicality of the Situationists." ARCHIS, February 1999, 72–78; Ruyters, Domeniek. "Playstation, Constant's New Babylon." MetropolisM, January 1999, 28–33.

8   Koolhaas, Rem. "Junkspace." In Content, by Rem Koolhaas, 162–71. Cologne: Taschen, 2004.

9   See note 1.
10   PROVO was an ungraspable movement, something between a series of "happenings" inspired by Fluxus and the situationists, and a spontaneous mass movement of mainly young people. In the course of time, stimulated by the repressive forces of the authorities before "repressive tolerance" was invented, it had an important impact on local politics in Amsterdam. On a national level, it greatly influenced the mentality of a whole generation.

11   See Wigley, note 6.

and instead cultivates the myth about himself that he produced with his autobiographical "novel" S,M,L,XL.[9] That myth begins with his architectural training at the AA School in London and the writing of Delirious New York, as if nothing had happened before. In fact, Koolhaas already had two interesting careers behind him when he decided to become an architect – one in journalism, the other in filmmaking. To better understand Koolhaas's position towards Constant, it is important to have more insight into the particular Dutch cultural context of the 1960s, where the activities of these two figures intersected.

Constant

Constant was an influential voice in the Netherlands in the sixties – a kind of conscience for progressive architects and regarded as a guru by the PROVO movement.[10] New Babylon – the project he spent 20 years developing through drawings, paintings, maps, texts, and most strikingly, through models of soldered metal, wire, and plexiglass – was presented, at various phases of its evolution, in museums, in art magazines, in lectures, and even on television.

New Babylon is the model of a possible future city: completely covered, artificially climatized and lit, and raised high above the ground on huge columns. Inhabitants are "given access to 'powerful, ambience-creating resources' to construct their own spaces whenever and wherever they desire." Light, acoustics, color, ventilation, texture, temperature, and moisture are infinitely variable. Movable floors, partitions, ramps, ladders, bridges, and stairs are used to construct "veritable labyrinths of the most heterogeneous forms in which desires continuously interact." "New Babylonians play a game of their own designing, against a backdrop they have designed themselves."[11] The city itself consists of chains of these multileveled structures that are strung across the landscape. Underneath them are fully automated factories, cars, and trains. Above fly helicopters. These means of transportation allow the inhabitants to dwell in this city in a radical dérive: they do not want to live in a fixed place, but drift and roam through the vast urban landscape with its multiple changing ambiences. Since technology has made work obsolete, energy is channeled into "collective creativity." According to Constant, it is "not the laborer but the player, not 'homo faber' but 'homo ludens' to whom the future belongs."[12] And New Babylon is the playground for this ludic society.

Often, Constant presented his vision of the future through cinematically conceived slide shows, accompanied by sound collages, that even today produce an eerily believable effect: "Only a few human figures are visible, perched on the edge of a vast space, but the soundtrack fills the auditorium with a metropolitan jumble of voices, traffic noises, machines, animals, and strange music. We hear the sounds of a life we cannot see, a life we are forced to imagine."[13]

Architect or artist

Mark Wigley calls Constant a "hyper-architect": "Indeed, he took on and exaggerated so many traits of the architect's typical behavior that he became – more architect than any architect."[14] But however central the tools and methods of the architectural profession were to his work, how spatial his proposals, however much he lectured and theorized, how intensively he engaged with architects like Aldo van Eyck, how far he went in his personification of the architect – lecturing, theorizing, and so on; Constant came from art and was seen as an artist in the 1950s and 1960s. That he was taken so seriously by architects at the time was a result of the CIAM debates in the 1940s and 1950s, in which modern artists – with their supposed ability to provide the city with new monumental symbols of communality – were considered crucial to the urban design process. After the Second World War there was a feeling that modern architecture had lost terrain in the thirties and forties, because the neoclassical revival in that period, which involved large scale employment of artists, had been much more successful in providing exactly such symbols – albeit reactionary ones.

Believing that they had completely overlooked and underestimated these issues in their drive for functionality and sobriety,[15] Dutch CIAM members introduced Constant – still a member of CoBrA at the time – to their meetings. Some of the Dutch CIAM groups were – apart from Le Corbusier – more open to collaboration with artists than others. This may have a historical background, because De Stijl originated in painting, but after the war also CoBrA painters like Karel Appel were regularly invited to realize important works in buildings by J. J. P. Oud, H. A. Maaskant and others. Aldo van Eyck was even in close contact with COBRA. For Constant, his contacts with architects may have been impetus to

12 Idem.
13 Idem.
14 Idem.

15 See i.a. Lootsma, Bart. "Kunst onder de vleugels van de architectuur." ARCHIS, no. 12, 1987.

rethink communality in a more drastic way, resulting – after his first contacts with the situationists – in whole urbanistic proposals. At the peak of the successful realization of the postwar reconstruction of The Netherlands, Constant provided not only a critical reading of modern architecture and urbanism, but also a much further-reaching vision of the future, that was visionary, optimistic, idealistic, and artistic in nature.

The Haagse Post

When Rem Koolhaas started working for the Haagse Post in 1963, he was 19 years old. It was then a rightwing liberal magazine – especially by Dutch standards – whose editor in chief, Mr. G. B. J. Hilterman, is still notorious today for the bronze voice he uses to deliver his Sunday radio-column, "The Situation In The World," in which he polemically defends capitalism and the free market. But even more than conservatism, Hilterman valued independence, both for himself and for the magazine. His wife, Sylvia Brandts Buys, personified this independence but was more adventurous. Seeking a younger audience, she wanted to model the "HP" – as it is generally known – on L'Express and Time, and recruited a series of non conformist younger journalists, a strange mix of intellectuals and ragamuffins, that were all to become part of the sixties avant-garde. In general, HP was a strange and often schizophrenic mix of conservatism and eccentricity. It happened that one editor refused to work at a certain desk, because another had made love on it the night before.[16]

Many editors and journalists at the Haagse Post had second careers in art, literature and film.[17] In fact, the magazine was almost a cover organization for the Nulbeweging ("Zero Movement," the Dutch variant of the German ZERO movement and the French Nouveaux Réalistes), and "De Nieuwe Stijl" ("The New Style"), the corresponding literary movement. Armando, head of the magazine's cultural section, was already a known painter and writer, but also a boxer who played the violin in gypsy bands. At the time, he was painting with industrial paints on sheet metal in place of canvas, to produce minimalist monochrome surfaces. He would wrap these surfaces with barbed wire, or carefully screw a few bolts to make simple geometric patterns. His sculptures consisted of simple stackings of car tires. Other members of the Nulbeweging and

16 Jansen van Galen, John, and Hendrik Spiering. Rare jaren. Nederland en de Haagse Post 1914–1990. Amsterdam: Nijgh & Van Ditmar, 1993.

17 For example Jan Cremer is now a known bestseller writer and painter, Jan Vrijman is a filmmaker, Trino Flothuis and Cherry Duyns became famous as makers of unconventional documentaries and the latter of absurdist programs for VPRO television, together with Armando.

18 Armando and Sleutelaar themselves deny by the way that De Nieuwe Stijl is a reaction to Cobra en De Vijftigers is. See Armando + Sleutelaar. "Aanwijzingen Voor De Pers (1965/66)." In *De Nieuwe Stijl, 1959–1966*, edited by Sjoerd Van Faassen and Hans Sleutelaar. Amsterdam: Bezige Bij, 1989.

19 Armando. "Een internationale primeur", 1964, published again in *De Nieuwe Stijl, 1959–1966*, see note 19.

20 Rem Koolhaas was one of the initiators and judges of a competition for a "House With No Style," organized by Japan Architect magazine in the early 1990s.

21 See note 14.

22 Armando, "Aanwijzingen voor de pers", see note 19.

De Nieuwe Stijl who also wrote for HP included Hans Sleutelaar and Hans Verhagen, both poets with a sharp eye for everyday life and culture.

Nul and De Nieuwe Stijl were clear reactions to the emotive style of CoBrA and to the corresponding Dutch literary movement, the Vijftigers, with their strong emphasis on individual expression and childlike innocence.[18] The Nul-members at HP were known as "de Heertjes" (the Gentlemen), because they refused the "alternative" style common to artists and journalists, and instead wore elegant suits, like Koolhaas does in the vague photograph illustrating the interview with Constant. Armando's manifesto, "Een internationale primeur," summed up what the Nulbeweging stood for: "Not moralizing or interpreting (art-ificing) the reality, but intensifying it. Starting point: an uncompromising acceptance of reality. (…) Working method: isolating, annexing. Thus: authenticity. Not of the maker, but of the information. The artist who is no longer an artist, but a cold, rational eye."[19] The meaning of Nul and De Nieuwe Stijl was, in other words, to work "with no style," to use an expression Koolhaas later applied in architectural terms.[20]

The new style of journalism that was introduced in the Haagse Post tried to do something similar. "Write it all down in a *deadpan* manner, with the amazement of someone who has just arrived from Mars," Armando instructed Betty van Garrel.[21] In the manifesto "Instructions for the press," written with Sleutelaar for De Nieuwe Stijl, he went even further: "Facts are more interesting than commentaries and guesses." "Historical conscience is the only reliable guidance;" "Information remains necessary: not by means of opinions, but by means of facts;" "It has to become evident as soon as possible that most critics are the bastards of journalism;" "These bastards have to leave the stage."[22]

So, the journalists of HP did not so much give their opinions, but tried to describe, with precision and neutrality, what happened. The tape recorder became an indispensable tool: in interviews, they wrote down as literally as possible and with a minimum of editing what their subjects said. In fact, Trino Flothuis developed a method of interviewing in which he

23 Jan Kuitenbrouwer, as quoted in *Rare Jaren*, see note 16.

24 Koolhaas, Rem. "Architectuur/Een woonmachine, Le Corbusier kreeg f 5000,–." *Haagse Post*, October 3, 1964, 24.

25 See note 17.

26 Lootsma, Bart. "Rem Koolhaas, In Search of the New Modernity." *domus*, January 1998.

stopped asking questions altogether and just waited with the microphone on for whatever his victims might say. Another rule for the Nul-journalist was that the "official" order of facts was arbitrary and therefore could be almost completely neglected: the waitress at the press conference of the prime minister was just as relevant as the prime minister himself.[23] In the cultural section, there was no distinction between high and low art: both were treated in the same way.

Indeed, Koolhaas's first ever published larger article in 1964, on Le Corbusier, consists largely of his observations of a restless audience that has to wait because the architect's flight is delayed. Than a portrait of the architect: "Le Corbusier, 76, with a dry, snappish appearance, a face in which only the under lip moves and pale blue eyes, makes an embittered impression. The largest part of his life he has worked on revolutionary plans that, when they were worked out, were mostly ridiculized, but have a great influence today." And after that an original but adequate resume of Le Corbusier's works and ideas.[24]

Writing With No Style

In this new kind of journalism, the choice of the subjects became crucial: what was isolated? What was annexed? Armando considered poetry as the result of a (personal) selection from Reality.[25] In the mid-sixties there was hardly a difference between the journalistic and the literary work of some of the contributors to the HP; it became far removed from a news magazine. At a time when tape recorders were still uncommon, this method of journalism could not only work as a tool, but also as a weapon, allowing for a certain amount of manipulation. Koolhaas, for instance, was a master at coloring the facts – and probably invented a few too. His detailed descriptions of the clothes worn by his subjects revealed much about what he thought about them. But most important in Nul-journalism was the act of "putting a topic on the agenda" rather than reacting to what was already on it. To call attention to what was otherwise neglected or considered trivial or unpopular became a new critical act. It exactly is this kind of critical act that distinguishes Koolhaas today when he puts topics like the Pearl River Delta, Africa, or Shopping on the architectural agenda.[26]

The most impressive result of the symbiosis between the Haagse Post and Nul is undoubtedly the book "De SS'ers"

27 Armando + Sleutelaar. *De SS'rs:.* Amsterdam: Bezige Bij, 1967.

(The SS members) by Armando and Sleutelaar, first published in 1967. It consists of a series of interviews with Dutch volunteers in the German army during the Second World War. The interviews are hardly edited; the words of the subjects have been written down exactly as spoken. In their foreword, Armando and Sleutelaar write that the book was conceived out of curiosity; until than only the victims and the resistance had been heard. They also point out a similarity between the volunteers that fought on the right side and the ones that fought on the wrong side: both hoped that their country would come out better off than it had been before.[27]

Even before it was printed, the book caused an immense upheaval; many considered its approach dangerous and morally wrong. At the time, the Dutch were just trying to forget that a considerable segment of the population had actually voted for the Dutch National Socialist party before the Second World War and that many collaborated, or had simply looked the other way. In fact, because the Dutch were generally obedient and efficient, providing the Germans with perfect registers, they ultimately deported a higher percentage of the Jewish population to concentration camps than any other European country. But the Dutch had gone on to create a myth about a small but heroic people that had stood up against a more powerful diabolic suppressor, and in which it seemed that everyone had been active in the resistance or at least in hiding Jews. This myth was even taught in history classes at school and associated with the resistance to the Spanish in the sixteenth century, after which The Netherlands had become an independent state.

In the 1960s, the Provos exploited this myth when they accused the right wing "establishment" of being a secret continuation of fascism. This led to one of their most notorious actions – setting fire, in 1966, to the headquarters of De Telegraaf, a newspaper that had appeared throughout the war and was critical of Provo, unlike other newspapers and magazines, which, having originated in the resistance, were more sympathetic towards the movement. The riots were instigated by a report in De Telegraaf on the killing of a worker during a demonstration: the report attributed the death to a stone throw by one of the demonstrators, when in fact the man had been killed by the police. But mostly, the incident stood out for its raw violence and destruction in the name of good intentions. Cynically, the Provos' actions could be read as the mirror image of similar activities carried out by the Nazis.

From their offices, the editors of HP had an excellent view of the riots; Koolhaas, who happened to be working in the printing office in the Telegraaf building at the time, found himself trapped in the middle of them, and climbing over roofs and through a barbershop to escape. Hiltermann and Brandts Buys regarded the riots as the culmination of a series of incidents in which the establishment, the royal family and the church were tarnished. Though some articles in HP sided with that campaign, Hiltermann himself, in his weekly columns, had criticized it in the most reactionary way. Brandts Buys ordered Hans Sleutelaar to write a very critical story on the riots, but he refused and was fired.[28] Instead, Koolhaas did the job, together with his colleagues Flothuis and Van Wansbeek. It was the Provos' use of violence, in particular, that led Koolhaas to attack them in the most cynical and sarcastical way. Entitled Boredom and Leisure and placed under the special new heading Sociology/ Politics, the interview portrays the Provos as a bunch of spoiled adolescents who have taken Constant's ideas about homo ludens a bit too literally. Appearing confused about their own motives, the Provos paradoxically come across as reactionary, rather than progressive. By recording their answers literally, the interviewers enhance this effect: "HP: No wonder sociologists call you reactionary: you resemble the people that lamented when in 1825 the first train rode between Stockton en Darlington in England.

Tuynman: No, individual man is definitely threatened by civilization. Sorry, I drop cigarette ashes in the microphone of the tape recorder. Man is threatened in his individuality by the developments in communication and in the sciences. And on this threat of the individuality our feeling of collectivity is founded. I admit, it sounds like a paradox."[29]

In the photograph that accompanies the interview, we see an elegantly dressed Rem Koolhaas in the center, suspiciously eyeing a group of long-haired, dirty, bearded and smoking Provos. From this article onwards, Koolhaas became much more prominent in HP, notably with a series of articles that criticized Provo, Hippies and people that inspired them – like Constant – or sympathized with them – like writer Harry Mulisch.[30]

28   See note 14.

29   Koolhaas, Rem, Trino Flothuis, and Van Wansbeek. "Sociologie/Politiek Verveling & Vrijetijsbesteding. HP-gesprek door Flothuis, Van Wansbeek en Koolhaas met de Provo Actiegroep." Haagse Post, July 9, 1966, 6–7.

30   See i.a. Rem Koolhaas, see note 25; Rem Koolhaas, see note 3; Koolhaas, Rem, and Trino Flothuis. "Politiek/ Literatuur, Honingbijen & Horzels, HP-gesprek met Harry Mulisch." Haagse Post, Sept. 24, 1966, 8; Koolhaas, Rem. "Amsterdamse Hippies: Liefde voor iedereen." Haagse Post, July 29, 1966, 8–9.

1, 2, 3 enz.

Like many of his colleagues at HP, Rem Koolhaas had a second career: he was in film, as a member of the group called 1, 2, 3 enz. 1, 2, 3 enz. ("1, 2, 3 etc.") was a brat pack including Rene Daalder, Rem's friend since high school, and a group of his friends from the Amsterdam Film Academy. Rem's father, Anton Koolhaas – a Dutch writer and novelist famous for his stories featuring animals – was director of the Amsterdam Film Academy at the time. The composition and size of the group changed (hence the "enz."), but the most notorious other members were Frans Bromet – a cameraman who became nationally famous as the maker of innovative TV documentaries; Kees (now: Samuel) Meyering, who became rich as the inventor of the Rolykit, a special folding toolbox; and Jan de Bont – now known as the cameraman of Black Rain, and the maker of Hollywood blockbusters like Speed, Twister, and, most recently, The Haunting. Director Pim de la Parra and cameraman Robbie Muller – now known for his work with, among others, Wim Wenders and Jim Jarmusch – were also transient members.

1, 2, 3 enz. mocked anything considered fashionable in the sixties – especially anything that was personal, artistic, idealistic, or intellectual, like the art house cinema and notably the Cinema d'Auteur. For a film to have only one author seemed to them a nineteenth-century idea. In three manifestoes, that were printed parallel above each other on the pages of the Dutch film magazine Skoop (as a reaction to earlier, negative critiques of Jack Clayton's 1965 film The Pumpkin Eater), Kees Meyering, Rene Daalder and Rem Koolhaas argued that films should be judged as teamwork – that actors, director, cameramen, screenplay writers and so on made equally important contributions to the final result.[32] They saw all of these roles as specializations in the filmmaking process, and believed that one person could combine several roles, or people could even switch from one role to another. That made it possible to adapt a crew to a budget and, as in a jazz band, to spontaneously start improvising and working. In their first film, 1, 2, 3 Rhapsodie from 1965, each participant shifted from cameraman, to actor, to director. But it was not all play and anarchy; on the contrary: the group was quite ambitious, believing that a film industry in Europe, similar to that of the US, could emerge.

31 Meyering, Kees. "Naar Een Vérité."; Daalder, Rene. "Naar een kompromisloze bioskoopfilm-avantgarde"; Koolhaas, Rem. "Een Delftsblauwe toekomst"; all three in Skoop, May 1965, 14–21; See also Daalder, Rene. "Rond Een Misverstand: Greta Garbo." Skoop, June 1965, 32–33.

The filmcombo

1, 2, 3 enz. saw a chain of evidence that filmmaking was a collective effort. In the three interwoven manifestoes in Skoop, Kees Meyering spoke of a new type of director – one who was not necessarily interested in making personal films, as Michelangelo Antonioni would be[32]; Rene Daalder emphasized the creative role of individual actors and how the director could get the most out of them[33]; and Koolhaas emphasized the importance of the screenplay writer. He thought that Dutch film had more in common with British film than with the French Nouvelle Vague and talked mainly about Harold Pinter.[34] A few years later, Jan de Bont analyzed the organization, the camerawork and the special effects on the set of Guy Hamilton's The Battle of Britain and published his findings in an extensive article in Skoop.[35] With their interest in teamwork and a professionalism, it is no coincidence that photographers like Jan de Bont and Frans Bromet developed into complete filmmakers, and director Rene Daalder became one of Hollywood's pioneers in digital technology.

Also in 1965, Rem Koolhaas published one of his longest articles in HP, on Federico Fellini – one of the directors Kees Meyering had mentioned as the representative of a new type. The occasion of the article was Fellini's latest film, Giulietta and the Spirits, around his wife Giulietta Masina, who had appeared earlier in La Strada. Koolhaas's piece is one of the finest examples of sixties HP journalism. It had to be, because, as it is revealed in the course of the article, Fellini did not really want to talk with Koolhaas at all. Koolhaas therefore puts all his energy into extensive and bizarre descriptions of Fellini's appearance, his office, the way in which he corrects an interview in Playboy, and his manner of dealing with other people – notably his barber, a lawyer and Koolhaas himself, who is sent out while the master is doing apparently senseless things in his room. "Mystery, probably Fellini's most loved attribute, comes into play …"

Because Fellini himself is not willing to speak, Koolhaas interviews Masina, adding plenty of malicious gossip, and Fellini's "master decorator" Piero Gherardi, who also appears "to be completely filled with the most false gossip" and "apart from that celebrates his honeymoon with his false teeth, so that his lisping gives him something even more vicious."[36] All in all, Fellini is portrayed as an enigmatic, obstinate genius, surrounded by idiots and

32 Idem.
33 Idem.
34 Idem.
35 De Bont, Jan. "The Battle of Britain." Skoop, March 1969, 24–37.

36 Koolhaas, Rem, and Lili Veenman. "Film. Een dag Fellini. "Hij doet altijd dingen die men niet verwacht."" Haagse Post, December 31, 1965, 39–41. The article has some similarities in approach with Koolhaas' later portrait of John Portman in "Atlanta, Journalism, 1987/1994." in S,M,L,XL, see note 1.

37 Hermans, Willem Frederik. *Het Sadistische Universum*. Amsterdam: Bezige Bij, 1964.

38 Hermans, Willem Frederik. "Antipathieke Romanpersonages." In *Het Sadistische Universum*. See note 38.

39 Idem.

40 Hermans, Willem Frederik. *De donkere kamer van Damocles*. Amsterdam: Van Oorschot, 1958.

parasites, who strangely enough seem to have a great influence on his work – for better or for worse.

A sadistic universe

Apart from the group's ideas about film as a collaborative effort, there was most certainly one other important influence on Koolhaas's thinking: the works of the Dutch writer Willem Frederik Hermans. Considered as the most important postwar Dutch writer, has built up a body of work in which the human existence is characterized by uncertainty: a chaotic, Sadistic Universe,[37] as one of his most provocative collection of essays is titled, where man cannot distinguish his friends from his enemies, and where his enemy today could become his friend tomorrow. Heroes are people who have been reckless without being punished; idealism is a gamble – and it could very well be a wrong bet. It's no wonder, that Hermans was one of the few to praise Armando and Sleutelaar's De SS'-ers: he himself had been the first to question the myth of Dutch heroism during the Second World War in many of his novels, short stories, and plays.

In the fifties and sixties, several Dutch filmmakers chose to base their screenplays on novels by Hermans. Generally very critical about those attempts, Hermans was prompted to write a series of polemical articles on Dutch film that were greatly enjoyed and admired by 1, 2, 3 enz.

Apart from Wittgenstein, whose Tractatus he would translate into Dutch in 1975, Hermans was influenced by Freud's discovery of the existence of the subconscious and its role in human behaviour.[38] According to Hermans, we could be hypnotized by the commercial media, but even our resistance to this "posthypnotic influence" is compulsory "as a superficial investigation of alcoholics, vegetarians, abstinents, idealists, criminals, and artists learns." "Not one eccentric could come up with something completely new and by the way, who would appreciate that? Resistance is accepted within the framework of the docile whole. The traditional society carries the artists' society like some skyscrapers bear a baroque tower or a Morish villa on their roof."[39]

Hermans' novel De donkere kamer van Damocles (The Dark Room of Damocles) from 1958 is about the weak adolescent Henri Osewoudt, who, during the German occupation, gets to know a character called Dorbeck.[40]

Dorbeck is Osewoudt's counterpart in everything; they look similar "like a negative of a photograph looks like a positive," according to Osewoudt's wife. Because of him Osewoudt becomes a hero of the resistance – or at least he thinks he does. Because, as it is typical in the work of Hermans, in the end the plot contains a crucial reversal or twist: immediately after the war, Osewoudt is imprisoned on accusation of betrayal. Only Dorbeck can prove his innocence, but he is not to be found. Osewoudt's last resort is a photograph that he had taken of Dorbeck and himself in front of a mirror. But when the film is found and he is finally allowed to develop it, the only picture on it is one of himself and an SS Obersturmführer. When he runs away in disbelief and despair, shouting that his prosecutors should try to find Dorbeck, he is shot by the prison guards. The prosecutors laugh, the SS prisoners yell "murderer!" and only a priest will believe Osewoudt and come to his aid. We are left to wonder whether Osewoudt has been a hero, a collaborator, or has done it all for his own reasons. All evidence – even though it is circumstantial – is against him. In fact, the book never actually explains why Osewoudt follows Dorbecks orders without question; indeed the Dutch reader – conditioned by the myth of Dutch heroism – takes it for granted that Osewoudt's actions are intended as an act of resistance to the Germans. In the end, the novel tests the reader's stand on this myth; is he a pessimist or an optimist?

De donkere kamer van Damocles opens with a story told by a school teacher to a class about a shipwrecked man, who has saved himself on a raft, but without anything to drink. The man resents the salt water that surrounds him, because he can't drink it. But when lightning strikes his mast and catches fire, he doesn't know how quickly to use the hated water to extinguish it. The teacher and the class laugh with the understanding that whether or not he succeeds in putting out the fire, he is doomed to die anyway. It is a parable that returns only a little bit different as Koolhaas's decadent plastic version, the "Raft of Medusa," which plays such an enigmatic and crucial role in the fictional conclusion of Delirious New York. This time, Koolhaas explains in a photocaption, the shipwrecked soldiers only had wine to drink and in a premature and drunken panic started to cannibalize each other already on the second day of their journey. "Saved on the 7th day of the shipwreck, they could easily have survived without eating anything at all."[41] In Delirious New York, The "Raft of Medusa" finally collides with the Pool of the constructivists. "Optimism vs. pessimism.

41 Photocaption – The Raft of Medusa, in Koolhaas, Rem. "Welfare Palace Hotel (1976)." In Delirious New York: A Retroactive Manifesto for Manhattan. New York: Oxford University Press, 1978.

The steel of the pool slices through the plastic of the sculpture like a knife through butter," Koolhaas concludes.[42]

Rem Koolhaas greatly admired Hermans in the nineteen sixties and the influence Hermans had on his thinking can hardly be overestimated. In his manifesto "Een Delfts blauwe Toekomst" in Skoop, Koolhaas already suggested that one of Hermans' novels should be made into a film.[43] When Hermans' novel Nooit meer slapen (Never Sleep Again), came out in 1966, Koolhaas visited the author in Groningen ad praised the book in a review in the Haagse Post where he applies the same twists in plot that are so characteristic of Hermans' plots.[44] Not long after that, in 1967, Hermans became a regular columnist of the Haagse Post; his first contributions were mainly about film, which could hardly have been a coincidence.

Rene Daalder

Driving force behind 1, 2, 3 enz. was Koolhaas' youth friend Rene Daalder. His first short films were widely praised, both in the press and at festivals; in fact he and cameraman Jan de Bont were widely considered the greatest talents Dutch cinema had ever known. Daalders first short movie, Body and Soul (1966), is set at a party given by a group of intellectuals, who ridicule one of the guests, a bodybuilder, because of his obsession with the corporal. They force him to undress – or better, they rip off his clothes – and make him pose as Atlas, bearing a study globe on his shoulders. But when the party gets out of hand and their bantering becomes violent, it is the bodybuilder that saves the globe from being destroyed. The film has no dialogue, but a voice over that comments on the events. The film won several prizes at Dutch film festivals at the time and as such paved the way for the financing of larger projects.

Body and Soul 2 (1967), about a woman and her younger lover, won even more praise. In the reviews of the film, critics mentioned the work of W. F. Hermans, not only in reference to the film's use of melodrama, but also because of the reversals in the plot, that in de end save the movie from being a parody, and instead make it into a satire of a satire. What intellectuals would consider to be kitsch and clichés thus appear as people's deepest and most real desires, which are hence beyond mockery.

Daalder's most ambitious project, The White Slave, became the most expensive Dutch film produced to that day. The

42 Koolhaas, Rem. "The Story of the Pool", see note 41.
43 See note 31.
44 Koolhaas, Rem. "Ik ben heel zielig. W. F. Hermans en zijn 'Nooit meer slapen.'" In Haagse Post, March 12, 1966, 22.

scenario was written by Daalder and Koolhaas together; director of photography was Oliver Wood, who worked more recently on films such as <u>Face Off</u>; and cameraman was again Jan de Bont. It premiered in 1969 at Amsterdam's Tuchinsky Theater (the producer rented a camel as a stunt), but Daalder and Koolhaas were not allowed to take their seats in the front row, because the security attendants thought they looked way too young to be the real director and scriptwriter.

The protagonist of <u>The White Slave</u> is a "good German" with the unlikely name Günther Unrat (= filth), played by the then well-known German actor with the similarly unlikely name Günther Ungeheuer (= monster). Unrat, who had gone into hiding in the Netherlands during the war, returns, at the beginning of the film, to his former underground address. He is a sort of Simon Wiesenthal, searching not for more war criminals, but for other "good Germans." This proves not to be easy, but Unrat is determined to compensate for all the bad things the Germans had done during the war. A drama develops – or better a melodrama – with a plot reminiscent of novels by W. F. Hermans, especially in the reversals. Unrat is persuaded by a mysterious Easterner (who claims to be a former assistant to Albert Schweitzer and is played by the Israeli actor Issy Abrahami) to help him select girls who will be sent to an African brothel, where they will work as white slaves. Unrat and the girls are of course ignorant of their fate: they think the girls will be trained as nurses to work in overseas aid projects – a wonderful ideal. After a short training session in Berlage's hunting lodge at the Hoge Veluwe, that involves what is for Unrat a confusing course in naturism, the girls are taken away by Abrahami and brought to an Arab brothel in the desert, where they perform belly dances to the score of Antoine Duhamel, known from i.a. the films of François Truffaut. The film also features sex between people older than fifty – a provocation – and a gun in a drawer that is never used – a mortal sin in scriptwriting according to Hitchcock, but also an inside joke referring to an essay W. F. Hermans wrote on Dutch film.[45] In fact, everything ultimately turns out differently than one would expect, but it comes as no surprise that all Unrat's ideals are shattered, and at the end of the film, his hair turns gray in one night.

Although there is a general consensus today that <u>The White Slave</u> marked the moment Dutch cinema became mature, and Jan de Bont's camerawork was widely praised, it was an enormous flop commercially. In a way, the film's failure

45 Hermans, Willem Frederik. "De filmmakers en de Witte Paters." In *Het Sadistische Universum*. see note 38.

46 See note 14; Koolhaas, Rem, and Henk Meulman. "Sex in Nederland, Deel 1." *Haagse Post*, August 5, 1967, 6–8; "Sex in Nederland Deel 2, De Adviseurs. Straks voorlichting via tv." *Haagse Post*, August 12, 1967, 14–15; "Sex in Nederland Deel 3, De Afwijkingen." *Haagse Post*, August 19, 1967, 16–17; "Sex in Nederland Deel 4, De Meisjes." *Haagse Post*, August 26, 1967.

47 See note 2.

itself was the ironical proof of its underlying idea that ideals can always result in the opposite effect one might have hoped, because it is impossible to know the real motives on which people act.

Architecture

So nothing indicated in 1966 that Koolhaas was interested in becoming an architect when he went to interview Constant. But only one year later, when the Haagse Post hired a new editor-in-chief, Koolhaas resigned after his series of four large articles on Sex in The Netherlands, based on intensive research, was heavily criticized.[46] He found new inspiration in a seminar on film and architecture at the university in Delft. One of the tutors there, Gerrit Oorthuys, had invited the 1, 2, 3 enz. group to participate, confessing that he was jealous of the work they did and of their – as he presumed – wild lifestyle. Koolhaas tried to convince him that filmmaking was actually an even more difficult, painstaking, and boring process than architecture and that architecture was in fact a more important occupation. Perhaps he went so far that he started to believe this himself; shortly after, he went to London to study at the AA School.

As a student at the AA, Koolhaas would still occasionally write scripts with Rene Daalder. In an interview with AMC Koolhaas once stated that they collaborated, during this period, on projects with Russ Meyer, the "King of Soft Porn" (in Koolhaas's own words), but this was more myth than reality.[47] Meyer made a series of films that play with the genres of pornographic, detective and exploitation movies, but in which everything turns out the other way one would expect: women with gigantic breasts appear as a kind of Nietszchean superwomen: absolute heroes, that are in complete control of the situation, both physically and mentally. Meyer often was not only the director, but also the cameraman and screenplay writer of his own movies. So in many ways, for Daalder and Koolhaas, he was almost the personification of the ideal filmmaker in the 1960s and 1970s. Daalder collaborated with Meyer for several years and definitively settled in Hollywood. Occasionally Koolhaas would visit him in there and in the beginning of that period; Daalder and Koolhaas collaborated on a treatment for a film to be called Hollywood Tower. In that film Russ Meyer was supposed to play the last movie mogul. According to Rene Daalder, who even talked to Chet Baker about doing the music, "the story dealt with a pivotal moment in the future of Hollywood when real actors were going to be made obsolete by lifelike computer generated performers. Along, of course with digital studio back lots, lighting, etc. – all of which would become artificial. Russ Meyer – the 'King of the Nudies' himself – represented humanity's last stance. Edy Williams, his super busty sex goddess girlfriend at the time, and Tippi Hedren (of Hitchcock's The Birds and Marnie) were going to be the last human movie stars in Russ's film within the film."[48]

From then on, Koolhaas and Daalder more and more went in increasingly separate directions. Koolhaas was not particularly fond of Los Angeles and Hollywood. He wrote his Delirious New York, established his name in architecture and finally returned to The Netherlands. Daalder decided to stay in Hollywood, where he collaborated with people like for example Malcolm McLaren and the Sex Pistols, but also made several films that gained a cult status and pioneered in music and digital technology.

A novelist

Although Koolhaas rarely mentions this part of his personal history since producing his autobiographical novel S,M,L,XL, the cultural climate of the Haagse Post, filmmaking and the writings of W. F. Hermans made a lasting impression on his work and thinking, that is essentially journalistic and literary in nature. For Hermans, by the way, the only difference between "journalistic" and "literary" is that the journalist writes what the masses think and that the writer disputes what the masses think and brings to light what the masses do not dare to think. This does not mean he stands above the masses, but that there is a deeply hidden solidarity between them; a writer despises the masses as much as he despises himself: "The reader hates himself in the writer, the writer hates himself in his protagonists."[49] In that sense Koolhaas is more a novelist than a journalist.

The echo of Armando's manifesto can be heard when Koolhaas speaks about the method of OMA as a "systematic idealization – a systematic overestimation of what exists."[50] One of Koolhaas's earliest descriptions of the city as "a plane of tarmac with some hot spots of intensity on it"[51] is almost a description of a gigantic Armando painting; in his laudatory text

48 Rene Daalder in an e-mail to the author Aug. 7, 1999.

49 Hermans, Willem Frederik, see note 38.
50 See note 1.
51 Rem Koolhaas in an unpublished paper for the Architectural Association School of Architecture, London, 1969, as presented in a lecture by Elia Zenghelis in a lecture at the Architectural Association School on the occasion of AA 150, London, 1996.

52 Koolhaas, Rem. "Typical Plan." see note 1.
53 Hermans, Willem Frederik. "Een Nederlandse detectivefilm." see note 38.

54 Wigley, Mark. see note 6.

<u>Typical Plan</u> in <u>S,M,L,XL</u> he even hints at the hidden affinities between this kind of plan, that was so characteristic for the anonymous American skyscraper typical of the 1960s, with other contemporary movements in the arts: "It is zero-degree architecture, architecture stripped of all traces of uniqueness and specificity."[52]

About Koolhaas's background in filmmaking a lot has been said, but here it is maybe good to emphasize that the most important contribution to architecture that originates from that field is the <u>scenario</u>. This scenario not only organizes the program of a building in a story with a <u>plot</u>, but the building itself is also part of a larger <u>plot</u>. A plot is a story that grows organically through what the protagonists of a novel or a film do. A plot is a literary rather than a visual influence – a story that grows organically through the actions and reactions of protagonists of a novel or a film.[53] It gives a possible, mythological order to reality – but it is never reality itself, which is essentially chaotic. The awareness of this unreal literary order is expressed in Koolhaas's preference for the paradox and the oxymoron that both connect seemingly different or even opposite phenomena.

Research

The impression made on Koolhaas by Constant and the Situationists was filtered through his experiences prior to becoming an architect. So, however tempting it may be to speak about the influence Constant and the Situationists may have had on Koolhaas's thinking as an architect through the obvious visual correspondences between some of the work of OMA and the models and drawings of New Babylon: the continuous folding floor planes, the use of constructions to define spaces instead of walls and the appearance of existing city plans in collages of designs for other cities; though one could also point out the sculptural qualities of many OMA models that in their handcrafted detailing, their use of materials, and their scale come close to some models of New Babylon; however important it may seem to mention that many of OMA's models were built to be shown as photographs, rather than as objects, like those of Constant which "were carefully constructed to reinforce the sense of the transitory;"[54] and despite the fact that they share(d) an interest in the rise of mega cities, a development that Constant already foresaw in the sixties; these parallels are all superficial.

Though these correspondences exist, they are caught up in completely different plots, in different readings of similar realities. Constant's New Babylon is an idealistic and artistic proposal for an architecture and urbanism for a future society, based on a reading and extrapolation of aspects of the present and an optimistic belief in the basic goodness of mankind – even if in some of his texts he does refer to criminality. His aim is to set free man's individual creativity – the ultimate proof of his goodness –, which was suppressed by a contemporary society that focuses on work and was reinforced by modern architecture and urbanism as promoted by the CIAM charters. He believed that his proposals could make a difference for the better.

Koolhaas's architecture and urbanism consist of a reading and extrapolation of tendencies he reads in the present reality, but he is much more concerned about the subconscious forces that are at work than about good intentions and ideal orders. His criticism consists of putting these forces on the agenda in the way a journalist or a writer would do it with a forgotten war or the cover-up of a political scandal: by going there, doing research and reporting his findings. More and more, this research is becoming his most crucial contribution to architectural thinking, rather than the concrete architectural and urbanistic proposals and buildings of OMA – however interesting they may sometimes be. Of course these projects contain research just as well, but this research is hidden by the final result: the design proposal or the building. And it is difficult to say how that building will function in reality.

Because of the many ungraspable and uncontrollable forces that are at work – forces largely related to sociology and psychology – and even a skepticism towards his own personal motives (which could very well be influenced by the same forces), Koolhaas realizes that it is meaningless and impossible to predict or control the future – which paradoxically is exactly what architecture tries to do. Reality can only be given a possible explanation in retrospect; Delirious New York is a retroactive manifesto and the conclusion is a fictional, literary proposal; S,M,L,XL is a novel, that concludes with a film scenario and a P.S. in the form of a project – the Jussieu Library – that was never built.[55]

55 Koolhaas, Rem. see note 8 and note 40.

In a short introduction to the Haagse Post article of 1966,
Koolhaas portrays Constant – with a deadly overdose
of irrelevant details, as was so characteristic for his style
of writing at the time – as a hilarious caricature of the
prototypical artist the Heertjes loved to hate. We learn
that Constant drives a "Duck" (from Ugly Duck, the Dutch
name for a Citroën 2CV, the stereotypical car for people
with an alternative lifestyle in the sixties); that he is an
"enthusiastic, dark-haired, beer-drinking erudite" who lives
with his wife and daughter in an apartment on the ground
floor in a petty bourgeois neighborhood in Amsterdam; that
they share this apartment with a German Shepard named
Hertha, a big hairy monkey that "unfortunately became
lifethreateningly dangerous," some parrots, and three cats;
that he plays harp, violin, dulcimer, balalaika, and especially
guitar in his spare time; that there is no television in the
house; that this "son of a civil servant who sometimes quotes
Marx" went to a Jesuit high school and believes that in
New Babylon people will not space out on drugs, because it
will be a kind of paradise in itself.[56] The style of this portrait
is similar to the one Koolhaas's former brother-in-arms,
the cameraman Frans Bromet, would use in later years when
shooting interviews for the VPRO television: not filming
the talking head, but focusing on silly movements of his
hands or stupid details in the interior and by doing so
completely undermining the speaker's authority. This also
means that Koolhaas clearly envisaged Constant as such
an authority. The only remarkable thing we learn about New
Babylon in Koolhaas's introduction in the Haagse Post is that
Constant is building his giant model to make a film, which
"according to him is the ideal way to get near the reality of
New Babylon."[57]

The interview itself opens with cynical questions like
"What would be the use of a world in which everyone could
play and be creative if people wouldn't want that?"
and: "We can imagine that if you can and may go everywhere,
in the long run it wouldn't be a challenge to move anymore. Especially if the differences in nature disappear.
Wouldn't traveling become so senseless then, that nobody
would have the spunk for it anymore?" In this sense,
the interview with Constant foreshadows the critique of
sixties radical architecture that Koolhaas would present in
Exodus, his final project at the AA. In fact, Exodus can be
seen more as a critique of New Babylon than of Archigram:
a series of sectors projected over London, each with

56   See note 3.

57   Idem.

58 Koolhaas, Rem. "Exodus." see note 1; "Superstudio.
Gli Dodici Città Ideali." *Casabella*, January 1972.
59 Koolhaas, Rem. The Generic City, see note 1.

a strong, artificially created "ambience," where "happenings" could take place. Exodus is caught in a literary plot that pays tribute to both W. F. Hermans and Superstudio's The Twelve Ideal Cities in the way it puts both itself and the expectations and presumptions of the reader into question.[58]

But then a shift occurs in the interview. As the conversation develops, Constant brilliantly manages to turn their sarcastic questions around: New Babylon, he explains, is not designed to change the world, but is an answer to, or an outcome of, how the world – and lifestyles – would actually evolve. During the course of the interview, New Babylon becomes less a Utopian project and more an inevitable reality something that is already happening, even without a design. Suddenly, it comes close to the acceptance and intensification of reality that Armando demanded in his manifesto. It also comes close to what Koolhaas would write 30 years later about the Generic City: that it "is sociology, happening."[59]

Now reverse the film

But, The Generic City can also be read as a remake – in movie terms – of Society of the Spectacle, written by Constant's former situationist brother-in-arms Guy Debord and first published in 1967.[60] Even the way the aphorisms and pieces of text are numbered is similar, though it is void of Debord's moralistic interpretation and criticism. In 1973 Debord made a film with the same name that was based on this text, and at the end of The Generic City Koolhaas asks us to "imagine a Hollywood movie about the Bible" set in "a city somewhere in the Holy Land."[61] As in a scenario concept he paints us a hilariously lively and chaotic market scene, laden with minutiae ("hairpieces dripping with glue") and couleur locale, that can be understood as a metaphor for Debord's film. And just as in many Hollywood remakes of European films, the moral of Generic City is quite different than of the "original," although it deals with the same issues. At the end, Koolhaas asks us to switch off the sound and to reverse the film. "The now mute but still visibly agitated men and women stumble backward; the viewer no longer registers only humans but begins to note spaces between them. The center empties; the last shadows evacuate the rectangle of the picture frame, probably complaining, but fortunately we don't hear them. Silence is now reinforced by emptiness: the image shows empty stalls, some debris that was trampled underfoot. Relief ... it's over. That is the story of the city. The city is no longer. We can leave the theater now ..."[62]

60 See note 6.
61 See note 6.
62 Idem.

63 De Tocqueville, Alexis. "Literary Characteristics of Democratic Times and Why the Americans Raise Some Insignificant Monuments and Others That Are Very Grand." In *Democracy in America, Volume 2*, translated by Henry Reeve. New York: Vintage Books, 1990.

64 See note 6.

65 Idem.

This is no longer a Hollywood movie about the city as seen by Debord, but a Hollywood movie about a city as seen by a kind of contemporary Alexis de Tocqueville. Didn't Tocqueville ask us to "turn down the picture" he paints of a mediocre American literature in <u>Democracy in America</u> and "consider the other side of it," that its authors spring "from the bosom of the heterogeneous and agitated mass" of the new democracy? And didn't he suggest that if the Romans had been better acquainted with the laws of nature, they wouldn't have produced their monumental cities? "A people that left no other vestige than a few leaden pipes in the earth and a few iron rods on its surface might have been more the master of nature than the Romans," he even says in his defense of American architecture.[63] The Generic City will leave almost nothing behind for archeologists. Koolhaas already warns us in the first chapter: "It is superficial – like a Hollywood studio lot, it can produce a new identity every Monday morning."[64] In the Generic City, Debord's <u>Society of the Spectacle</u> has become reality (without anyone complaining). But Constant's New Babylon has become reality as well, only the artificially created ambiances and collective creativity have resulted in commercial *junkspace* (TM), and the overall sculptural design is lost. This must be the zero degree of urbanism: "Nietzsche lost out to Sociology 101."[65]

REALITY BYTES

THE MEANING OF RESEARCH IN THE SECOND MODERNITY

Reality Bytes

The Meaning of Research in the Second Modernity

In the history of architecture, periods in which the autonomous rules of the discipline were being sought, consolidated, and refined have probably always alternated with periods in which the rules were subjected to discussion because of changes outside the field, whether social, economic, technological, or cultural. At the same time architects are, of course, also part of any given social constellation. Thus one may assert with equal justification that changes come from the very depths of the discipline, from the way in which the architectural profession is organized, the role society assigns to it, how clearly defined it is, and the degree of co-determination that society accords architects or that they are able to obtain for themselves.

The Second Modernity

There is some indication that architecture today is under pressure and that the role of the architect is in a state of flux. Social life is undergoing new upheavals in the post-industrial age, and there is already talk of a new modern age. As in the first wave of modernization brought about by the industrial revolution, today, too, technological innovation goes hand in hand with social transformation. The two are so closely intertwined that it is difficult to say which came first. The direction that this second modernization may take is also far from certain, for we find ourselves in its very midst. Precisely for that reason we urgently need to analyze certain individual aspects of this modernization, and to formulate and test hypotheses. Globally speaking, architecture and urban planning represent a sort of cast of the social. This is also what Rem Koolhaas means when he writes that the "Generic City is sociology happening."[1]

To be sure, the relationship between society and architecture and city planning is complex and not as direct and unambiguous as we might wish. It is also certain that life today largely takes place in buildings that were constructed in the distant or recent past for quite other ways of life. The tensions and frictions that occur, for instance, between the original program for a building or city and present-day demands, however, always provide a point of departure for new designs. Every design is a hypothesis that can be verified or falsified and that must have been preceded by extensive preliminary studies and fieldwork. The increasingly

1   Koolhaas, Rem. "The Generic City." In S, M, L, XL, by Rem Koolhaas and Bruce Mau, edited by Jennifer Sigler. Rotterdam: 010 Publishers, 1995.

rapid, and in some parts of the world virtually explosive, growth of cities forces us to consider our point of departure precisely. With 70 percent of its buildings constructed after the Second World War the Netherlands surely represent an exception in Europe, but this figure pales in comparison to the situation in Asia, Africa or South America. To keep on building according to tried and true methods, with smaller or larger ad hoc adaptations in typology and urban structure is no longer a guarantee of success. Berlin's Friedrichstrasse is a case in point, behind – and, in places, under – whose facades lurks a network of shopping malls that has nothing whatsoever to do with the historical structure of the city. Another is Stefano Boeri's study of the Milan region, in which he takes the methods of morphological and typological analysis to their limits.[2]

Esprit Nouveau

Research also played an important role during the first phase of modernism. We need only think of the gigantic undertaking that Le Corbusier intended to promote in Esprit Nouveau. "The spirit that dominates the work of this journal is one that welcomes all scientific study," one can read in the programmatic statement that accompanied the journal's first number.[3] Although the statement continues with a manifesto-like declaration of faith in an experimental aesthetics comparable to experimental psychology, the program of Esprit Nouveau was tar more broadly conceived, and encompassed contributions on designs by others as well. As Le Corbusier himself wrote in L'Art decoratif d'aujourd'hui, "The wondrous development of the book, of printing, the labelling of the entire preceding archaeological period has crowded our brains and dazzled us. We find ourselves in an entirely new situation: everything is familiar to us."[4] All available knowledge had to be deployed for the renewal of the visual arts, of design, architecture, and urban planning. This went far beyond the photographic displays of automobiles, airplanes, and ocean steamers with which Le Corbusier sought to shake up his contemporaries in Vers une architecture. It included a vision of history, inspired by evolutionary theory as it was presented in museums of natural history: a political and economic vision based on the triumphal march of industry; and it included statistics on urban life, to which he devoted an entire chapter in Urbanisme. "Statistics show us the past and foreshadow the future: they provide us with the necessary figures and interpret our graphs and curves. Statistics help to formulate the problem."[5]

2   Boeri, Stefano, Arturo Lanzani, Edoardo Marini, and AIM (Milano). Il territorio che cambia: ambienti, paesaggi e immagini della regione milanese. Milan: Abitare Segesta, 1993.

3   "Domaine de l'Esprit Nouveau." Esprit Nouveau, no.1, October 1920.
4   Le Corbusier. L'Art décoratif d'aujourd'hui. Paris: Éditions Crès, 1925.
5   Le Corbusier. Urbanisme. Paris: Éditions Crès, 1924.

6 See Lootsma, Bart. "Kunst onder de vleugels van de architectuur, Le Corbusier en de Synthese des Arts." *ARCHIS*, no. 11, 1987.

7 Van Rossem, Vincent. "Introduction." In *Het idee van de functionele stad: een lezing met lichtbeelden 1928 = The idea of the functional city: a lecture with slides 1928*, by Cornelis van Eesteren and Vincent van Rossem. Rotterdam: NAi, 1997.

All of these preliminary studies culminated in a hypothesis, which took shape in the temporary <u>Pavillion de l'Esprit Nouveau</u> at the 1925 Exposition Internationale des Arts Decoratifs in Paris. Here all of the sub-fields of art, design, architecture, and city planning came together in a preliminary synthesis. This preliminary, fragmentary synthesis was no new *gesamtkunstwerk*, and also no "*synthese des arts*," but rather a "*synthese de pensée*" as Le Corbusier noted in the 1930s.[6] It was a synthesis that needed time to mature, which was often rather hastily referred to as a "Manifesto". The only thing really manifest about it was a faith in research.

Similarly, Van Eesteren's and Van Lohuizen's statistical study played an important role in the genesis of the 1935 General Expansion Plan for Amsterdam, on which the city planner C. van Eesteren and the empiricist T. K. van Lohuizen collaborated intensively. "Van Eesteren had come to the conclusion in 1927 that one could only find new rules for city planning through careful study of those factors decisive for the continued existence of settlements," writes Vincent van Rossem. "Pointing to the at once highly functional and aesthetically very satisfactory nature of old settlements and cultivated landscapes, he concluded [in a lecture given in Berlin in 1928] that human beings act intuitively when they shape and equip their environment ... Van Eesteren considered it quite possible to master the chaos of the modern city without rendering urban life impossible. This was, however, possible only under one condition: that one be prepared to throw all unusable design theories and the accompanying aesthetic prejudices overboard. The city planner is thus compelled to begin all over again, just like those who many years before had done pioneering planning work by creating the first cultivated landscapes with human settlements ... Van Eesteren did not create a 'modern' style, but rather merely tried systematically to exclude even the tiniest trace of aesthetic bias. He presented [in his Berlin lecture] elements of the modern world which, according to all architectural and urban planning norms are absolutely formless, not in order – pour épater le bourgeois – to call them very beautiful, but rather because they are necessary. He conveyed an image of the modern city as an urban planning debacle, a chaos. At the same time, Van Eesteren noted, there was no reason to assume that modern elements such as railways, industrial zones and leisure facilities offered fewer possibilities for satisfactory urban planning than polder dykes, windmills and canals."[7]

An integral part of the work of Van Eesteren and Van Lohuizen is the scholarly analysis of existing cities that were facing the stresses of modernity. The analysis and the resulting norm could be deployed for the design of wholly new towns or at least of major urban extensions, or in the context of the adaptation of existing cities. Van Lohuizen placed great hopes in these studies and the norms that could be derived from them. He believed that these norms could promote "the unity of city planning," although of course some experts would have to be consulted as part of the teamwork. "A number of questions arise and lend direction to the socio-economic and demographic survey. At the same time the study begins to provide guidelines: sometimes it substantiates the correctness of an idea that developed intuitively, while at other times it demonstrates its untenability or suggests a modification that will permit a better adaptation to the actual situation, or even reveals wholly new possibilities. In any case it facilitates precise concepts of the necessary extent of the plan and shows the desired surface relations and the concrete measurements required for the design, which is then fixed in exact measurements and figures. Thus there is a continual interaction between intuition and knowledge, a growing depth of insight and with it a maturing of the design form. It is a game in which the relationship between the reflection of the perceived and the creative capacity of the artist is constantly being reversed. And so in the end the multiplicity of the facts and circumstances that determine the design yield a synthesis in which all of the aesthetic, technical, social, economic, and psychological factors have taken shape in an internally and externally harmoniously formed organism."[8]

The influence of Van Lohuizen and Van Eesteren, at least upon Dutch urban planning, is inestimable. In 1948 they both became professors in Delft, Van Lohuizen in the field of survey issues and Van Eesteren as a city planner. Their investigation would affect a number of planners and architects. The method devised by a group of Rotterdam architects to study leisure behavior in order to lend new substance to such a traditionally artistic task as park design shows how improvised and uninhibited the modes of investigation developed in the 1930s could be. "In 1935 the 'Opbouw' decided to study the problem of leisure in the city of Rotterdam. Over a period of two years they took walks through the city in order to record the recreational preferences of the Rotterdam population in photographs. They collected valuable material from which they derived

8   Van Lohuizen, Theodoor Karel. "De eenheid van het stedebouwkundig werk." Inaugural speech, TU Delft, Rotterdam, February 11, 1948.

9   Van Gelderen, Wim *De 8 En Opbouw*, August 1939, quoted from Louwerse, David. "De wederopbouw en de vormgeving van het stedelijk groen." In *Nederlandse Landschapsarchitectuur: tussen traditie en experiment*, edited by Gerrit Smienk. Amsterdam: Thoth, 1993.

leisure needs, organized according to age groups. They then studied the minimum distances for recreational areas of individual age groups and the intensity of use of these areas. The population was divided into age groups and then norms were established for the space per capita that was needed for the various types of recreational areas. The results were then elaborated for a 'conceptual plan' in which the facilities that were considered necessary for Rotterdam were listed, divided according to neighborhood, quarter, and city parks. Finally, three transformation plans were set up for the three types of park to clarify the conceptual plan."[9]
The Opbouw method was presented at the CIAM congresses held in La Sarraz in 1936 and Paris in 1937.

Institutionalization

Without mentioning him by name or actually discussing him explicitly, Van Rossem describes Van Eesteren as a precursor to Rem Koolhaas and OMA, and although this connection has never been made before, it appears to me that there is much truth in it. The desire to avoid all bias – and above all a style – the embracing of modernity and a form of plan that consists above all in the overlaying of various layers of plans. And yet, however tempting it may seem, it is too simple and even dangerous to make this connection so directly. The difference lies in the fact that Rem Koolhaas and OMA began to work in a situation in which the norms that Van Eesteren and his successors had formulated had long since become institutionalized. I do not merely mean that they had been realized in countless modern residential areas, cities, and rural districts, but also that the norms had become rigidified as laws that fixed architecture and city planning, from the location of gas and electricity meters to the type and number of certain types of residence – mainly family apartments, recreational facilities, building systems, access to natural light, etc. – to such a great extent that every design had to follow these guidelines, and that society had changed drastically in the meantime.

Admiration and criticism for the tradition of Van Eesteren and Van Lohuizen are expressed in Rem Koolhaas' confront-ation with the Bijlmermeer district, first in the context of a student project at the Technical University of Delft and later (1986–87) within the context of a commission for a design intended to save the district from disrepair. The district, built in the 1970s as Amsterdam's last large-scale Modernist urban extension, had degenerated into a frightening ghetto. According to OMA, the problem lay not so much in what was visible – the Modernist apartments and their honeycomb arrangement, but rather in the almost complete absence of facilities for the new social, commercial, and cultural life of the community. The type and number of such facilities had been determined by the results of studies undertaken in the 1930s, while leisure behavior had changed radically in recent decades. "For these reasons, Bijlmer's central problem is the homogeneity of the land's surface. Never before in history had anyone tried to make an urban population of 50,000 people [and more] happy with an urban life that consisted of taking walks arm-in-arm, foot baths, fishing, playing games, etc.: in other words, with nothing but innocent activities. Conclusion: the spectrum of urbanity that Bijlmer offers, determined by the form of the land's surface, is too limited. It is disconnected from contemporary culture, consumer society (culture of congestion) and is a pure anachronism in relation to the diversity characteristic of the current situation. It is absolutely essential for a vibrant Bijlmer that this spectrum be broadened."[10]

Old and New Modernity

In the past two decades, both external and internal influences have brought about drastic changes in social life. The full impact of the effects of globalization and individualization is becoming visible, no longer only in the large cities, but, under the influence of international media networks and a sharp increase in individual mobility, literally everywhere. The city is no longer synonymous with the spatial manifestation of a community with a clear – preferably hierarchical – structure.

This also means that one can no longer draw conclusions about the structure of a society based on the morphological structure of a city. The city can no longer be simply the enumeration of the same things. I would like to use the word *city* here in the broad sense of an "urban area". A number of smaller and larger communities find space side by side and in continually changing combinations in this sprawling, practically unbounded area. The communities are no longer defined here by their consistent spatial proximity within a limited territory. Increasingly, communities are formed by active conscious choice and by proximity measured in time periods. This goes beyond the half-baked and vague hints of something that is called "multicultural society", which, however well intentioned, inevitably connotes the "invasion" of aliens, of foreigners.

10 Office for Metropolitan Architecture. *Studie Herinrichting Bijlmer*. 1987.

11 Geuze, Adriaan, and Onze Flat. *Jaarverslag stimuleringsfonds voor architectuur 1994*. Rotterdam, 1995.

12 See Lootsma, Bart. "Designing for the New Communities." In Adriaan Geuze, *West 8: Landscape Architecture*, by Bart Lootsma and Inge Breugern. Rotterdam: 010 Publishers, 1995; Geuze, Adriaan. "Accelerating Darwin." In Gerrit Smienk, see note 9; Geuze, Adriaan, "Wildernis." In *De Alexanderpolder, waar de stad verder gaat*. Edited by Anne-Mie Devolder. Bussum: Thoth, 1993; Lerup, Lars. "Stim and Dross: Rethinking the Metropolis." *Assemblage*, no. 25, 1994.

13 Beck, Ulrich. "The Reinvention of Politics: Towards a Theory of Reflexive Modernization." In *Reflexive Modernization: Politics, Tradition and Aesthetics in the Modern Social Order*, by Ulrich Beck, Anthony Giddens, and Scott Lash. Cambridge (UK): Polity, 1994.

In a text on the history of the inhabitants of the Maaskantflat in Rotterdam, Adriaan Geuze has shown enormous differences in the homogeneity and sense of community between the original inhabitants and those who have moved into apartments that became vacant in recent years. Here he is speaking not of people from different countries, but merely of mainly young people with a more individualistic way of life.[11] The communications media that are everywhere individually accessible and the strong increase in individual mobility play a central role in shaping new and by no means only temporary communities, as Adriaan Geuze and Lars Lerup have clearly shown.[12]

Sociologists such as Ulrich Beck and Anthony Giddens view individualization as an unavoidable and necessary intermediate phase on the way to new forms of social life. While in classical industrial society there were direct connections among class, family, sexual roles, the division of labor between men and women, familial and architectural typologies, today many more people have the opportunity to replace the standard biography with one they have chosen themselves – a *do it yourself biography* as Ronald Hitzler has called it or, as Giddens puts it, a *reflexive biography*. According to Ulrich Beck, individualization also means "first the disembedding and second, the re-embedding of industrial society's ways of life by new ones, in which the individuals must produce, stage, and cobble together their biographies themselves."[13] In this case, the reflexive element consists above all in the confrontation with others. Naturally, this always plays a more central role at those moments when social life is becoming more compact at the same time.

All of this turns our conception of culture in the broadest sense of the word on its head, particularly when it is a matter of those aspects of culture, such as architecture and the visual arts, which take effect in public space and owe their legitimacy to the public sphere. Traditionally, architecture mediates between the individual desires of a person commissioning a work and the public interest. Art in public space traditionally produces symbols in which society as a whole is supposed to be able to recognize itself. However individual, this expression is, after all, legitimated by the particular position of the artist. Architecture and art are always legitimized on the basis of a constantly changing discourse on "art" and "architecture," which is interpreted from above as a possible part of "culture." Today everyone can receive twenty or thirty television stations at home, and there are at least that many subcultures. Each of these cultures seeks its own program or creates its own mixture out of various programs. Each of these cultures listens to its own mix of music and dresses in its own combination of articles of clothing, which, individually or together tell a story about the wearer's position in life. The same holds true of the cars people buy – often specially equipped with significant accessories – as well as their interiors, gardens, and homes.

Roemer van Toorn has characterized this new society as the Society of the And in contrast to the Society of the Either/Or. "Thinking in terms of good and evil no longer legitimates our civilizatory process. Either/or categories such as East/West and left/right have dissipated. The end of the Cold War has precipitated a crisis of victory in the West, which is why the question of a social sense of possibilities now has to be posed in a completely new way. Previously, the dominant criteria were differentiation, specialization, transparency, and predictability; now, we speak of the quality of simultaneity, of a multicultural society, of uncertainty, alienation, chaos, theories, networks, hubs and nodal points, interaction, hybrid ambivalence, paradoxes, schizophrenia, liquefiable space, cyborgs, and so on.[14] The Society of the And is a great rhizome, defined by endless libidinous couplings produced by technological means.

Rem Koolhaas

The shift from the Either/Or Society to the Society of the And is clearly legible in the work of Rem Koolhaas. Initially, in the 1970s, Koolhaas' interest was directed above all toward "either/or" conditions such as the Berlin Wall; yet he quickly discovered the problematic nature of this approach: "The Berlin Wall was a very graphic demonstration of the power of architecture and some of its unpleasant consequences. Were not division, enclosure (i.e. imprison- ment), and exclusion – which defined the wall's performance and explained its efficiency – the essential stratagems of any architecture? In comparison, the sixties dreams of architecture's liberating potential – in which I had been marinating for years as a student – seemed feeble rhetorical play. It evaporated on the spot."[15]

14 Van Toorn, Roemer. "The Society of the And. Constructing Progressive Reflexivity in the And." Unpublished manuscript, 1998.
15 Koolhaas, Rem. "Berlin Wall." see note 1.

16 Koolhaas, Rem. "Exodus, or the Voluntary Prisoners of Architecture." see note 1.

17 Koolhaas, Rem. *Delirious New York: A Retrospective Manifesto for Manhattan.* London: Academy Editions, 1978.

18 Koolhaas, Rem. "Die erschreckende Schönheit des zwanzigsten Jahrhunderts." In *OMA. Rem Koolhaas,* edited by Jacques Lucan. Paris: Electa Moniteur, 1990; Milan: Electa, 1991; Zürich: Verlag für Architektur, 1991.

In the polemical project Exodus or the Voluntary Prisoners of Architecture, Koolhaas ruthlessly settled accounts with the architecture of the 1960s. The project envisioned strips extending across London, inhabited by "voluntary prisoners" who lived in the kind of paradoxical, ecstatic freedom also expressed in the projects of Archigram.[16] Koolhaas then moved to New York in order to compose a "retroactive manifesto" for this metropolis, a work that was not taken seriously by the architectural profession at that time. Delirious New York was conceived as a "blueprint" for a Culture of Congestion.[17] It was the first book to attempt to come to terms with a culture defined by the consumer society, technology, concentration, and chronic instability – in other words, with everything now considered essential to the Second Modernity. Koolhaas' New York virtually epitomizes the Society of the And: elevators, traffic, underground tubes, and high-speed railways – for Koolhaas, the subconscious of the city – generate a situation in which new forms of behavior such as the famous "eating oysters naked with boxing gloves on the nth floor" can emerge.

And just as Le Corbusier's study in Esprit Nouveau ended with a hypothesis in architectural form, Koolhaas also concluded his book with a series of architectural hypotheses, models that were to be applied later to other situations and allowed to ripen in them: The City of the Captive Globe, Hotel Sphinx, New Welfare Island, Welfare Palace Hotel, and The Story of the Pool. The designs for the Parc de la Vilette and the world exposition in Paris in 1982 and 1983 were the first opportunities for Koolhaas and OMA to apply these hypotheses to concrete commissions outside of New York. In the practice of OMA, research had been an integral part of the design process for years. "If there is a method to our work, then it is that of a systematic idealization, a spontaneous overestimation of the existing situation, a theoretical bombardment in which even the mediocre is comprehended in retroactive conceptual and ideological advances," wrote Koolhaas in 1985.[18]

The work of OMA can largely be described as "designing research" or "researching design." In this process, the marginal conditions for every design – building codes, laws, programs – are precisely mapped out in order to explore the outer limits of the possible. Within these boundaries, then, a design is prepared that is specific to the context while at the same time introducing a new typology within the limits of the possible. The concrete results of such investigation consist, in part, of realized projects, but above all of

19 OMA. "Point City/South City." In *De Alexanderpolder: waar de stad verder gaat*, by Anne-Mie Devolder. Bussum: Thoth, 1993; OMA, and NYFER. *MAASVLAKTE*. Den Haag: Sdu Uitgevers, 1997.

20 Koolhaas, Rem. "Atlanta."; "Singapore Songlines."; "The Generic City."; all see note 1.

a series of new architectural concepts and typologies that have been put into practice either by OMA itself or by others, the most important example of which is the large building as a folded and stacked continuation of the landscape.

Although in many cases these projects are explicitly based on designs from the first phase of modernism, renewed attention should be paid to the pitfalls of a situation in which the first modernity is institutionalized and thus not only exists as a "toolkit," but is also imposed in laws and regulations. In addition, a series of special polemical designs were created in the context of design studies, projects such as Point City/South City for Architecture International Rotterdam and MAASVLAKTE for a study of the Rotterdam harbor.[19] These projects generate information not only through the research performed by OMA itself, but also through political and social reactions.

The Harvard Project on the City

In recent years, a clearer distinction has emerged between the "design research" of the architectural office and the more foundational architectural and above all urbanistic research of Rem Koolhaas himself. One reason for this distinction may lie in the fact that the realization of buildings necessitates specific compromises, which prevent the in-depth exploration of more general themes in the context of specific commissions. Examples of more in-depth studies are found in S, M, L, XL as well as in essays and newspaper articles such as Atlanta, Singapore Songlines, and the The Generic City.[20] In recent years, Koolhaas has intensified this research – along the lines of Delirious New York, but without the architectural Fictional Conclusion – within the context of the Harvard Project on the City. The project, "unofficially known as 'The Project for What Used to be Called the City'," researches the effect of modernization on the urban condition in student groups and is intended to produce a series of lectures, books, and exhibitions in the coming years. Topics of investigation known at present include "China – The Delta of the Pearl River," "Shopping," "Africa," and "Rome." Though the project is accompanied by much discussion, rather impressive and curiosity-arousing prototypes of the books are circulating, and many are craning their necks for a glimpse of the first results; nonetheless, Rem Koolhaas has managed to prevent too much material from slipping to the outside.

21 Koolhaas, Rem. "PEARL RIVER DELTA." In *Politics, Poetics: Documenta X, the Book*, by Catherine David and Jean-François Chevrier. Ostfildern-Ruit: Cantz, 1997.

The most conspicuous presentation of initial research results was the exhibition and catalogue text Pearl River Delta at Documenta X in 1997. The exhibition showed an impressionistic collage of countless photos of new cities in the Pearl River Delta along with statistics and texts. The catalogue text PEARL RIVER DELTA consisted of a series of conceptual definitions derived from phenomena characteristic of the Pearl River Delta: "The PEARL RIVER DELTA project is based on fieldwork: it consists of a series of interrelated studies that, together, attempt to give an initial overview of the emerging condition(s) in a Chinese region that, according to reliable predictions, is destined to grow to 34 million inhabitants by the year 2020, and through its sheer size alone, to play a critical role in the 21st century ... Together, these studies describe a new urban condition, a new form of urban co-existence that we have called CITY OF EXACERBATED DIFFERENCE, or COED. Beyond the particularities of each condition that we found, the COED project introduces a number of new, copyrighted concepts, that, we claim, represent the beginning of a new vocabulary and a new framework to describe and interpret the contemporary urban condition."[21]

The need to explore the essence of this COED results from its definition: "The traditional city strives for a condition of balance, harmony and a degree of homogeneity. The CITY OF EXACERBATED DIFFERENCE, on the contrary, is based on the greatest possible difference between its parts – complementary or competitive. In a climate of permanent strategic panic, what counts for the COED is not the methodological creation of an ideal, but the opportunistic exploitation of flukes, accidents, and imperfections. Though the model of the COED appears brutal – to depend on the robustness and primitiveness of its parts – the paradox is that it is, in fact, whole to reassert the equilibrium of complementary extremes."[22] In other words, this new form of urbanism demands a continual process of measurement and regulation, whereby the regulation consists of ad hoc interventions based on studies that resemble marketing research. The Shopping project was presented in a less conspicuous form in context of the exhibition Cities on the Move. The catalogue text – presented separately from OMA's contribution on "hyperbuilding" – consisted of 198 bibliographic references related to shopping, a collage of photos of shopping malls, and a collage of sections of large shopping mall projects in Seoul, Jakarta, Shanghai, Fukuoka, Tokyo, and Osaka. The motivation for the study of shopping derives from its status as an area which, according

22 Ibid.

23 Hanru, Hou, and Hans Ulrich Obrist. "Harvard Project on the City: Shopping." In *Cities on the Move*. Ostfildern-Ruit: Hatje, 1997.

24 Lootsma, Bart. "Rem Koolhaas, In Search of the New Modernity." *domus*, January 1998.

to the initiators of the project, has remained relatively invisible to the "official" architectural and urban professions, an area "with its own internal logic, language, velocities. In researching these logics, what is revealed is an idea of the city that is more prolific, more powerful, more efficient, and responsible for an exponentially greater percentage of urban fabric than the theories familiar to the professions of architecture and urbanism. Inherently mutable, parasitic, and resilient, shopping is proliferating to the point that it is becoming analogous to the development of cities – a phenomenon that finds a particularly uninhibited medium in the Asian city, where the vertical proliferation, sectional mutations, popular fascination and smooth pervasiveness of shopping supports the thesis that modernization must now be understood in Asian terms."[23]

Although few concrete results from the Harvard Project on the City have been published, it has already exercised considerable influence on the profession. For Rem Koolhaas, this influence – the way the designs call attention to new problems and approaches – is already in itself an important critical aspect of the project, one that appears to have been successful.[24] Exhibitions and publications on metropolises are projected in rapid succession for the coming years. Already in recent years, the Dutch Fund for Individual Subsidies has organized a series of study tours of Japan, Los Angeles, Brazil, and Southeast Asia, in which groups of 20 architects trace Koolhaas' footsteps. Such tours have already given rise to a series of lectures, publications, and exhibitions. Under Koolhaas' influence, the Berlage Institute in Amsterdam plans to devote itself to research in the coming years even more than previously, in particular to the comparative study of the Dutch city of Randstad, Los Angeles, and Tokyo. No less significant are the former colleagues from OMA as well as those with close ties to OMA, architects who have founded their own offices and are not only extensively pursuing "designing research," but are cultivating research as an independent activity as well.

Datascapes

An example of one such office is MVRDV. It continues the designing research/researching design methods introduced by OMA, where Winy Maas and Jacob van Rijs both worked for some time. In the design process, MVRDV draws up a precise inventory of all codes, laws, regulations, and desires that influence the design. All these factors are also visualized in spatial containers superimposed on one another, creating

25 Maas, Winy, Jacob Van Rijs, and Richard Koek, eds. *MVRDV – FARMAX: Excursions on Density*. Rotterdam: 010 Publishers, 1998.

an abstract form that defines the outer limits of the design. Subsequently, the office proposes spatial concepts, and wherever possible negotiations take place with the various parties involved. In this way, the design gradually develops. To this extent one can speak of an expansion of what is usually referred to as "the site." However, MVRDV also pursues independent research that flows directly out of their working methods. The recently published book FARMAX, Excursions on Density offers a foretaste of this approach.[25] FAR stands for Floor Area Ratio, the relation between the total floor space in a built area and the dimensions of the building plot, while FARMAX refers to a series of studies on maximum-density building, i.e. building that accommodates the maximum number of persons within a limited area. Maximum density is often defined and limited at least partially by legislation, building regulations, and profitability calculations. FARMAX presents a series of examples from MVRDV's own office, a series of projects and studies based on the methodology of "datascapes" as developed by MVRDV, to which their next book, due out in the coming year, will be devoted.

Datascapes are visual representations of all the quantifiable forces that can influence or even define and control the architect's work. These influences could be planning and building regulations, technical constraints, natural conditions such as sun and wind, but it could just as well be jurisprudence, for example about minimum working conditions, or political pressure from interest groups from both inside and outside the organization that provides the commission. Every datascape deals with only one or two of these influences and reveals their impact on the design process by showing their most extreme effects. For that reason, normally a site contains more than one datascape. In studios conducted by Winy Maas at the Architectural Association School of Architecture and at the Berlage Institute, students developed such datascapes within a cubic city of 100×100×100 meters and a Floor Area Ratio of minimally 10, which is the equivalent of Hong Kong. Datascapes reveal the extent to which Van Lohuizen's dream – in which statistics and norms constitute the integrating factor of urbanism – has become reality. The dream has in fact been institutionalized and takes on tangible form at the moment of concentration of social life.

But datascapes are more than mere illustrations. They constitute visualizations of what the sociologist Anthony Giddens calls "expert" and "abstract systems": bureaucratic systems in which trust in the system is grounded in assumed expertise in a particular area.[26] The status of a person in one system says nothing about his or her status in another. Moreover, even the information of the various expert systems is debatable. Modern-day society is dominated by a multiplicity of such "abstract systems."

Market Democracy

Along with the striving for as free a market as possible and a minimum of state intervention, the new legislation will perhaps be characterized by deregulation, but also by the effects of protest procedures and the ability of individuals to register complaints against initiatives taken by the state or by private persons. State and industry reach agreements on production norms, while self-organized interest groups negotiate norms and regulations with both state and industry. In addition to state legislation, investors develop "laws of experience" based on economic analyses and prognoses, rules that to a not inconsiderable extent are definitive for the shaping of social life. All these parties use "scientific" research to support their arguments in an effort to make them as "objective" and convincing as possible. Opposing parties dispute each others' methods and findings; the only thing they share is their mode of presentation in series of numbers, statistics, and graphs. Even emotions, insofar as they affect decisions, are quantifiable – for instance, when arguments are made on a collective basis, as in the case of referendums, opinion surveys, and marketing research. With a certain amount of cynicism, one could describe this situation as a market democracy.

Quantification is the new language of this internationally prevalent political form. The computer is not only an appropriate tool for quantification, but transforms this language into an international standard as a means of communication. The new market democracy has consequences for everyone, but especially for architects and urban planners. Their field of activity has become increasingly complex, indeterminate, and unstable. Numerous parties are involved in the process of architectural or urbanistic design and realization. Some of them – the clients or their representatives, the municipality, the urban planner, the various technical consultants, the contractor, and subcontractor – can sit at the same negotiating table with the architect. Others exert their influence behind the scenes and turn up at unexpected moments, catching the architect red-handed, as it were. These can be the residents of an

26 Giddens, Anthony. "Living in a Post-Traditional Society." see note 13.

urban district or future employees of the client, utility companies, journalists, local politicians, or others involved directly or indirectly.

In addition, architecture also implicates a whole range of laws, norms, experiential values, and jurisdictions. Thence have enormous influence on architecture – greater, perhaps, than the individual architect or urban planner. What makes the datascapes so fascinating is that in many cases they actually generate schemes that seem to come close to something that might be called an architectural project. As such, they certainly have an aesthetic appeal of their own. Also, the method and the results sometimes are very similar to, for example, some of Greg Lynn's designs. Datascapes are not architectural projects, however. The difference is that in the case of Greg Lynn the input is chosen by the architect in order to produce a specific spatial or formal effect, whereas the datascapes are given, so that every architect has to work with them, if he wants to or not. "What makes datascapes wholly unlike the 'normal' architectural project today is their deliberate denial of the endless negotiation between competing forces, regulations, planning criteria also known as the planning-procedure by which all space is administered today; in the sense that Tafuri has written, a complex managerial task that largely characterizes the profession of architecture and defines its principal forms of labour."[27] The visualization of the often contradictory datascapes that play a role in a project provides the starting point for the process of negotiation with all the participants – a starting point that might finally lead to the project or at least help show what is possible if the architect wished to choose a different starting point.

The superimposition of the various datascapes relevant for a particular place – configurations that not infrequently have completely contradictory consequences – gives rise to a complex spatial structure that demonstrates not only the limitations, but also the possibilities and outer margins of the design. Moreover, as Detlef Martins puts it: "It is here at the limits of the possible that architecture must take a stand, at the point where the reasonable becomes unreasonable, the normal abnormal and vice versa."[28] Brett Steele, on the other hand, points out that the datascapes themselves might provide a way out, an opportunity more or less suggested in the name. He suggests that in the end, they offer a chance to deal with space as a kind of product, one that can be dealt with by appropriating the usual tactics of product design and marketing.[29]

27 Steele, Brett. "Data-Escape." Unpublished manuscript, lecture, AA-150, London, 1997.
28 Detlef Martins to Winy Maas, letter, 1997, unpublished manuscript, London.
29 See note 27.

In this context, the role of the architect undergoes considerable shift. Clearly, the architect has largely forfeited his erstwhile power and is no longer the visionary he might still have been at the beginning of the century. The architect's range of action appears to be narrowed to one of the following two roles: either he becomes an expert who offers designs or specializes in form – the role that Greg Lynn and a few other American architects appear to be striving for – or he attempts, through intensive cooperation and skilful negotiation with the various parties involved, to become a kind of manager, the last generalist in a society of experts – the role that MVRDV seems to have chosen.

THE STYLE OF CHOICE

1   Koolhaas, Rem. "The Generic City." In *S, M, L, XL*, by Rem Koolhaas and Bruce Mau, edited by Jennifer Sigler. Rotterdam: 010 Publishers, 1995.

"The style of choice", Rem Koolhaas writes in <u>Generic City</u>, "is postmodern, *and will always remain so*. Postmodernism is the only movement that has succeeded in connecting the practice of architecture with the practice of panic. Postmodernism is not a doctrine based on a highly civilized reading of architectural history but a method, a mutation in professional architecture that produces results fast enough to keep pace with the Generic City's development. Instead of consciousness, as its original inventors may have hoped, it creates a new unconscious. It is modernization's little helper. Anyone can do it – a skyscraper based on the Chinese pagoda *and/or* a Tuscan hill town." Koolhaas continues: "All resistance to postmodernism is anti-democratic. It creates a *stealth* wrapping around architecture that makes it irresistible, like a Christmas present from a charity."[1] In other words: Postmodernism has become the global vernacular in architecture an urbanism, our new folklore. How did this happen and how should we deal with it? Acceptance of the situation is only the first step in any therapy.

Whahappened & Whodunit

2   Canguilhem, George. *The Normal and the Pathological*. New York: Zone Books, 1991.

Indeed, postmodernism, as an architectural style consisting of collages and assemblages of building elements belonging to different historical styles, and including its derivative branch deconstructivism, has become the dominating style in the world in a similar move that made capitalism the dominant political and economic operating system. Wherever one goes, be it to the remoteness of the Inlay Lake in Myanmar, a country that tries to resist globalization with almost all means, or anywhere else: one is certain to find postmodern buildings. The current state of architecture seems to be torn apart between rarely brilliant and exceptional designs that stand out in their context and this context, whereby it is completely unclear, to speak with Georges Ganguilhem, what is <u>The Normal and the Pathological</u>.[2] Do these aberrations teach us anything about what is normal, does the normal actually define these aberrations or should we understand them as a drug, cure or therapy (a kind of acupuncture or homeopathy than)? It has become impossible to say. The work of the artist Dionisio Gonzalez, images and videos consisting of crude Photoshop montages of postmodern structures amidst shantytowns or vernacular architecture in remote parts of the world, is therefore hardly a caricature or a vision: it just brings the global status quo in architecture to a point as quasi an illustration to The Generic

City. In a world in which more than 50% of the people live in shantytowns – a percentage that is still increasing – it is clear that individual architectural interventions based on appearance – in whatever style – cannot really change anything to this situation and are doomed to appear desperately lost. Remarkable is the virtual non-appearance of the recent digital architecture inspired by Greg Lynn, Asymptote, KolMac and their more mannerist followers in this context. But when it appears, it appears in a similar manner as described above, as the Culture Village in Dubai proves. The real success of the digital age in terms of appearance until now is not to be found in the possibilities of generating new and unknown shapes, but in the worldwide presence and availability of images in the media, from printed media, film and television to Google Image Search, Flickr, Youtube and so on.

New developments in the media accompanied and supported postmodernism from the very beginning. First, at the end of the nineteen seventies, its success was boosted by the sudden drop in costs of colour printing. Overnight, architectural magazines changed their dull and grey appearance as full colour portfolios replaced grainy black and white illustrations of brutalist buildings and scenes of urban decay. In the midst of a severe economic crisis, architects previously unknown and with almost no built work at all were enabled to publish their painfully detailed and carefully coloured pencil drawings and paintings. With the new presence of architecture in the media something changed in its nature. Architectures' traditional association with building became less obvious. "Architects don't build, they design", different architects and theoreticians like Robin Evans and Bernard Tschumi stated. However correct of course as an analysis of the division of labour, all of this had much further reaching consequences. Architecture became a communication medium itself in the first place. The question remaining only exactly *what* architecture communicates.

"For all their differences, the architects mentioned here, Moore, Venturi, Rossi, and Ungers, share a common goal. Not only do they want to present symbolic and typological forms in the foreground purely as a way of communicating content, they also want to use them as the material of fiction, allowing a building to become a work of art once again, a *fair illusion*." Heinrich Klotz writes in an article that appeared in connection with Die Revision der Moderne, in 1984 the opening exhibition of the Deutsche Architekturmuseum in Frankfurt and meaningfully the largest retro-

3 Klotz, Heinrich. "The Revision of the Modern." In *De Collectie: Architectuur 1960–1988*, by Herman Kossmann, Reyn van der Lugt, and Niña Bos. Utrecht: Veen Reflex, 1988.

4 Wigley, Mark. *Constant's New Babylon: The Hyper-architecture of Desire*. Rotterdam: Witte De With, 1998.

spective of postmodern architecture at the time and maybe even to date. "They play an essential part in bringing about a structure not of function but of fiction. (…) The motto of postmodernism, directed against the *builders functionalism* (…) can be summarized thus: Not just function, but fiction."[3]

How detailed the drawings of many early postmodern architects were, in many cases it hardly seemed to matter whether the projects were actually built or not. In this sense, the movement was in many ways an immediate continuation of the speculative drawings of the radical architecture of the nineteen fifties and sixties. Indeed, this early multimedia variant of the architect, as someone who draws, lectures, publishes, exhibits, makes films and lives from teaching has become the standard idea of contemporary practice, to such a degree even that Mark Wigley can call one of the forerunners of radical architecture, Constant Nieuwenhuys, an artist who was indeed one of the first to build up an architectural oeuvre solely consisting of drawings, paintings, models, multimedia installations, texts and lectures, a *hyper-architect*, as "Indeed, he took on and exaggerated so many traits of the architect's typical behaviour that he became more architect than any architect."[4]

But than, suddenly, at first almost unnoticed, the clones of the radical and postmodern architects, having seen the work of the earliest generation, started to build. Today, after the building boom of the last decades, they have sprawled all over the world. The results look as if they took the lessons from Las Vegas almost too seriously. Already at the end of the nineteen eighties, Dietmar Steiner could write in Baudrillardesque manner about the city on the occasion of the Heavy Dress project of Matteo Thun, an architect and designer, member of the Italian postmodern collective Memphis from the first hour, who in 1987 came out with a fashion collection for buildings and skyscrapers. "Real houses are no longer under discussion." Says Steiner. "All that we see are vague silhouettes. The over-fatigued eye has been conditioned by the vibrating quadrature of the screen, slow and meaningless images are eliminated without reflex. Only now and then does the eye stand still, interrupting its automatized speed, begins to see and stops for the beautiful dress. This is the situation when a skeleton risks its concealed skin. This is the Heavy Dress. That is our position today. This transformation, this suicide of houses has taken place with imperceptible speed. This is

5   Steiner, Dietmar. "The Heavy Dress." *Forum* 32, no. 1, 1988.

6   McLuhan, Marshall. *Understanding Media: The Extensions of Man.* New York: New American Library, Mentor Series, 1964.

happening in a unique conjuncture or architecture which was previously not possible. Architecture is in! The best architects are like opera stars, juggling with engagements and the planning of their agendas. The cities are yearning for the great magicians of their image who can be used in the advertising strategies of the *intercommunal competition*. Everything everywhere must be more beautiful because nothing can be improved anymore." Steiner continues. "Matteo Thun's Heavy Dress Collection is the first realistic answer to the present day and future role of representations in the city. It argues strongly for fashion. Fashion, the manifestation of the surface, liberates the representations of the buildings from their one-sided application and significance."[5] Today, with ever cheaper and energy efficient solutions to turn complete buildings into video screens, the facades fashion may enter a next phase.

The consequences of these developments can be seen in many of the works in the exhibition Insiders organized by arc en rêve in Bordeaux in 2009. Even in the buildings of Gramazio & Kohler und Hildundk, almost the most tectonic contributions to the show, we can see an emphasis on decoration and a certain pixilation in the facades – the pixels being replaced by bricks. But there is also a tendency in which buildings become more ephemeral containers for ideas. Anna Galtarossa & Daniel Gonzalez' Chili Moon Town Tour, for example, is a floating installation in the form of a city block formed by skyscrapers. "Chili Moon Town is a utopian floating city of dreams that knows no boundaries." Galtarossa & Gonzalez write. "It was born as a free city without frontiers. Its citizens do not migrate; the city itself migrates, carrying the dreams of its people." Speaking about the ephemeral, here is a surprising return of inflatables, the icons of the nineteen seventies, in MMW's Kiss The Frog Gallery and Raumlabor's Küchenmonument. There are also teams like Interbreeding Field, who with projects like Jello Maze again realize psychedelic multimedia environments to train us in dealing with the bombardments coming in through our *extended faculties*, as Marshall McLuhan would say, in the tradition of Haus-Rucker-Co and Coop Himmelblau.[6] Most certainly a next phase in architecture becoming a *fair illusion* are the parallel worlds in Second Life and the like. Stephan Doesinger's Bastard Space and Speedism's Whitehouseparadise are examples of projects that take these developments, including their superficiality and speed, as a starting point for further explorations.

From the nineteen nineties on, the increasing influence of new electronic media and the Internet, coinciding with the explosive growth of the world's population and the concentration of it in cities produces endless seas of built stuff, in which difference and differentiation are only perceptible on the spot but on a larger scale disappear in an endless sea of houses and buildings. In an installation representing the 800.000 individual houses the Dutch government was foreseeing to build until the year 2005, Adriaan Geuze demonstrated already in 1995, that with such quantities any attempt at individualization would completely dissolve. We can see similar things happening in the photographs Kai Vöckler took in Prishtina and the documentations of the rooftop buildings and river boats in Belgrade by Dubravka Sekulić & Ivan Kucina. Orientation in the new cites and megalopolises that emerge today is only possible with the help of Google Earth and Google Maps or Tomtom. Very different from the nineteen sixties and seventies, when the architects' main enemy laid in boredom and monotony created by the industrial housing production, today a similar boredom is produced on an even bigger scale by the desperate attempts of people – not necessarily architects any longer – to produce individual objects different from anything else. In his video Thinking Hanoi from 2009 Dionisio Gonzalez suggests the similarity between the sea with its waves and the city as a rolling back and forth in a constant movement.

"The Generic City is what is left after large sections of urban life crossed over to cyberspace." to quote Koolhaas again. "It is a place of weak and distended sensations, few and far between emotions, discreet and mysterious like a large space lit by a bed lamp. Compared to the classical city, the Generic City is *sedated*, usually perceived from a sedentary position. Instead of concentration – simultaneous presence – in the Generic City individual *moments* are spaced far apart to create a trance of almost unnoticeable aesthetic experiences: the colour variations in the fluorescent lighting of an office building just before sunset, the subtleties of the slightly different whites of an illuminated sign at night. Like Japanese food, the sensations can be reconstituted and intensified in the mind, or not – they may be simply ignored. (There's a choice.) This pervasive lack of urgency and insistence acts like a potent drug; it induces a hallucination of the normal."[7]

7 See Note 1.

Therapies & Strategies

The consequence of postmodernism being the worldwide default style is that it will never again be possible that any avant-garde will be able to reset the values in architecture and urbanism as a whole on a global scale in the way Modernism, and particularly modern architecture and urbanism, did. One may of course argue that even Modernism never managed to do so because, how successful it may have been, there were always and immediate counter reformations that favoured local and national interests, traditions and, not in the least, straightforward monumentality – modern architectures biggest enemy. Avant-gardes were replaced by stardom, merely in the service of the protagonists themselves.

Today however, after a period in which architecture had more resemblance with the culture industry than anything else and *starchitects* could come to unprecedented fame, stars fade quicker and quicker. Students in architectural schools have forgotten the names of Pritzker Prize laureates from just a few years ago already. Probably the most fascinating contemporary publication on architecture at the moment, the BLDG BLOG, hardly deals with this kind of architecture and if it does, there is no difference in the way it is treated in comparison to other articles on the built environment. Basically, BLDG BLOG shows that the built environment is just as fascinating and spectacular without starchitects or an architecture d'auteur.[8] Roland Barthes' demand for the death of the author, a position defended by the sword by many architects and theoreticians (who at the same time present themselves proudly on paparazzi – like snapshots casually folded into the highbrow Log magazine), is happening just by itself in the sense that signature architecture is drowning in the sea of images that surrounds it.[9] This architecture, the architecture that makes out Generic City, is therefore in many ways our new vernacular, our contemporary Architecture without Architects.

Thirty years after Laurids Ortner's essay we seem to need again something like a new "Amnesty for constructed reality". In 1978, after more than ten years of wild and fantastic experimentation with the Austrian collective Haus-Rucker-Co, of which he was a founding member, Ortner wrote: "The discussion about our constructed environment has become primarily a problem of aesthetic judgement. It is the visually perceptible criteria, far more than the factors of physical threat, which give us difficulty: what we

8 Manaugh, Geoff. BLDGBLOG. 2004. Accessed April 25, 2016. http://www.bldgblog.com/.

9 Barthes, Roland. "The Death of the Author." In *Image, Music, Text,* translated by Stephen Heath. New York: Hill and Wang, 1977.

10 Ortner, Laurids. "An Amnesty for Built Reality." *Forum* 31, no. 1, 1986.

11 Debord, Guy. *The Society of the Spectacle*. New York: Zone Books, 1994.

12 Baudrillard, Jean. *Les Stratégies Fatales*. Paris: Grasset & Fasquelle, 1983.

can generally observe as our environment is characterized by adjectives which, according to their level of sophistication, vary from emotionally loaded words such as *ugly*, *dreary* and *chaotic* to so-called objective terms as *inaccessible* and *monotonous*." Basically, nothing has changed since then: architecture is still mainly judged on its visible appearance. The only thing is that the postmodern regime seeded some more colour. Ortner's manifesto – like conclusion that "it will be necessary to accept the totality of this unpleasant reality and to deal with further development with an unprejudiced state of mind" and that "the trivial potential present here is the raw material from which the culture of the new epoch will be made", still stands.[10]

Koolhaas' The Generic City is a text written fifteen years ago as a "détournement" of Guy Debord's The Society of the Spectacle – including a treatment for a film at the end.[11] Instead of Debords complaints and critique, communicated in a depressive voice-over in his film, Koolhaas suggests, to "switch off the sound (...) and reverse the film". People now stumble backward, leaving the chaotic market scene that they had originally built up, "probably complaining, but fortunately we don't hear them". "Silence is now reinforced by emptiness: the image shows empty stalls, some debris that was trampled underfoot." Koolhaas style of critique is known as "hyperconfirmation", a "Fatal Strategy" in the words of Jean Baudrillard.[12] Still it is clear that for now Koolhaas wants us to forget about the market, capitalism and all artificial excitement that belongs to it and focus on essences that lay behind it and that may appear as a kind of temporary Pompeii – one of his all-time favourite references.

The architects exhibited in Insiders accept the new conditions in which architects have to work and their much more humble role in it to a large degree. They work with the raw material of the city and its debris in many different ways. Their style of choice is a choice of style as in choosing from a catalogue, choosing in a shop or selecting a television channel or website. Alexander Brodsky builds his Vodka Pavilion completely out of used windows, for example, and Richard Greaves manic production of totems and houses – that appear as a mix between Buster Keaton's house in One Week, Kurt Schwitters' Kathedrale des erotischen Elends and the architecture in the Kabinett des Dr. Caligari – seems to be completely built from waste and garbage. Harbour me, Celia!, the conversion of a Bavarian farm house by Peter Haimerl, takes up the Smithson's *As Found* principle by building the new house in the existing ruin.

The view the participants in Insiders have on the city is largely defined by perception through the media. Even the authenticity of the old farmhouse Harbour me, Celia! is presented in ironical photographs remembering of lifestyle magazines, with a woman reading a book in an uncomfortable pose as if she is praying and walking through the door as if she is drunk with a vase on her head. Fujimori Terunobu's Tagasugi-an or Too-High Tea house reminds, how poetic and fairy-tale-like it may appear between the cherry blossoms, of the Efteling, the fairy tale park in a forest in the Netherlands designed by Anton Pieck in the early nineteen fifties, that was apparently the inspirational source for Disney to build Disneyland. Thereby, the position of the Insiders is further and further removed from both the utopianism and the bitter criticality of the generations before them. Instead they display attitudes that range from euphoria and irony over therapeutic to a sheer acceptance or Gelassenheit. Their work shows indeed in many ways a kind of amnesty for both constructed and virtual reality.

Understanding and accepting a situation is the best starting point to begin working and improving it. Still, beyond the reuse and transformation of the everyday and beyond a general amnesty there are other layers that could and should be addressed. There are other fields that define architecture in which changes and improvements are very well possible, desirable and necessary: politics, financing, distribution, organization, in short: everything that runs megalopolis behind the scenography the postmodernist city presents us with.

Architecture and urbanism are not just about aesthetics and experiences but, in the first place, organize stuff, people and material in hopefully intelligent ways. There are however few offices in this exhibition that show an active and further reaching ambition in this field. Gramazio Köhler organize building process using robots. But they use them too much as a tool in the service of ideas or ideals of other architects – and often rather conservative ones – instead of really going to the bottom of what the computerization of the building process could mean in our society. Crimson seems the only practice with an interest in organizing the city on a larger scale and on a deeper level that involves urban planning, governance and everyday municipal politics. Crimson's attitude remains too ad hoc and curatorial, choosing different architects (NL, FAT) and urban planners (MaxWan) to achieve their rather eclectic goals. They present their WIMBY! IBA project in Hoogvliet in a panorama that shows striking similarities with Dionisio Gonzalez' photomontages.

Many of the offices in <u>Insiders</u> look at exemplary practices from the second half of the twentieth century, particularly the history of radical architecture from the nineteen sixties and seventies like Archigram, Archizoom, Ant Farm, Haus-Rucker-Co, early Coop Himmelblau, the Whole Earth Catalogue, Global Tools, Memphis and Alchymia. In all their playfulness, it is not probable however that they have the same investigative goals as their predecessors. There is a *retro* aspect in the countless quotes of radical architecture. They are drenched in irony and melancholy, the architects obviously realizing that radical architecture – whether it was carelessly positive or critically dark – appeared against the background of a period of naive optimism based on an unprecedented economic and technological growth that is forever gone. The first report of the Club of Rome from 1972 followed – and thus underlined – by the first oil crisis of 1973 put an end to it, thereby also largely ending the era of radical architecture. Today, we are even more aware of the environmental threats that were announced in that period. But with these quotes or radical architecture we can at least temporarily revive some of the hope of the period and withdraw in its comfort – or see if there are still hidden opportunities in it.

Conclusion

There are also new tasks and challenges for architecture and urbanism. The need for more sustainable lifestyles presents some of those. The others arise as consequences of the postcolonial era. Globalization does not just consist of increasing flows of people, data, money and goods all over the world. It also means that we cannot blend out the increasing percentage of settlements in the world that consist of shantytowns any longer. They are part – and with over 50% of the world population living in them a large an ever increasing part it most certainly is – of the context of architecture. Therefore it is unavoidable that architecture and urbanism will have to rethink their roles in the world, putting themselves in the service of the people who live there. Large-scale modernist housing programs, like they were still successful in Hong Kong and Singapore in the nineteen fifties and sixties, are not possible any more today because the immense investments needed. Looking at the increasing amount of quasi temporary camps in our cities – the refugee centres, the homeless sleeping in tents in Paris and in the

United States, the Roma in Italian cities, the victims of earthquakes in Italy and Turkey, the victims of Katrina in New Orleans; or looking at the explosive increase of informal settlements in Turkey and in the former Yugoslavian countries, etc., etc. – this context inevitably comes closer and closer. Retroactive legalisation of illegal and informal extensions of cities, as largely financed by institutions like the World Bank and the European Union, is an unavoidable task. It is however only the first step in the direction of another form of mental amnesty that will allow us to start working on them in proactive ways.

More than any other historical example, today Otto Neurath and the Viennese Settlement Movement from the period immediately after the First World War might help us to find new perspectives for dealing with this situation. In 1919, Vienna was in a desperate state and hundreds of thousands of families, both from outside the city and from the city itself, sought refuge around allotment gardens and in the periphery to avoid starvation by growing their own food. "For many observers of the city, these Zigeunersiedler or gypsy settlers were the ideal citizen-planners in that they relied on know-how and instinct, utilizing everything around them, from urban refuse to trees and captured prey, in order to assure their survival. They illustrated the power of community as an agent of urban reform, and as a force that had the potential for improving life in the metropolis more broadly."[13] The governing Social Democratic Party accepted and supported this movement from the beginning, as it knew it could never afford any collective infrastructure. As a key player in the Austrian Settlement and Allotment Garden Association, the Public Utility Settlement and Building Material Corporation (GESIBA), the Settlement, Housing and Construction Guild of Austria and later on the Research Institute for Gemeinwirtschaft, Neurath looked for Converse Taylor System, in which he tried to combine *bottom up* and *top down* strategies borrowed from industry.[14] As long as Neurath could, he maintained an economy in kind, in which people paid for their houses by performing collective duties, for example building roads. Architects like Adolf Loos, Margarethe Schütte-Lihotzky and many others were also involved in this ambitious and successful undertaking, which unfortunately disappeared into oblivion after the nineteen thirties, when Neurath and his friends were obliged to seek refuge outside of Austria.

13 Vossoughian, Nader. *Otto Neurath: The Language of the Global Polis*. Rotterdam: NAi Publishers, 2008.
14 Idem.

Information and communication, in the form of newspapers and exhibitions were a crucial aspect of Neurath's approach. Together with the artist and graphic designer Gerd Arntz he developed Isotype, a sign language that allowed communicating statistical data about the city – and later on about the world – in a simple and striking way, in order to make the citizens understand the complex organization of their city.

In Insiders, EqA's study of the PREVI Experimental Housing Project in Lima, Peru, one of the most ambitious housing projects ever realized, with the participation of famous architects like Aldo van Eyck, Charles Correa, James Stirling, Christopher Alexander, and Atelier 5, Candilis, Josic and Woods, among others, is the only project that consciously deals with such themes. EqA shows how, similar to the projects by Candilis, Woods and others in Casablanca in Morocco, the inhabitants continue building and expanding their property in the course of time once they have been provided with the basic house as a starting capital.

Communication may also be a key issue today. Whoever has visited shantytowns, has been struck by the immense amount of satellite dishes. Mobile telephones and mobile computing are, even if often still unaffordable for many, opportunities for the inhabitants these cities, as they demand far less investments in infrastructure than traditional communication systems. In these almost inevitably chaotic cities, GPS offers the next potential for orientation.

Innovations in production are still possible and necessary, if not necessarily only in the form of CAD CAM processes which, replacing mass production by mass customization, has retained too many of the values and goals of the industrial society. The improvised structures of textile industry in Turkey, with their just-in-time organization, seem to offer serious alternative for mass production in Asia.

All of his has not immediately to do with either the appearance of buildings and city quarters or with building styles. "There is a choice," Koolhaas remarks almost between the lines of Generic City.[15] Our style of choice should be a different lifestyle. It will hardly be a choice, by the way.

INDIVIDUALIZATION

Individualization

1 Beck, Ulrich. "Je eigen leven leiden in een op hol geslagen wereld." *ARCHIS*, no. 2, 2001.

From at least the nineteen sixties on, individualization has been one of the implicit, secret driving forces of the architectural debate. However, the perspective on this phenomenon has largely changed. In the sixties, seventies, eighties, and even largely today, individualization was seen as something that had to be achieved. The main task of progressive architecture was to find and create aesthetical and organizational differences or even to provoke them. Today and in the next decades individualization will become something that has to be dealt with, that has to be accommodated. That is a completely different program and we are already struggling with it. Some of the biggest problems in architecture and urbanism, like urban sprawl and the uncertainties about what public space is, are immediately related to individualization. But individualization is doing more than that: it is threatening the very nature of what we have learned to consider as Architecture (with a capital A) and urban planning. Now, in itself that may be not a problem, but there are some essential responsibilities and tasks in society that would have to be reshuffled, particularly in the field of urbanism and urban design. This is an enormous task ahead of us that is still taken too lightly, particularly by architects. It is such an enormous task because, as Ulrich Beck writes, "any attempt to come up with a new concept that would provide social cohesion must depart from acknowledging that individualism, diversity and scepticism are rooted in Western culture".[1]

What is individualization?

According to Ulrich Beck, together with globalization, the phenomenon of individualization is one of the greatest changes to have occurred in the western European society in recent decades and one that can be expected to continue in the foreseeable future. Globalization and individualization are related in many ways. To a certain extent, they are different sides of the same coin. Both are processes. Put very simply, individualization means that people are getting more individual – but you already guessed that.

As such, it seems to be something very nice, something that is right and something that has to do with freedom. In the Western world, we have all been raised to see people that way: as individuals, with equal rights maybe, but each with his or her own particularities. It explains our fascination for portraits, for example: not just the portraits of emperors and kings, generals and philosophers, but also the portraits of people as collected in exhibitions as The Family of Man, the portraits of people that we see in the newspaper and the portraits of our loved ones that we collect in our living room and on our desks. These photographs seem to convey emotions that we consider highly individual.

But, unavoidably, individualization also creates many smaller or larger conflicts, as it becomes very difficult to grant someone's individual freedom if it conflicts with someone else's. Than suddenly, we can use people's individuality in passports, police photographs, fingerprints, iris scans etc. for our security and for control.

These are however not aspects of individualization I want to talk about here, although many values that are attached to them most certainly play a role in the background. I want to speak about individualization as a sociological process, which means that I want to focus much more on human relationships and the way they are organized, because that is also where architecture and urbanism come in. In architecture and urbanism, human relationships are organized spatially.

One thing has to be clear: individualization does not mean people get more and more autarchic, even if this sometimes seems a goal. Individualization is much more about being part of multiple networks and multiple abstract and caretaking systems, as Anthony Giddens calls them.[2] It is because of this, because of the fact that people rarely use the same mix of networks, that individualization takes place. Media and mobility play a crucial role in this process. When we look at individualization this way, there are some enormous changes between the industrial society and the society we live in today.

Until recently, individualization seemed to be something to fight for. Wars were literally fought in the name of individual freedom. And I do not just mean wars in the name of capitalism. Left-wing intellectuals from the sixties and seventies also fought for individual freedom and they meant something very different.

But today there is also a difference, as we realize more and more that individualization is forced upon us somehow – be it by the soft seductive strategies of the media industry and politicians or by the economic and political forces that create migration. Paradoxically, the basis of individualization is formed by both the eternal desires for the dream worlds

2   Giddens, Anthony. "Living in a PostTraditional Society." In Reflexive Modernization: Politics, Tradition and Aesthetics in the Modern Social Order, by Ulrich Beck, Scott Lash, and Anthony Giddens. Cambridge (UK): Polity Press, 2007.

of freedom and the fear of poverty, starvation, and war. It is produced by prosperity and high levels of education that make people able to choose and to come up for themselves, just as well as by economic deprivation that tears people away from their traditional bonds, families, and communities. The neo-liberal market ideology forces atomization, with all political consequences.[3]

Reflexive Modernization

Political theorists as Antonio Negri and Michael Hardt[4], but also sociologists such as Ulrich Beck and Anthony Giddens view individualization as an unavoidable and necessary intermediate phase on the way to new forms of social life. They speak of a *First Modernity* that was linked to the effects of the Industrial Revolution, and a *Second Modernity* that is linked to such events as the emergence of the computer, post-Fordist production methods, biotechnology and worldwide communication and transport networks. While in classical industrial society there were direct interconnections between class, family, marriage, sexual roles, the division of labour between men and women, and architectural typologies – the factory, the station, the tenement block today, many more people have the opportunity or are forced to live biographies that deviate from this pattern: *doityourself biographies*, as Roland Hitzler has called them, or, as Giddens puts it, *reflexive* biographies. In this case, the reflexive element consists above all in the confrontation with the other. According to Beck, individualization also means "first the dis-embedding and second, the re-embedding of industrial society's ways of life by new ones in which the individuals must produce, stage, and cobble together their biographies themselves".[5]
It is interesting to note here, that Ulrich Beck, in the English edition of the book Reflexive Modernization that he published together with Anthony Giddens and Scott Lash in 1994, is still quite optimistic about the re-embedding of society and has a great belief in the self-organizing potential of the individuals. Beck believed that if society grew denser, people would be faced with problems that would force them to come up with new, collective solutions. As an example he mentioned the sign that Munich motorists can read at a heavily congested location: "You are not in a traffic jam, you are the traffic jam". He believed that this change of awareness would change collective behaviour, that people would organize themselves again from bottom up.[6] It was an optimism that corresponded with the attitudes and strategies some

3 See note 1.

4 Hardt, Michael, and Antonio Negri. *Empire.* Cambridge, MA; London: Harvard University Press, 2007.

5 Beck, Ulrich, Scott Lash, and Anthony Giddens. "The Reinvention of Politics: Towards a Theory of Reflexive Modernization." In *Reflexive Modernization: Politics, Tradition and Aesthetics in the Modern Social Order*, 1. Cambridge: Polity Press, 2007.

6 Idem.

7   Lootsma, Bart. *Superdutch – New Architecture in the Netherlands*. New York, NY; London: Princeton Architectural Press; Thames and Hudson, 2000.

8   Beck, Ulrich. see note 5, but than the edition of 1996.

9   See note 1.

10 Bird, Colin. *The Myth of Liberal Individualism*. New York: Cambridge University Press, 1999.

Dutch offices, like OMA, West 8 and MVRDV, developed in the same period, in which they confronted the Dutch society and politicians with the effects of their desires.[7] Beck was heavily criticized for his opinions and accused of being a neo-liberal. OMA and MVRDV are increasingly faced with similar criticism.

To my surprise, I found out that in the later German edition of Reflexive Modernisierung of 1996, Beck replaced his original text by a completely different one that is much more pessimistic in nature. In this text, Beck does not speak any more about the self organizational potential of the society. Instead, he is much more concerned about the side effects of the Second Modernity: social insecurities, lack of safety due to pollution, criminality, and violence, uncertainties caused by the belief in progress, science and experts.[8] In another recent text, Beck also speaks of risk-biographies and broken or interrupted biographies.[9] The way illegal immigrants live is a good example of this. It is certainly an example of self organization. But it operates literally in the margins or better: on the back side of the society and is linked to it in many ways.

Americanization

Individualization is often associated with Americanization and indeed the process of individualization in Europe seems to have speeded up after the collapse of the communist world in Eastern Europe and the fall of the Berlin Wall, as if Western Europe has suddenly lost its traditional counter-balance. The main goal of the European Union seems to be the development and expansion of a free trade zone that can compete with that of the United States. The ideological basis of the American political and economic system has always been liberal individualism. That is the belief that individual freedom in the sense of the guarantee of a private sphere and individual entrepreneurship go hand in hand and that instead of a strong state an *invisible hand* will regulate society in an *organic* way. However, as Colin Bird puts it in his book The Myth of Liberal Individualism, we can believe that society is organic, but that does not help us to make the numerous decisions we have to make every day in that same society. "If a jellyfish is organic, that does not give the animal the moral status that is generally attributed to people."[10] This argument particularly suits architecture and urbanisation. What nobody seems to realize is that the abolition of rules and laws only causes a shifting to jurisprudence, for everybody appeals to the judge or the media in every conflict.

It simply causes chaotic inequality in justice, and even stickier decision-making processes than we are already familiar with. Nevertheless, now that the decision making processes in the Netherlands are slowing down in the same period massive deregulation and privatisations take place, in a Pavlov reaction everyone still immediately points at the state and the government. These processes create a schizophrenic world that is paradoxically smooth and fragmented at the same time: the kind of food you would not like to eat.

But, even though aspects of Americanization do play a role in the process of individualization, what is more manifest in Europe is the crisis of the Welfare state and social democracy. In fact, one could say that it is the Welfare state itself that produces its own crisis. We are so rich and so well educated that the middle class has become the dominant class. It feels secure and now wants to capitalize on its own wealth.

Social democrats were never interested in a revolution. Instead of that they always propagated a better distribution of wealth in the society. Social housing, education, medical care and social security were used to give people a better starting position in a society that remained basically capitalist.

It is interesting to see how social democratic strategies don't work any more in a country like the Netherlands, as is demonstrated in the policies Armand Akdogan has investigated in Rotterdam. Immigrants that want to start their own individual businesses get a subsidy to renovate shops in the 19th century housing estates at the Binnenweg. However, the shops in the city centre are booming because bigger and bigger attractors create a flow of people from the Central Station to the heart of the shopping centre. At the Binnenweg, no such attractors are planned and there is a big gap between the Binnenweg and the Lijnbaan, the main shopping district. That means that the immigrants may start their own small businesses, possibly because the whole family works in them, but that at the same time the segregation increases – how proud the politicians may be of their multicultural street.

After the collapse of the Communist empire, there was never a real choice in Europe, as Slavoj Žižek writes, never a real free choice in the sense that the existing situation could be transcended. The inhabitants of the European welfare states may very well see the risks and side effects Beck is speaking about, but the politicians of the Third Way give them the feeling that they are strong enough to deal with them. Who would like to admit that he or she is really a coward?

11 Žižek, Slavoj. "Was kann Lenin uns heute über die Freiheit sagen?" In *B&K+, Political Landscape.* Proceedings. Cologne: Walther König, 2001.

12 Appadurai, Arjun. *Modernity at Large: Cultural Dimensions of Globalization.* Minneapolis, MN: University of Minnesota Press, 1996.

13 Deleuze, Gilles, and Félix Guattari. *Capitalisme et schizophrénie 1 : L'Anti-Œdipe.* Paris: Les Éditions De Minuit, 1972.

14 Boeri, Stefano, and Multiplicity. "USE Uncertain States of Europe." In *Mutations*, Barcelona: Actar, 2000.

Žižek makes a plea for a reinterpretation of Lenin's What is to be done?: to take the courage to make dirty hands again.[11] It seems indeed as if the politicians from the Third Way do not want to make dirty hands, but of course, in reality, they do when they produce the side effects Ulrich Beck is referring to, even if they manifest themselves in other parts of the world.

But, apart from scepticism on a more general level, individuals do organize themselves. If one thing has become clear, it is that individualization has nothing to do with the individual as a unique individual. I mean: the individual as a face, as a fingerprint or whatever. At best he is a DNA structure, in which the genes come from many different places. He is a moment in a landscape, as the complex individuals the anthropologist Arjun Appadurai describes. Appadurai uses many different approaches, but basically when reading his book Modernity at Large, the general impression of landscape paintings remains.[12] In the case of Appadurai, they have a kind of Biedermeier character, painted with warm overtones, describing Indian people that have become internationally successful and still maintain strong family bonds. It is not so difficult to see them in a different light as well however, as Romantic landscape paintings, with small, less successful individuals in front of, or surrounded by, a sublime nature, on top of a mountain that they have just climbed with great difficulty, near a ravine in which they almost fall, caught in the ice that has frozen an ocean. Whereby in the case of Appadurai the landscape is a complex construct of cultural, financial, ethnic, technological and many other overlapping and often conflicting *scapes* and the small figure in the foreground is a machine attached to different flows that he can connect to or cut off like the Deleuzian schizo.[13] In architectural and urbanistic terms, the many different case studies Stefano Boeri has collected in his Multiplicity/USE project for the exhibition and the book Mutations, follow a similar approach, just as many research projects the Berlage Institute has produced over the last couple of years.[14] Where Boeri focuses on territories, the Berlage Institute focuses more on the processes of organization themselves. These case studies demonstrate also that individuals do organize themselves in very different ways than they traditionally would when they were limited to a particular territory all their life. Networks of media and mobility increasingly allow them to do so, even across national borders, as Diego Barajas' study of the Cape Verdeans learns. Cape Verdeans have spread over the world, but the interesting thing is that the organizational structures that connect them are still very similar to those of the original islanders. There are a few larger settlements of Cape Verdeans, traditionally in larger harbour cities like Oporto, Lisbon, Rotterdam, Paris and Boston. However, what connects these settlements is their own system of banks, travel agencies, radio stations, magazines, hairdressers, music groups, etc. The music groups travel along the different cities, for example, like they would originally have done by boat from island to island. But also within the cities themselves the organizations, shops and institutions are scattered and linked like smaller archipelagos. The Cape Verdeans, like the Chinese do on a much larger scale, operate like a transnational community and almost like a transnational society. In the case of Ben Laden's Al Qaida network, we realize that such networks today can achieve a quite considerable political and military power; that they can transgress traditional spatial relationships and in the most extreme case can even destroy architecture.

Urbanism

Individualization means for the city that it is no longer synonymous with the spatial manifestation of one community with a clear – preferably hierarchical – structure. This means that one can no longer draw conclusions about the structure of a society based on the physical, morphological structure of a city like we used to do and neither can we expect that the traditional society or traditional forms of communality will return when we build the city according to traditional typologies. The city is no longer simply the enumeration of more of the same things and programs; it is the enumeration of many different things and programs. Many of these new programs are hidden within the existing, traditional structures, mutating and converting them from within. Indeed: the city is many cities and these cities are bound in many different networks themselves.

But, with the growth of the world's population, the consequences of individualization become most visible and tangible in the new parts of the built-up environment. Architecture and urbanism always dealt with how these things and programs relate to each other. But what happens to architecture and urbanism when they are torn apart between the small, intimate scale of the highly individual and the huge, abstract scale of global networks of media, mobility and economy? How do people deal with that? How do they organize themselves?

If I still use the word "city" here, it is just because better or more specific words do not yet exist. I would like to use it here in the broadest sense of "urbanized area". A number of smaller and larger communities find space side by side and in continually changing combinations in this sprawling, practically unbounded field. These communities are no longer defined here by their consistent spatial proximity within a limited territory. Increasingly, communities are formed by active conscious choice and by proximity measured in time spans. This goes beyond the half-baked and vague hints of something that is often referred to as the *multicultural society*, which, however well intended, invariably connotes the *invasion* of aliens from outside.

Instead of looking for difference, we will have to look for *sameness* again, but maybe on a very different level than we used to do. The analysis of the Royal Flying Doctors in Australia by Peter Trummer and Penelope Dean is a good example of this. The Australian Outback is a metropolis that lacks the traditional appearance of a city. The traditional infrastructure of roads and telephone lines is completely replaced by an infrastructure of airplanes and an open radio system. The city government is replaced by a huge caretaking system: that of the RFDS. But in the analysis of Trummer and Dean this seemingly shapeless city, this city that does not even seem to be a city, appears to have a very distinctive, collective form on a higher, abstract, virtual level. It is a form that can be visualized though and it can be altered by changing the parameters on different levels. That means it is a form that can be designed and is actually designed. The tools or means to do this are however radically different from the traditional tools of urban planning.[15]

Architecture

Instead of looking for new forms of *sameness*, over the last four decades or so, architecture has focused on finding all kinds of techniques to create difference. This was a reaction to Modern Architecture.

Modern architecture was – and is – blamed for causing monotonous quarters and cities, in which one couldn't even recognize one's own apartment, because they were all the same. After the Second World War, Modern Architecture that began as a liberating movement had become part of a system that was criticized more and more for being oppressive. In fact, it had become so much part of this system, that it was – and sometimes is – regarded as not only the perfect

15 Trummer, Peter, and Penelope Dean. "Time Sharing Urbanism." *Daidalos*, no. 69/70, Double Issue, December 1998/January 1999; see also "The Need for Research." *OASE*, no. 53 (2000).

symbol of this system, but also its most important tool. And, even though particularly during the eighties, officially the belief that architecture could change society was largely abandoned, architects of course secretly believed it could. From postmodernism to deconstructivism, this was the secret agenda of architecture. So, architecture had to be deconstructed. In terms of plans and sections, irritations had to be built in the form of in-between zones and unexpected confrontations of programmes that traditionally excluded each other. And if these confrontations were not forced, smooth, folding open plans were proposed on which populations could organize themselves more or less spontaneously.

Apart from these general approaches, in the architectural debate, individualization is almost solely discussed in relation to the issue of the housing production and the market. This debate is politically completely overloaded with ideological issues that are still related to the good old left-right debate from the Cold War. The arguments from the left are that individuals should have the right to live their chosen lifestyle against the disciplinary oppression of the *system* and to express their culture and creativity in their immediate environment. The arguments from the right are based on the liberalist-individualist position that is both related to the inviolability of the private sphere and on the basis of the economy in private ownership as the start of individual entrepreneurship.

No wonder that in countries that are ruled by politicians from the Third Way, like Great Britain, the Netherlands, Germany and soon Austria, the issue of individual home ownership is subject to *grandstanding* in which politicians can score easily. The most extreme case of this grandstanding and the political momentum it can create is without doubt the propagandistic debate around Het Wilde Wonen (Wild Habitation), as it was triggered by architect and former BNA-chairman Carel Weeber in the Netherlands in the mid-nineties. It was immediately taken up by politicians from the left like Adri Duyvestein, to break the power of the housing corporations and the building industry, and by his colleagues from the right like Secretary of State Remkes, to increase individual home ownership. The propagandistic aspect of this debate is given further profile by semi governmental cultural institutions like the Dutch Architecture Fund and the Architectural Institute, who encourage architects to develop seductive plans and images for individual houses. At this moment, there is an exhibition in the Netherlands Architectural Institute that for the first time in Dutch archi-

16 *Domestic Delights, The finest examples from the Nai's collection of house architecture,* Exhibition, Netherlands Architecture Institute, Rotterdam, October 14, 2001–January 27, 2002.

tectural history wants to show the great tradition of individual homes, whereas this was always considered only a minor or even politically incorrect issue. A market was even organized, where potential clients could find their architect.[16] Counterarguments, like they could still be heard in the early nineties, that this development would swallow large parts of the landscape and ruin the ecology, that it would create a new segregation and an increased mobility, have been almost completely silenced. In the next years, the percentage of homes that are to be commissioned by individual clients is to be raised to 30 percent of the total production.

Charles Bessard has analyzed how these new individualized quarters are produced in Almere. In fact, Almere is the city where individualization has been an urban planning and design strategy from the beginning. Driving through Almere one doesn't even realize one is in a city. Housing quarters are hidden from the road by dikes and bushes. They are separated from each other by dikes, bushes and canals. Almere purposely has no centre: there is a lake. The new quarters with individual lots are divided into simple themes: farm houses, traditional houses, and modern houses, as in the beginning sometimes a modern house in the middle of traditional ones caused a curse. As there is a shortage of plots, people can inscribe for a lottery. If they want a modern house, they inscribe for the modern quarter and so on. But because of the shortage, they also inscribe in other quarters. Thus, it can happen that someone who wants to build a modern house ends up in a quarter dedicated to farms or the other way around and has to use all kinds of tricks to more or less realize his or her dream. In the end, everything looks more or less similar of course. Bessard also investigated the real dreams the people had and discovered that they were always related to holiday destinations far away: a farm in Africa, a mansion in Scotland, an apartment in New York... It is painful to see than what really came out of it. In the end, what the building industry has to offer for the money the clients have is more than ever decisive for the final result.

Cultural Implication

In the cultural debate, one can see similar developments. We witness a shift from a policy in which Culture was written with a capital C and people were educated to understand this culture to a policy that tries to take different cultural expressions equally serious by distributing subsidies as broadly as possible. Again, arguments from the traditional left form a coalition with arguments from the traditional right, for both multicultural initiatives as well as commercial initiatives are supported. In this context, subsidies have become more like prizes, official governmental blessings of cultural initiatives. From steering devices, subsidies have turned into tokens that show that as many different initiatives as possible are officially recognized by the state or city government. Rotterdam is Many Cities, is the carefully chosen official slogan of the Cultural Capital 2001. Just as in the case of the new housing policy, cultural politics take the form of a general amnesty. I am OK, you are OK, as we used to say in the seventies. It is interesting to note however, that when we were to judge the Cultural Capital as an event that one would expect it to produce, be it in the form of unique events or in terms of something that is more than the sum of its parts, nothing seems to be happening that wouldn't be happening in Rotterdam anyway.

So, on an official political level, individualization is accepted and even encouraged and everyone seems happy. No one would like to be called an elitist, would one? No one would like to be accused of discrimination, would one? No one would like to restrict anyone's personal freedom, would one? But why then does this current policy seem so toothless and tasteless, why does it create such mediocre results in itself and why does nobody seem to be interested in the side effects? Antonio Negri and Michael Hardt write in Empire that "in this regard, Guy Debord's analysis of the society of the spectacle, more than thirty years after its composition, seems more apt and urgent. In imperial society (the current global society Negri and Hardt describe, B.L.) the spectacle is a virtual place, or more accurately, a *non-place* of politics. The spectacle is at once unified and diffuse in such a way that it is impossible to distinguish any inside from outside – the natural from the social, the private from the public. The liberal notion of the public, the place outside where we act in the presence of others, has been both universalized (because we are always now under the gaze of others, monitored by safety cameras) and sublimated or de-actualized in the virtual spaces of the spectacle." According to Negri and Hardt, and with a similar optimism Ulrich Beck originally had, "the end of the outside is the end of liberal politics".[17] That remains to be seen of course and remains unclear what kind of society they imagine will replace the current one. It will not simply happen by itself. This is exactly why, for now, it is necessary to investigate the phenomenon of individualization more deeply. Andreas Gursky's monumental photograph Montparnasse shows an enormous modernist apartment

17 Negri and Hardt, see note 4; Debord, Guy. *The Society of the Spectacle*. New York: Zone Books, 1994.

building from the nineteen seventies in Paris. The façade is a regular grid, reflecting the apartments inside, that all have more or less the same size and plan. A list of the names of the inhabitants shows that this building that was made for average French families of two parents and one and a half child is now inhabited by people coming from a wide range of different countries. When we look at the photograph more closely, we see that each inhabitant uses his or her apartment in a completely different way. In reality, the crisis of this kind of modern public housing is even more manifest and shows itself in a chaotic and kaleidoscopic mix of different lifestyles. Charles Bessard, who used to live in this building, told me that, because of the poor sound isolation, one is constantly confronted with the musical tastes of one's neighbours, a mix in a way not even the coolest Parisian DJ could achieve. Maybe cool, maybe annoying, but what this demonstrates at least is that individuals have the tendency to expand their private sphere beyond the actual borders of their private domain.

One of the case studies in the Mutations exhibition in Bordeaux examines a similar case. Here the modernist Italie or les Olympiades slab in the 13th Arrondissement in Paris contains a Chinatown that uses the building in an incredibly creative way, using the underground parking as a public space and market and the apartments for sweat shops and restaurants during the day and as sleeping quarters during the night. The elevators work overtime, connecting different apartments and functions within this city within a city; moving people, products and furniture quickly in order to escape from the control of the Parisian police. However, these examples are only part of the story. The real multi-cultural society develops just as well from within. In a text on the history of the Maaskantflat in Rotterdam, one of the highlights of the modern post-war reconstruction of the city, Adriaan Geuze[18] has shown enormous differences in the homogeneity and sense of community between the original inhabitants and those who have moved into apartments that became vacant in recent years. Here he is speaking not of people from different countries, but merely of mainly young people with a more individualistic way of life. If one visits the Donaucity and the Copa Cagrana in Vienna or the surroundings of Graz and Linz one can see similar phenomena happening. In all these cases, we can see the result of an aggressive individualism that nests itself in a parasitical way in the public architecture and urbanism that are so typical of the Western European welfare state. Very often, this individualism also manifests itself in an aggressive

18 Geuze, Adriaan. "Onze Flat." In *Over Rotterdam*. Rotterdam: 010 Publishers, 1994.

capitalist entrepreneurship that, in a seemingly paradoxical way, shows similarities with the mentality of squatters and hackers, that we always associated with an anti capitalist, anarchist attitude. Joep van Lieshout's AVL-Ville is the most radical expression of this tendency: an artist that has developed his practice to a larger firm that becomes a village that he wants to turn it into a Free State, gates and guns included.

We may be fascinated by this kind of developments and experiments, as we are fascinated by the vital processes of self organization in China, in Lagos, in the shanty towns in South America, Africa and India and by the Walled City, but aren't they just the larger flipside of the tendency that creates Common Interest Developments, the themed and often gated communities that the new rich middle class builds?

Individualization has far reaching consequences for the way in which we think about culture. This is currently being expressed chiefly in debates between the cultural relativists, who accept a variety of cultures (ethnic, religious, *high* and *low*) existing next to one another and value this variety as an asset in its own right, and the cultural pessimists who at the very least wish to preserve certain (*Western*) values and attainments that, whether they actually say so or not, they deem superior to others. Some say individualization has gone too far, others say it is not going far enough, because it is unavoidable that in the future, in a unified Europe and in general in a globalized world, individuals will have to take larger responsibilities.

The cultural implications of individualization, however, go farther than this debate. This is particularly true for those aspects of culture, such as architecture, urbanism and the visual arts, which take an effect in public space and in fact largely owe their legitimacy to the public sphere. After all, architecture traditionally mediates between the individual desires of a person commissioning a work and the public interest. Public art has to be understood by larger parts of the community. Urbanism largely creates the physical conditions for the public sphere. Sooner or later, therefore, the concept of public interest, some kind of sameness, will need to be reformulated. However this is increasingly difficult in a globalized world in which national borders become increasingly meaningless and therefore national policies become increasingly meaningless.

19 See the E-mail correspondance of Jonah H. Peretti with Nike about his wish to have a Nike shoe with "Sweatshop" embroidered on it produced for him.

Multinational companies seem to have found part of the solution in terms of the design of their products, as another photograph by Andreas Gursky (Untitled V, with Nina Pohl from 1997) demonstrates. The photograph shows a year's collection of countless different sports shoes in a PRADA vitrine. Originally, these shoes were made for particular sports, but nowadays people wear them to show an aspect of their identity and for the purpose of fashion. Basically, in a kind of democratization process, they have taken over the role fashion brands like PRADA used to have to enable people to distinguish themselves. Different brands of sports shoes carry many different styles next to each other. Today, only a few years after the photograph was made, most sports shoes are not even made with the purpose to use them for sports, but just to provide a cultural identity. At the Nike website, you can even design your own shoe – to a certain degree: Nike keeps the right to refuse some designs.[19] It is interesting that OMA's new PRADA shops use a similar strategy as Nike does in its larger stores.

Sooner or later, therefore, we will be forced to re-formulate the concept of public interest, a certain form of uniformity. In a globalized world in which national borders and thus national political initiatives become less and less important, this shall prove increasingly difficult.

What the long-term architectonic and urbanistic consequences of this will be is still open to speculation. Architects like Greg Lynn, Lars Spuybroek and Kolatan/McDonald develop ways to design, produce and market non-standard individual-ized housing types, in an attempt to use similar strategies as Nike does.

Even if they share certain common interests and charac-teristics, like the intensive use of the computer in the design process, the latest flexible production and marketing techniques and the relationship between architecture and the natural environment, all three of them approach the issue of individualized housing in their own way.

Greg Lynn has been conducting specialized research, both in his own firm (FORM) and at Columbia University, UCLA, and ETH in Zürich, into the possibilities of applying the computer-operated flexible manufacturing technologies that have been developed in the car industry to the construction of housing. In the car industry, it has long been common practice that a single factory is not limited to manufacturing a single kind of car. Instead, several different models and even different brands will be produced on the same production line. What is more, the models are entirely custom built to suit the wishes of the customer so that practically no two identical cars are ever produced. This production method requires the cars to have a more or less similar *genetic code*, e.g. an equal number of basic parts. This would also have to apply to houses: they would have to be composed of a standard number of parts. In Lynn's case, these are 2,048 panels, 9 steel frames, and 72 aluminium ribbings. If this condition is met, houses can be constructed in an almost infinite variety of shapes and sizes. Just as with cars, the construction of these houses is based on a self-supporting monocoque, thus the project's name is embryological housing. Sulan Kolatan and William McDonald (Kolatan/McDonald Studio) emphasize the marketing of homes. The various types they have developed are geared to the various existing lifestyles as seen on the American housing market, examples being The Golf Course House, the Hot Tub House, the Infinity Pool House, the Ramp House, the Bungalow House, and the Shingle House, but also allow the inhabitants to express their individuality within the given types. Like Greg Lynn, Kolatan/McDonald belong to the first generation of architects conducting research at Columbia University into the use of computers in architecture. They present their work by way of *product placement*, inserting them into commercials for various products as is the custom in the American film industry: the commercials remain the same, but somehow one of the Kolatan/McDonald homes has been inserted into the familiar suburban environment.

In the project entitled Off-the-road 5-speed created by Lars Spuybroek (NOX), the focus is on finding a new system for building an urban district that consists entirely of individual, different, industrially produced homes geared to various lifestyles and living arrangements but that still form a single unit in terms of urban development. In fact, the point of departure for the project was an urban planning problem: the original commission by the Stadsbeeld Committee involved designing an acoustic baffle. However, using a computer model NOX was able to show that a careful arrangement of houses, taking into account the way in which sound travels, would make an acoustic baffle unnecessary. The contours thus developed made it possible to create a district in which each building plot and the building shape on it would be completely different. The Trudo housing association liked this idea so much that they asked NOX to develop the plan further. The result is a district containing only individual homes that are nevertheless generated by means of a single design principle – that of the *fluid grid*. Research is still being conducted into the best industrial method for constructing these homes; however it seems at the moment that the project would only be realizable if many more houses would be constructed with the same machines to reduce the costs.

Very different from the period in which the nation states controlled the housing production and in which architects played an important role in the housing production, this kind of approaches is more and more marginalized. One of the things that have changed due to the process of individualization is that Architecture with a capital A will not be able any more to achieve the kind of power modern architecture had. The large bulk of the market production goes in a totally different direction. The fact that architects like the ones mentioned above will hardly play a role in that development is in itself not the issue. There will certainly be a niche market that is big enough for them to survive. The question is if the market system that we are collectively embracing really offers the individual freedom it promises. When we see Charles Bessard's analysis of Almere we can answer: no, not really. Lynn, Spuybroek and Kolatan/McDonald will remain the PRADA's of built production.

But how do individuals organize themselves in, be dependent of or link themselves with groups and how does this manifest itself spatially, in representation and aesthetically for example? What kinds of organizations are desirable and what kinds of organizations, like the aforementioned gated Common Interest Developments for example, are not? These are largely political decisions.

What role can architects and urban designers play in that process in the future? That is also a question that is very difficult to answer at this point. One thing is clear for me however: the real changes in architecture and urbanism we are looking for do not so much depend on individual design proposals by architects, as also these approaches become more and more individualized that they simply get lost in the quantity of proposals and realized projects. I think however that at a level of urban planning much more care should be given to bureaucratic measures than design. At least in the faster growing parts of the world we will simply not be able anymore to design and control everything.

But when we are able to simulate the growth of cities, as we can for example with models based on <u>Cellular Automatons</u> like the one Keith Clarke has developed[20], we should also be able to figure out where to intervene to avoid problems or to stimulate certain other developments.[21] We should be able to present these simulations to democratic bodies that can make a choice.

But also in architecture, a lot of care will have to be given to regulations, norms and new building technologies. New building technologies will have to be developed to answer the demand for individualization and non-standard products. That is however not so easy, as the current regulations, norms and technologies were all developed during the rise of Modern Architecture. Technologies were often subsidized by nation states and the laws were implemented by the same nation states, within the social housing policies in order to reduce the housing shortage as soon as possible. That means that our current norms and regulations are intrinsically linked to the industrial production. They are intrinsically linked with standardization. If we want a different architecture and urbanism, large investments in the building industry will have to be made again. But who will make them? And why should they? Therefore architectural policies will be a crucial keyword for the next decades, but in a very different way than the policies we have known the last decade.

20   Clarke, K. C., S. Hoppen, and L. Gaydos. "Methods and Techniques for Rigorous Calibration of a Cellular Automaton Model of Urban Growth." In Proceedings of the Third International Conference/Workshop on Integrating Geographic Information Systems and Environmental Modeling. Proceedings of Third International Conference/Workshop on Integrating Geographic Information Systems and Environmental Modeling, 21–25 January 1996, Santa Fe, NM.

21   See i.a. Tack, Frank. "Emulating the Future. An Approach to Simulating Urban Growth for Long Term Planning and Policy Decision Making." Master's Thesis Berlage Institute, Amsterdam/Rotterdam, 1999.

THE NTH TYPOLOGY

THE TYPOLOGY OF THE AND, OR THE END OF TYPOLOGY?

The nth typology

The typology of the And, or the end of typology?

Traditionally, in dwelling, ideas about the collective have been
expressed in types, both on the level of the individual
dwelling as well as on the level of urbanism. Today however,
this relationship is not as obvious any more as it used to
be. In his famous essay The Third Typology, Anthony Vidler
distinguished in 1977 between three different kinds of
architectural and urban typologies. First there is one, dating
from the 18th century, that tries to return architecture
to its natural origins. Laugier's primitive hut is one example.
The chaotic Paris of those times being a forest; the ideal city
would be a garden-making André le Nôtre, designer
of among others Versailles, the ideal urbanist. The second
typology, dating from the 19th century, belongs to the
industrial revolution. One prototype is Bentham's Panopticon,
a machine that produces behaviour. But also the buildings
themselves become industrially produced, consisting of
standardized parts. One might add to this that this typology
is also related to nature, but sees the emergence of ideal
types at the end of an evolutionary chain, that can be
speeded up by the machine and by industrial production.
"L'homme type a des besoins types", Le Corbusier wrote.
And so *objets types*, *meubles types*, and *maisons types* were
needed. In both of these typologies, there is a clear relationship between the whole and the parts.

The third typology Vidler distinguishes is very different from
the first two in that it does not take nature as a reference
in any way, but the city itself. From the nineteen seventies of
the 20th century, the city is seen as a whole that embodies
both its history and its presence in its physical structure.
This whole can be taken apart in fragments, *Urban Facts*,
as Aldo Rossi calls them, that can be types. These fragments
can be recomposed in many different ways. Thereby a
certain type can also be used for other functions that it was
originally designed and made for, just like what used to be
the Diocletian Palace in Split is housing a complete city
quarter today. However, this reassembling, as a conscious act
of design, produces meaning. First, derived from the
originally ascribed meaning of the fragment; second, derived
from the specific fragment and its boundaries; and third,
proposed by a recomposition of the fragments in a new
context. Particularly in Aldo Rossi's work this enabled
the architect to introduce critical and cultural comments, by
using typologies like the prison for, for example, a public

building. "The Dialectic is as clear as a fable." Vidler writes. "The society that understands the reference to prison will still have need of the reminder, while at the very point that the image finally loses all meaning, the society will either have become entirely prison, or, perhaps, its opposite. The metaphoric opposition deployed in this example can be traced in many of Rossi's schemes and in the work of the Rationalists as a whole, not only in institutional form but also in the spaces of the city." In opposition to the fragmentation caused by the elemental, institutional and mechanistic typologies of 20th century modernist architecture and urbanism, this typology originated in a critical position that wanted to stress a continuity of forms and history. It is this typology that is still most present today in Switzerland and Austria, be it in a milder, subtler and more nuanced way. This restraint also means that the critical suggestions that defined the buildings and projects of Aldo Rossi and many of his contemporaries have almost disappeared.

Today, thirty years after Vidler's essay, we can observe the fragmentation the Rationalists drew our attention to proliferating even further – particularly outside of the political borders of the cities. We know, at least since the analyses by Stefano Boeri, Arturo Lanzani and Edoardo Marini, as published in the book Il territorio che cambia, Ambienti, paesaggi e immagini della regione milanese, that we can certainly find certain new typologies crystallizing out in the new diffused urbanity as it is developing all over Europe. Some even more recent typologies – Common Interest Developments, Gated Communities, Holiday Resorts – also reflect new ideas about the collective. These ideas are however very different from those underlying the three typologies Vidler distinguished, which were – even if Vidler does not mention it – all related to the emancipation of new classes. In an intriguingly perverse way, the initially critical design method of Vidler's third typology, which plays with the cultural meaning of existing historical typologies, reappears here in the service of *theming*.

The crisis of the welfare state is a result of its own success. Programs of public housing, but also education, medical care and social security were developed to give people better starting positions in a society that remained capitalist in the end. This goal has been largely realized in Western Europe. Now assertive citizens want to capitalize on the starting position and seem to be prepared to take individual risks to do so, leaving the collective behind. Whereas in the classical industrial society there was an immediate relationship between class, family, marriage, gender, the division of labour and architectural and urban types – the factory, the railway station, the housing block –, today many more people have the opportunity or are forced to diverge from these basic patterns. These demand individual value for their individual money or they put it together individually out of existing material like real *bricoleurs*. Communality is organized and experienced in multiple networks that not necessarily manifest themselves spatially in an immediately visible way. Even if lately differences in income and wealth may increase, these developments put an end to large statistically more or less equal groups. This causes a crisis in collectively organized housing – and thereby to a crisis of dwelling in types.

It seems almost that the traditional cities are there for collectives and the former countryside for the individuals that build their own individual homes. It is intriguing to see that some of the more recent collective housing projects in cities in Austria and Switzerland react to that by offering more individualized forms of dwelling that at the same time have qualities that the potential inhabitants normally would find in the countryside. More in particular, these new typologies either relate to (living in) nature or reintroduce nature in new ways. Sustainability not only forms a strong argument for the collective aspects in these projects but can also become a generating principle for the design. Markus Pernthaler introduces different gardens inside his Marienmühle project in Graz. Miller & Maranta present their building in the Schwarzpark in Basel as a *tree-like* object and Splitterwerk not only camouflage their Black Tree Frog in Bad Waltersdorf completely with ivy, they even turn its interior into a mesmerizing artificial green garden. It seems that indeed, as Deleuze and Guattari predicted, nature and the city are folding into each other again in a process of *retroactive smoothing*. And, after a detour, typological thinking is back where it started: in the reference to nature, the park and the primitive hut.

THE NEW LANDSCAPE

The new landscape

A city is a plane of tarmac with some red hot spots of intensity.[1] Rem Koolhaas, 1969

1 Koolhaas, Rem. Unpublished manuscript, Architectural Association School of Architecture, 1969.

Thinking about the new urban landscape and public space and wondering where to start, I suddenly remember how, as a boy, I built my first crystal receiver. I must have been ten or twelve years old. It was a very simple device, built in an old cigar box from my grandfather, who also provided me with a pair of prehistoric headphones. I may be mistaken, but as I remember it a battery was not necessary. There were just the crystal, a long spiral antenna, a resistance, a potentiometer, the headphone and the wooden box to hide how clumsily everything was put together. You would put the headphone on, turn the potentiometer and you could hear all kinds of more or less vague noises from different radio stations. They would become clearer and faint away again. This produced a mysterious effect and it suggested that the sources were far away. The most stunning aspect of the experience was that they had always been there and that they had been there simultaneously. There were so many of them that the crystal receiver worked best at night, when most of the stations were out of the air. In the dark, intimate space under my blankets I would scan the air. It made clear that public radio, public space was everywhere and that you just had to plug in.

I don't know if ten year olds still build their own crystal receivers. I suppose it is boring when you can zap between at least twenty television stations or, if you are a whizz-kid, surf around Internet. Maybe the television did take over the role of the crystal radio. In the movie Poltergeist that is the case. After midnight, when the stations have closed and the adults have fallen asleep, the TV set functions like a crystal, receiving vague messages from another world. "They're here!", says the little girl with a strange fascination in her voice, something between triumph and resignation.

In David Lynch's film Lost Highway, all kinds of electronic devices seem to be bewitched as well. Video recorders start recording by themselves, for example, and cannot not only play back what happened in the past, but also what will happen in the future. The most stunning is however that a mobile phone seems to enable some people to be at different places at the same time, as the main character discovers when he is approached by a strange man at a party, who claims he has been inside his house. In fact, someone had been in his house, because he had received videotapes of the interior and even of himself and his wife, sleeping. But no one had broken in. "Actually, I am there right now" says the man, and invites the main character to dial his own number with a mobile phone right on the spot. Indeed, he is stupefied to hear the man's voice on the other end of the line. The man breaks out in a diabolical laughter.

Working late one night I had a ghostly experience myself. From the garbage can in our kitchen I heard strange noises. They appeared to be fragments of conversations on the police radio. When I opened the lid, the voices disappeared. When I closed it again, they slowly came back. At first I thought my neighbour downstairs, a district attorney, was following a police action he was involved in. But when I asked him the next day, he laughed at me of course, suggesting that I had watched too much television – which he in turn can hear from his bed. Months later it appeared that it was my other neighbour from next door, a lonely divorced housewife. Ever since she had to evacuate her house one night because the house next to it was on fire, she puts the scanner on at night, listening to the police frequencies. She sleeps lightly, but whenever the name of the street we live in is mentioned, she is immediately alert and puts her clothes on, waiting to be rescued. The dustbin in my kitchen must have worked as a kind of amplifier, very much like when you put a glass on the wall to be able to hear what people are talking about in the other room.

What is the point in these observations? First and most obviously, they are about how the media radically destroy the traditional urban and architectural spatial organization and notably the traditional distinction between private and public space. But secondly, they might also contain clues about a new, higher order of organization in the city. They are all about the paradoxical experience of both isolation, intimacy – the individual alone in its room –, while everyone is asleep, in a house surrounded by a vast darkness – and the awareness of the continuous presence of them, the others, far – or less far – away, trying to make contact, desperately trying to unveil their identity, to get in touch.

It is a slumbering awareness, but we share it all. Every one of us has this experience of jumping up when the telephone rings, even if it is in another room, in another house or on television. The disbelief and disappointment if it is not for you. To make sure anyone can get in touch with us anytime, we carry cell phones and beepers.

The radio and the television set function as media, as a kind of crystal balls, and the scanner is their institutionalized form. Still, at the same time, there is the disbelief and the doubt if they, the others really are or have been out there. "This program has been recorded in front of a live studio audience". If they hadn't said that, one would doubt if it had really happened. The laughter and the applause could have been dubbed in later, which often happens. The studio audience functions as a witness for the public at home. The police are the official, institutionalized witnesses that make it so fascinating to listen to a scanner: hearing about all the fears, the crimes, the uncertainties and getting an official confirmation that it all really happens – or not.

Here we enter the universe of Marcel Duchamp's Large Glass, in which the Bride in the upper part tries to draw the attention of the lonely Bachelors below by undressing herself, leaving the Milky Way behind, and the Bachelors in their turn desperately try to get in touch with her by means of the Oculist Witnesses.

The Large Glass has been used more often to describe, to find or to suggest a new coherence in urban life. It seems the only contemporary metaphor or myth that is complex enough to mirror the new complexity of the relations within the metropolis. As a metaphor or myth it possesses at the same time a schematic clarity and a desperate fuzziness, not in the least because it is unfinished. It offers a quasi mechanical hardware and a surrealist, disturbing software. Desire is the fuel of this Bachelor-machine.

Gilles Deleuze and Felix Guattari broadened the concept and the meaning of the bachelor-machine in L'Anti-Oedipe, the first part of their monumental study of Capitalism and Schizophrenia, of which Mille Plateaux is the second part.[2] They consider the schizophrenic not so much as someone who has problems with his parents – therefore anti-Oedipus –, but as someone who has problems with capitalist society. For the schizophrenic everything consists of processes that change one thing into another. They couple all kinds of processes like machines: production machines and desire machines. As opposed to these endless chains of desire machines is the "body without organs", that can't bear any kind of coupling any more. The bachelor machine is the model that links the two extremes of schizophrenic behaviour in a process of attraction and repulsion. It is especially this broader interpretation of the bachelor machine that seems suitable to describe the

2 Deleuze, Gilles, and Félix Guattari. Capitalisme et schizophrénie 1 : L'Anti-Œdipe. Paris: Les Éditions de Minuit, 1972; Capitalisme et schizophrénie 2 : Mille plateaux. Paris: Éditions de Minuit, 1980.

3   Koolhaas, Rem. *Delirious New York*. London: Academy Editions, 1978.

4   Lerup, Lars. "Stim & Dross: Rethinking the Metropolis." *Assemblage*, no. 25, 1994.

position and the behaviour of the individual inhabitant of the new urban landscape.

Rem Koolhaas, for instance, speaks in <u>Delirious New York</u> of the Downtown Athletic Club with its delightful sea breezes and commanding view, (…), an ideal home for men who are free of family cares and in a position to enjoy the last word in luxurious living, which means for example eating oysters with boxing gloves on, as a machine for metropolitan bachelors whose ultimate peak condition has lifted them beyond the reach of fertile brides'.[3]

Most recently it was Lars Lerup that used the Large Glass as a kind of underlying scheme for his fascinating paraliterary description of Houston at night as he sees it from his window in the article <u>Stim & Dross: Rethinking the Metropolis</u>.[4] Again, here is the sudden insight of an isolated individual, in the intimacy of his room, in this case looking out over the outstretched landscape of the city through the window, wondering what is out there. The room is a centre, but it is not *the* centre. Most important it is not the city centre, nor the centre of power. The individual observes, he is overwhelmed and is carried away. In fact Lerup describes an experience that reminds one of the experiences as they are put down in Romantic landscape paintings, like the ones of Caspar David Friedrich. With the difference however that the landscape described here is an urban landscape and that we still have this desperate urge to understand it in mechanical terms: *we want to know how it works*. The unfinished mechanical model of the Large Glass, with its sometimes hilarious and surrealist explanations, is not only such a desperate attempt, but *just because* it is so desperate it is also a metaphor for our misunderstanding, our missing the real point. It is an expression of our amazement and our agony.

In a kind of cartoon, Lerup attributes the names of aspects of the Houston cityscape to the different parts of the Large Glass. The Malic Moulds, for example, stand for the skyscrapers downtown. The chariot on which they stand he calls a <u>Chevy Suburban</u>, which is the typical car to cruise around. The bride is suspended in the air field, which is, according to the photographs that further illustrate the article, not only a sublime piece of nature, with sometimes heavy clouds and streaks of lightning, but which is also crowded by aeroplanes taking off and landing, heading for and coming from unknown destinations: the fourth dimension Duchamp refers to. The weather report is projected on the

5   Carrouges, Michel. "Mode d'emploi." In *Jungesellenmaschinen/Les Machines célibataires*, edited by Jean Clair and Harald Szeemann. Venice: Alfieri, 1975; See also Carrouges, Michel. *Les Machines Célibataires*. Paris: Arcanes, 1954.

6   Gibson, William. *Neuromancer.* New York: Ace Books, 1984; *Count Zero.* New York: Arbor House, 1986; *Mona Lisa Overdrive.* Toronto; New York: Bantam Books, 1988.

7   Bunschoten, Raoul. "The Skin of the Earth." *A + U,* August 1992.

bride's veil. The bachelors try to reach the bride by means of hitting golf balls on a nine hole course, much like Duchamp was using a toy cannon and matches dipped in paint. In the area below the Oculist Witnesses Lerup marks a place for car crashes. Because let us not forget: according to Michel Carrouges, a bachelor machine is "an uncanny image that transforms love into a death mechanism".[5] Lerup must have been aware of this aspect of the metropolis as he describes it, as the cover of the issue of Assemblage his article is published in, features a photograph of a stockcar race, in which cars desperately try to hit each other.

Rethinking the Metropolis means for Lerup in the first place changing a point of view and finding a new vocabulary. He introduces the terms *stim* and *dross*. Although his view of the new urban landscape is mainly dominated by the experience from the car, the introduction of these terms seems to have a broader importance. *Stim* comes from stimulation, as William Gibson uses it in his novel Mona Lisa Overdrive, where *stims* are a kind of mixture between the soap series we know from television and virtual reality. In the other books of the Neuromancer cycle, Gibson uses the term *simstim*, which is even more linked to computer technology and which makes the *stim* even more artificial, *simulated*.[6] But, as Lerup rightly says, the word stim also has connotations like *Stimme*, voice, and *Stimmung*, ambiance. *Dross*, on the other hand, is a waste product or impurities formed on the surface of molten metal during smelting, but it is also used in the meaning of worthless stuff as opposed to valuables or value, dregs.

With these terms Lerup offers a beautiful characterization of the new urban landscape as we can see it developing all over the world now. The idea of life as a bubbling hot metal with a dirty skin on it through which at some moments it breaks to the outside. It reminds us of the intriguing images of parts of a folding landscape Raoul Bunschoten isolates in his project The Skin of the Earth.[7] But again, it is also an image that reminds one of some of the methods Duchamp used to make de Large Glass: the dust breeding and the use of molten lead to fix it. Lerup seems to forget another crucial layer, however, which is formed by the media, but it can easily be understood as the vapours floating above this skin of *Dross*.

No need to say that most of our urban environment is Dross, Alike a television set tuned to a dead channel, to paraphrase Gibson again.[8] In a way it comes close to what Rem Koolhaas calls the Generic City, or maybe it is the ultimate experience of the Bigness.[9] We can also hear an echo of Guy Debord here, who talks in The Society of the Spectacle of the unification and trivialization of space due to the capitalist mass-production system that shattered all legal and regional boundaries, dissipating the independence and quality of places.[10]

But in this Generic City, Dross, Bigness or plankton, as Koolhaas sometimes also refers to it, in this endless addition of non-places, for the inhabitants it is the Stims that count however. They are somewhere out there and they have to scan them with all the electronic means that are available, picking out just the specific information they are interested in. In the heat of Lerup's Houston, the Stims are the cool spots. Places that are kept cool by means of a massive technological infrastructure, air conditioning and refrigerators. That is where people start to meet. It could be a bar or a restaurant, a shopping mall or an art party in a beautiful house. But when the party is over and the lights are turned off, the Stim becomes Dross again. "Like the surface of a lake during a rainstorm pocketed by thousands of concentric ripples", Lerup says, "the Metropolis is bombarded by a million Stims that flicker on and off during the city's rhythmic cycles. These Stims steam and stir, oscillate and goad, yet each specific Stimme, or voice, reverberates throughout the Metropolis in a most selective manner: the art party visited above draws a very narrow audience just as do the zydeco dance halls in East Houston. Both are essential, vital elements of the full-fledged Metropolis. The Stimmung, or ambiance, projected by each Stim is fully understood and fully had by insiders only. Although as a stimulus the zydeco dance occasionally draws a group of (slumming?) upper-middle-class guests (and they are graciously tolerated), they remain aliens, however touched and moved they may be by the dance and its inert stimulantia."[11]

In his programmatic text Accelerating Darwin, landscape architect Adriaan Geuze states that the difference between city and nature no longer actually exists: The new city is, in his words, "an airy metropolis with villages, urban centres, suburbs, industrial areas, ports, airports, woods, lakes, beaches, reserves and the monoculture of the high-technology agricultural areas".[12] The city has become an outstretched urban landscape. The city-dweller has changed too and he is

8 Gibson, William. Mona Lisa Overdrive. see Note 6.
9 Koolhaas, Rem, and Bruce Mau. S, M, L, XL. 1995.
10 Debord, Guy. The Society of the Spectacle. New York: Zone Books, 1994.

11 See Note 4.
12 Geuze, Adriaan. "Accelerating Darwin."
In Nederlandse Landschapsarchitectuur, tussen traditie en experiment, edited by Gerrit Smienk. Amsterdam: Thoth, 1993.

13 Geuze, Adriaan. "Wildernis." In *De Alexanderpolder: waar de stad verder gaat*, edited by Anne-Mie Devolder. Bussum: Thoth, 1993.

not limited to his immediate surroundings anymore.
In Geuze's vision he is not a victim of the situation, but he has adapted himself to it in an active way, he takes the situation in his own hands: "A minority of city-dwellers lives in a family situation. The city-dweller is not the pitiful victim of the city that has to be cherished and protected in a discreet and green environment. The city-dweller turns out to be a self-assured, exploratory individual, is extremely mobile, disposes over the achievements of technology and has access to several media. The surroundings do not always have to be adapted to the supposed desires of the city-dweller, it is he that adapts himself to his surroundings. The home is to the city-dweller no longer an individual world. He is continually changing his guise and surroundings, finds recreation on the Maasvlakte (an industrial area in the port of Rotterdam) and in the Alps, relaxes in dark alleyways, skims across the landscape, sleeps and works at various places and his friends and relatives do not live in the same street. The city-dweller makes use of the whole landscape, has several addresses and prefers to live in a water-tower, an old farmhouse or a warehouse rather than in a single family house".[13]

The image of the landscape corresponding to this is one with a pronounced differentiation of multiple densities and cultures. It is a landscape that until recently we tended to call the periphery, but which in the meantime has become so extensive that in this landscape the old town centres are no more than accents amongst others of equal worth.
As Adriaan Geuze has observed, the Maasvlakte is not just a forgotten industrial or port area, but it also houses an impressive family of orphans: "an artificial dune 25 metres high, that hides the oil drums facing the beach on the Hook of Holland, a uranium ore terminal, a shunting yard, a dozen experimental wind turbines, the sea inlet and the port dredging pump, a chemical waste dump, a container terminal, the explosives disposal service's explosion zone and a trout farm. The most bizarre set of structures is the World Disaster Centre, a site where copies of blocks of flats, a drilling rig, a train, lorries, a refinery, storage tanks, and suchlike are built and then set on fire with gas. Firemen and disaster teams train here 24 hours day. But that's not all. On holidays, masses of people flood to the area to practise new and adventurous forms of recreation: They see these sandflats as a practice ground for sledge dogs or for motocross, the dredging pump as a hang-glider slope, the rock dam as a source of fossils, the saltwater sand quarry as a place for deep sea diving".[14]

14 See Note 12.

According to Adriaan Geuze this neglected but very lively landscape holds the seeds for the future European city, in which the inhabitants no longer need illusions or stopgaps, but define their own exotic culture. Their behaviour can or need no longer be pre-programmed since it is based on anarchy, exploration, and self-expression. It is a landscape that comes close to Lars Lerup's description of Houston.

At first, the informal, seemingly chaotic nature of the dross and how the urbanites live in it in a kind of radical, almost situationist dérive, moving from one specific ambience to another, bring the action paintings of Jackson Pollock or even the piss paintings of Andy Warhol to mind. But again, it is not just the increased individual mobility that enables the urbanists to use their city in this way. They only know where to go because of the information they select from the media or that the media manage to shoot at them. It is the media that trigger the curiosity and generate the desire and it is the existence of many different media networks over each other that is crucial to understand that the schizophrenic behaviour of the urbanites is not as random and desperate as it seems and that actually new relationships and communities are formed every day.

Think about the homosexual community. Most of its facilities are still carefully hidden, almost invisible in the urban tissue. From the outside, they look like any other building and sometimes they even only have a back entrance in an alley. Once inside, one could expect the whole spectrum of places: from simple bars and restaurants, in which only minor differences with a regular bar or restaurant makes the place interesting for gays, to extravagant clubs and saunas with maybe even darkrooms or special SM-cellars, offering all the *stims* you could imagine. Nevertheless, how hidden and secret they may be for most people, if, as Jan Kapsenberg has analyzed, we would concentrate for example all Dutch gay facilities into one city, it would be as large or even larger than the city of Utrecht. And if we would use a more average density, they would even occupy almost the whole province of Utrecht.[15] Of course, if one has the nose for it, one might discover some of these places by simply drifting through the city or by hearing about them from a friend. But basically one needs a magazine, advertisements, a website or a special guide to localize the ones that suit ones particular interest. The Spartacus guide is for example such a guide that lists all the gay facilities with their particular features, gives their addresses and even small maps or route descriptions. Being listed in this guide is the first step in becoming a meeting

15   Kapsenberg, Jan. "Erotic Manoevres." Thesis, Berlage Institute, Amsterdam, 1998.

16 Ammann, Karl, and Giuseppe Mantia. "Nowhere,
Recommendations for the Analysis of Urban Reality."
Daidalos, no. 69/70, Special double issue 'Research',
December 1998/January 1999.

place for gays. One can imagine the lonely homosexual
that desperately tries to get the park in his neighbourhood on
the list. And in fact, these things happen. As a joke, some
gays wrote in a gay newspaper that the regular year market
in Bergen op Zoom in the Netherlands is a place where a lot
of homosexuals meet. Ever since it really is.

Think about techno-parties. They take place on specific
days, with irregular intervals and often in unexpected places.
Nevertheless, a refined system of flyers, distributed in
particular boutiques and record shops, attracts specifically
interested crowds of people each time.[16]

David Cronenberg's movie Crash is completely filmed in
non-places: on highways, car parks, looking out over an
immense intersection, on an airport, in a hangar and in a
deserted airport hospital, especially built to host the victims
of an air crash. One of the main characters, a stuntman,
even says he lives in his car. In Crash, the protagonists form
a very peculiar group of insiders that somehow find each
other. Most of them share the traumatic experience of a car
crash and they have discovered that they want to relive
this experience over and over again. In the movie it is
suggested that a car crash brings you even more close to
another person than when you are having sex, that dying in a
car crash is even better than an orgasm. Driving around
on the freeways in the Lincoln Continental Kennedy was shot
in, the protagonists constantly listen to a scanner that picks
up the police radio frequencies, in order to know where
spectacular fatal car crashes have happened and to be able
to get there as soon as possible. With voyeuristic fascination
they watch the wrecks and the victims, document them
with photographs in order to be able to re-enact the crashes
again, just as they do with the car crashes famous movie
stars died in and that made them immortal, like James Dean.
Here we are back in the universe of the Large Glass again.

The conclusion of all this is that the Metropolis is not
simply a matter of form or an addition of more of the same.
It is a mental state, a way of life and a new form of
community. A community that is formed by many different
communities. In the Metropolis new communities come into
being in places that no one would expect. Some of these
new communities do not even need a physical place.
On the Internet so-called Virtual Communities are formed in
which people are drawn together on the basis of shared
interests, ranging form child care to the Grateful Dead, from
political debate to electronic sex-chat. As Howard Rheingold

17 Rheingold, Howard. *The Virtual Community: Homesteading on the Electronic Frontier*. Reading, MA: Addison-Wesley, 1993.

puts it in his book <u>The Virtual Community, Homesteading on the Electronic Frontier</u>, answering the question what tempted him to log on to the WELL, the specific virtual community he describes, as often as he does: "There's always another mind there. It's like having the corner bar, complete with old buddies and delightful newcomers and new tools waiting to take home and fresh graffiti and letters, except of putting on my coat, shutting down the computer, and walking down the corner, I just invoke my telecom program and there they are. It's a place". Of course, Rheingold admits, "Many people are alarmed by the very idea of virtual community, fearing that it is another step in the wrong direction, substituting more technological ersatz for yet another resource or human freedom. These critics often voice their sadness at what people have been reduced to doing in a civilization that worships technology, decrying the circumstances that lead some people into such pathetically disconnected lives that they prefer to find their companions on the other side of a computer screen. There is a base of truth in this fear, for virtual communities require more than words on a screen at some point if they intend to become other than ersatz".[17]

In a footnote Lars Lerup says that "it is ironic that at the end of a century characterized by the most dizzying urban transformations in human history, academic readings (apart from writers like Banham and Koolhaas) and projects of the city (particular in post-war cities like Houston) remain haunted by the irrelevant ghost of the historically outdated European centre city. (...) The hegemony of the pedestrian, the plaza, the street and the perimeter block must be challenged not because the values they embody are no longer valid, but rather, because they are suffused with a set of fundamental misconceptions about the nature of contemporary civilization and its outside, leading to a false understanding of the whole. More pointedly, even the most sophisticated readings (and the occasional building) of the (...) city and its post-war extensions, whether haunted and paranoid (...) or openly nostalgic for the bourgeois pedestrian (...) are predicated on a more or less hidden positivity that, if fulfilled, would bring us community – or better, bring us back to the American version of the European city. Yet the City is forever surpassed by the Metropolis and all its givens (...)".[18]

18 See Note 4.

It is a misunderstanding to say that public space was neglected by the Modern Movement, as for example Rob Krier puts it in his book <u>Stadtraum</u> and Colin Rowe and Fred Koetter suggest

19 Krier, Rob. *Stadtraum in Theorie und Praxis.* Stuttgart: Krämer, 1975; Rowe, Colin, and Fred Koetter. *Collage City.* Basel; Boston; Berlin: Birkhaüser, 1984.

20 Giedion, Siegfried. *Architecture, You and Me: The Diary of a Development.* (Including Siegfried Giedeon, José Luis Sert, Fernand Léger, "Nine Points on Monumentality"), Cambridge, MA: Harvard University Press, 1958.

21 Sennett, Richard. *The Fall of Public Man.* New York: Knopf, 1976.

in Collage City.[19] Architects and urbanists have been struggling to give it a central position at least since the first World War: look at Bruno Taut and the Expressionists for example. After the Second World War it even became a central theme in CIAM. In the search for a New Monumentality Sigfried Giedion, José Luis Sert and Fernand Léger proposed an empty space in the core of the city. The (public) buildings and modern art surrounding it would function as scenery for whatever would take place there. Mass demonstrations, for instance, in analogy of the fireworks, water ballets and light – and sound shows that had taken place during the world exhibitions of Paris in 1937 and New York of 1939. Giedion already considered the influence of the mass media, such as radio and television, on public space, but he thought that the experience of communality as he imagined it could not be replaced by anything else.[20] He was wrong, as we know now. The most crucial change in Western society after the Second World War is the disappearance of the masses that would live in the streets and could suddenly organize themselves in a whole that could act collectively. The media, the increased mobility and the sprawling of the cities played a crucial role in this process. The only monuments where crowds come together that are built now are sports stadiums. And even the possibility to build the latter relies on mass media spectacles that are broadcasted all over the world, like the Olympics or the Soccer World Championships.

The problem about public space is not about the architecture or the empty space itself. Architects, with their fixation on their own discipline and physical spatial solutions, tend to put the cart before the horse. The problem was – and is – that it remains completely unclear what exactly would take place in this empty space. Therefore, hoping that when one would only return to a specific kind of architecture with a specific kind of public space the old sense of community would come back is an illusion. Society is always stronger than architecture.

Some critics, like Richard Sennett for example in The Fall of Public Man, see the source of the problem of public space in an narcissistic individualism that came up due to broad changes in capitalism and in religious belief.[21] To a certain degree this is certainly true, but again, the analysis is disappointing in its implicit longing for the reconstruction of a society that simply does not exist any more. The philosopher

22 Flusser, Vilém. "Nächstenliebe." *Kunstforum International*, March/April 1991.

Vilém Flusser on the other hand suggests that all this new technology of telephones and faxes is not so much a sign of alienation, but on the contrary the expression of the ultimate love of people for each other and their extreme desire to communicate.[22]

Therefore, to understand the contemporary urban landscape it would be much more interesting to study the rise of the new communities and what they might have to offer, what is so appealing about them and how they relate to new larger wholes instead of constantly talking about public life and community in terms of a loss of something that we are not even sure of what it was. The classical disciplines of architecture and urbanism are not enough to understand, plan and control this urban landscape and the behaviour of its inhabitants any longer. We need to understand the influence of the new media, not only to be informed and be able to avoid traffic jams, but also to know where we are and where we want to go. They trigger our desire. They tell us not only where to buy, but also where to meet and where to kiss. They are a crucial part of public space.

9 POINTS ON
PUBLIC SPACE

1: It seems that in the new urban landscape as it is now taking shape, there will be less public space, in the traditional sense, compared to the traditional European city centre. A series of shopping malls, frequently combined with indoor entertainment parks, parking garages, hotels, apartments, and above all, numerous restaurants and snack bars have entirely taken over the series of sequential streets and squares to which Rob Krier ascribed such enormous importance some twenty years ago in his book Urban Space.[1] If we were to be honest, we would even have to admit that the well-intended attempt to reconstruct Berlin's historical fabric of squares and streets will be buried under the increasing number of shopping arcades within buildings and underground.

The new urban space is not only roofed to the greatest possible extent, but also climate-controlled. And in the parts of the world where it is too cold or too warm most of the time, that is a blessing. Internal shopping arcades are not particularly spectacular or well-designed in and of themselves. Everything serves only to make the glut of articles in the storefronts as attractive as possible, and to maximize the area of rentable retail space. Only the stair-cases have been cautiously transformed into atria, sometimes even into sophisticated spaces dominated by a reflective or transparent escalator. The mezzanine is reserved for special product displays and for the oversized Christmas tree – sign of consumption.

But the actual spectacle occurs preferably in the lobbies and atria of the big hotels. John Portman is the champion of such spaces. His atria (he built three mega-hotels virtually side by side in Singapore's Marina Bay) occupy a middle ground between an intimate urban square, with various seating arrangements, bars, and fountains; a club; and a cathedral – a sociable and nonetheless really big cathedral at that. These are spaces whose atmospheres most closely approximate the broad maternal skirts under which children hide-only here, they are magnified several hundred times. "Close your eyes and imagine an explosion of beige. From its epicentre bursts the colour of vaginal labia (un-aroused), metallic, matte, eggplant, khaki-tobacco hues, mouldy pumpkin …"[2] In the atrium's midst, transparent elevators, at the forefront of technology, shoot up and down noiselessly like derricks. At night, they are aglow with golden light bulbs, and the atria are only dimly lit. You can usually hear the

1   Krier, Rob. *Stadtraum in Theorie und Praxis: an Beispielen der Innenstadt Stuttgarts.* Stuttgart: Karl Krämer, 1975.

2   Koolhaas, Rem. "The Generic City." In *S, M, L, XL,* by Rem Koolhaas and Bruce Mau, edited by Jennifer Sigler. Rotterdam: 010 Publishers, 1995.

muffled sounds of an orchestra in the salon. At this point, these spaces become unexpected hybrids of a night club and Piazza San Marco – as if in a dream.

Just how public these spaces in fact are, depends upon the deal cut by the city and the developer. Whatever it is that we are used to calling public space will become mainly transitory space, shaped and regulated by the traffic laws and the civil code. On the other hand, a vast new public space opens up parallel to the old one. Cyberspace needs design as well to allow us to navigate it – which poses yet another challenge to architects.

2: In those American and Japanese cities that seem to give an indication of how this new landscape will look, we see buildings become more and more introverted and isolated. I think it was Peter Wilson who referred to them as submarines floating in cyberspace.[3] Or better, as is the case with computers or other complex machines, there seems to be no relation anymore between the interior and its immediate surroundings. Spectacular public buildings like those in Japan by Philip Starck and Shin Takamatsu stand there like gigantic, enigmatic household appliances, independently plugged into the city's largely invisible infrastructure. They seem to be parked there temporarily. "With atria as their private mini-centres, buildings are no longer indebted to a particular site. They could stand anywhere. And if they could stand anywhere, why should they stand in the centre of the city?"[4]

3: Private homes are becoming more and more introverted as well. The reason for this is the scarcity of available land and subsequent increasing density in which we are obliged to build. The effect is visible in the new housing projects around Vienna and in The Netherlands. Another reason is of course that the home is becoming more and more just a base, where we sleep at night. When we are at home, it is dark outside. We don't gaze out the window then, we watch television. To see a pastoral landscape, we tune into the Landscape Channel. (The funny thing about the Landscape Channel is, by the way, that most of the time you tune in, it just shows a test image with abstract colour fields, like a simulation of a Mondrian painting or the Dutch landscape in springtime, with all the flower fields.)

4: Public space is literally the space left blank between buildings. It is ambiguous, permitting air and light to flow in between.[5] In Japan as well as in the United States, we see the rare, larger, public, or better, leftover space occupied by

3   See Verstegen, Ton. "Het tastende gebouw: de metaforische animaties van Peter Wilson. The Groping Building: The Metaphorical Animations of Peter Wilson." ARCHIS, no. 5, 1993.

4   Koolhaas, Rem. "Atlanta." see Note 2.

5   Toyo Ito in Roulet, Sophie, and Sophie Soulié. "Towards a Post-ephemeral Architecture. Interview with Toyo Ito." In Toyo Ito: Architecture of the Ephemeral. Paris: Editions du Moniteur, 1991.

fenced sports fields. In the US, they are used for basketball. In Japan, the green nets of the training centres for golf and baseball even dominate the skyline of the city. Sports seem to be the most important new reason for people to meet in public.

5: A public space will not necessarily be a beautiful square between public buildings in a city centre. It could equally well be a parking lot under motorways and railway lines near an important station. This year a design will be realized by Adriaan Geuze and West 8 Landscape Architects for such a place near the Sloterdijk Railway Station in the Teleport area near Amsterdam. It is a landscape for creative parking mixed with green areas planted with tree stumps which refer to the forest of concrete columns. A part of the tree stumps is made of cast iron and lit at night, which not only produces a surreal effect, but also enhances the strange artificiality of the situation.

6: Where we want to go in a city depends only on the specific quality and the amount of *Stim* a place has to offer. (*Stim* is a term introduced by Lars Lerup. It comes from stimulation, as William Gibson uses it in his novel Mona Lisa Overdrive, where *stims* are a kind of mixture between the soap operas we know from television and virtual reality. In other books of the Neuromancer series, Gibson uses the term *simstim* which is more closely linked to computer technology and which makes the stim even more artificial, *simulated*.)[6] Where we go has nothing to do with the fact that a place is public, semi-public or private. On the contrary: semi-public spaces like bars, restaurants, dance clubs, and shopping malls have gained importance in the city. In larger cities, complex semi-public networks are growing, which are used in a similar way to zapping through the different television stations. We use them intuitively and we are easily bored, constantly hunting for new, possibly even stronger experiences. "It is cool or it sucks," in the MTV-terminology of Beavis and Butthead.

The bars and discotheques realized by Alfredo Arribas in Barcelona illustrate this tendency perfectly. The interior of Network, a strange hybrid between hamburger joint, serious restaurant, bar, pool room, and discotheque, is inspired on the Ridley Scott movie Blade Runner. Another of his creations, Velvet, a mixture between nightclub, bar, and dancing, is inspired on David Lynch's Blue Velvet. The latter was so successful that a much larger version of it is realized now in an industrial area on the city's periphery.

6   Lerup, Lars. "Stim & Dross: Rethinking the Metropolis.." *Assemblage*, no. 25, 1994; Gibson, William. *Neuromancer.* New York: Ace Books, 1984; *Count Zero.* New York: Arbor House, 1986; *Mona Lisa Overdrive.* Toronto; New York: Bantam Books, 1988.

7   De Sola Morales, Manuel. "Openbare en collectieve ruimte. De verstedelijking van het privé-domein als nieuwe uitdaging." *OASE*, no. 33, Summer 1992.

8   Geuze, Adriaan. "Accelerating Darwin." In *Nederlandse Landschapsarchitectuur, tussen traditie en experiment*, edited by Gerrit Smienk, Amsterdam: Thoth, 1993.

7: Writing about public space in Barcelona, Manuel de Sola Morales states that it is important to connect these bars in some way or another with what we traditionally consider public space. This seems to be the only strategy to keep public space interesting and to help it survive.[7]

The Schouwburgplein in Rotterdam, designed by Geuze and West 8, is a large void on top of an underground garage topped by the city theatre, the concert hall, and a megacinema designed by Koen van Velsen. Geuze transformed the square into a gigantic stage. A quartet of movable, hydraulic lightning masts 35 meters tall changes configuration every hour. The general public can also change the position of the lights by inserting a coin. The lamps temporarily transmute the public space into a private territory. Whether inspired by one of the surrounding theatres or cinemas, momentarily, it is the theatre where they perform, and it could be the stage for marvellous scenes extending far into the night. Adriaan Geuze explains that "[...] new public space will manipulate its users to the extent that they will immediately be aware of their behaviour, that they can no longer revert to pre-programmed acts ... This space transforms anonymity into exhibitionism, spectators into actors. It is not a matter of design, of the beauty of dimensions, materials, and colours, but of the sensation of a discrete culture created by the urbanite."[8]

8: The same applies to public space and the media. In order to keep public space interesting, it has to be connected to the media. This makes me think of the biggest television screen in the world overlooking the square in front of the Shinjuku railway station in Tokyo. Although the Japanese don't have our tradition of public space, and the square itself is not uniquely designed, this is a most successful place for people to meet. Watching the television helps kill time. Toyo Ito's Tower of Winds in Yokohama seems to have a similar purpose, though the building is much more poetic in nature. In the oval tower that hides the airshaft of an underground shopping mall, thousands of small lamps flicker on and off, coordinated by a computer linked to sensors that react to light, sound, weather, and wind. It is an ephemeral image that, though reacting to natural sources, evokes the media nebula around us, making it suddenly visible. 220 Volt Electro Clips, a temporary installation by Christian Müller in the Museumpark in Rotterdam in the summer of 1995 combined aspects of both the Schouwburgplein and the

Tower of Winds. It involved a large wooden stage, surrounded by towers that projected both light and sound. The sound consisted of fragments of randomly selected radio and television broadcasts. By means of sensors in the floor, the public could play with the sound and the light, make it change and *move* in the space. It was extremely successful and attracted a large audience of all ages. With the latter, I return to the experiences with which I started this essay. Christian Müller's installation seems to be a kind of gigantic crystal receiver, one that can be enjoyed collectively while also serving as a stage for collective self-expression.

9: Only one thing remains to be said. If there is no place at hand for the activities or the Stims we are looking for, we use a place that was originally meant for something else, a leftover, and we just squat it or appropriate it. For city councils, the police, architects, and urban planners, this means, in order to survive, they must be extremely alert and flexible to the ways of life and the specific desires of small groups of people, not of everyone. Instead of designs based on top-down strategies that try to educate and reunite people and confront them against their will with what another small group of people considers to be *high culture*, it would be better to design places where the public can interact with the subcultures of their own choice and express themselves.

OF OTHER SPACES, (RE)VIS(IT)ED

ALL HETEROTOPIAS MELT INTO AIR

Of Other Spaces, (re)vis(it)ed

All heterotopias melt into air

A summary of the places appearing in Bas Princen's photographs has an effect which is strange and a little disturbing: a) muddy strips between a camping site and horticultural glasshouses in South Holland, b) a former production forest in Brabant which was also used as a military training area for a while, c) a canal which was intended for large ships but remained unused, d) a discotheque car park, consisting of former tennis courts, in the middle of a small village somewhere south of Nijmegen, e) a hill under which nuclear waste is buried, f) the sea, etc. Why should anyone care about photographing these places and compiling the results in a book? If we make a similar summary of the activities taking place in the photos, the effect is hilarious: a) people on motorbikes driving through the mud at high speed, b) people holding fishing rods and apparently fishing in a place where no water is visible in any direction, c) people sitting in a forest wearing strange masks and capes, d) people training cameras with long telephoto lenses onto an invisible bird, and so on.

They are enumerations that recall similar lists of seemingly disconnected entities in an unspecified text by Jorge Luis Borges, cited by Michel Foucault in his preface to Les Mots et les Choses as the inspiration for this imposing philosophical work. In that text, Borges quotes a "certain Chinese encyclopaedia" in which it is written that "animals are divided into: (a) belonging to the Emperor, (b) embalmed, (c) tame, (d) sucking pigs, (e) sirens, (f) fabulous, (g) stray dogs, (h) included in the present classification, (i) frenzied, (j) innumerable, (k) drawn with a very fine camelhair brush, (l) et cetera, (m) having just broken the water pitcher, (n) that from a long way off look like flies".[1] After allowing our laughter to subside, Foucault writes that in our amazement at this taxonomy, it becomes clear to us in one leap that what Borges' fabulous enumeration represents as the exotic charm of a foreign system of thought is actually a limitation of our own mentality: and that is something which is otherwise impossible for us to grasp.

Something similar is happening in Bas Princen's book Artificial Arcadias[2]. I do not mean only that I have noticed that when I present these images to people in lectures and tell them what is going on, it often draws a laugh; but also that Bas Princen regards his photos as architectural

1 Foucault, Michel. Les mots et les choses. Paris: Gallimard, 1966.
2 Princen, Bas. Artifical Arcadias. Rotterdam: 010 Publishers, 2004.

3 Rudofsky, Bernard. *Architecture without Architects: A Short Introduction to Non-pedigreed Architecture.* New York: Museum of Modern Art, 1964; Bernard Tschumi, *Advertisement for Architecture,* 1976

4 Foucault, Michel, see note 1.

projects, even though a feeling of incredulity that this could be architecture creeps up on us when we see this collection of photos. After all, hardly a single building appears in the photos, let alone a building with a certain aesthetic coherence or pretension. Perhaps these landscapes were once designed by someone, but now they are in transition to a new use and a new structure, or have simply been abandoned and forgotten; one can hardly speak of landscape architecture here. Still, maybe we could live with that. With Bernard Rudofsky, we could regard the spontaneous, informal structures we see now and then and which the people in the photos can themselves see, as a kind contemporary, minimal Western form of Architecture without Architects. Or we could appeal to Bernard Tschumi when he argues so convincingly that "Architecture is defined by the actions it witnesses as much as by the enclosure of its walls".[3]

Foucault notes that "The monstrous quality that runs through Borges' enumeration consists ... in the fact that the common ground on which such meetings are possible has itself been destroyed. What is impossible is not the propinquity of the things listed, but the very site on which their propinquity would be possible. (...) Where else could they be juxtaposed except in the non-place of language?"[4] It does indeed seem to be a similar sense of alienation that dominates the places and events we encounter in the book of Bas Princen's work. They are abandoned, orphaned places and events, *non-places* and *non-events* which at first sight seem to be devoid of any logic.

Naturally, there is a tradition in photography of photographers taking snapshots of unrelated subjects as a kind of anecdotes. We can amuse ourselves by thumbing through such books and occasionally pausing by some or other image that catches our interests. Perhaps we familiarize ourselves in this way with the photographer's personal outlook and style. But Bas Princen's photographs are not snapshots. They are meticulous compositions made with large-format negative cameras and printed in a large format. They are more akin to the branch of photography that seeks alignment with the landscape painting tradition, in which artists like Andreas Gursky, Thomas Ruff and Thomas Struth also belong. Princen's photos are allied to the Dutch landscape painting tradition of Ruysdael etc., with its wide perspectives, explicit horizon and cloud-studded skies. In the absence of hills and mountains, distinct places stand out within these empty, flat landscapes by virtue of a ray of sunlight or a different soil condition. Often we can see small, forsaken groups of figures in such places, while a distant church tower or windmill denotes the presence of organized human activity.

The concentrated photographic gaze of Princen's images enables them individually to elicit reflection. As a series, moreover, they research a theme which takes explicit shape through the act of juxtaposing the photos in a book. Collated as they are here, they challenge us to think all the harder about that integrating theme.

Foucault compares the taxonomy of Borges with the impro-bable constellation from the famous poem by De Lautréamont, in which a sewing machine encounters an umbrella on an operating table. What makes Borges' list so disturbing, he holds, is that now even the operating table has been whipped away from under it. He argues that it would be impossible to find a space that could contain all the elements enumerated by Borges, that there is no table in the sense of a clarifying framework – and that the very possibility of thinking and classifying is thereby annihilated. Only a Utopia, with its beautiful, smoothed-out spaces, could in Foucault's view bind the heterogeneous elements together.

In place of Utopia, Foucault introduces the concept of a heterotopia, which has a different way of combining diverse elements: "Heterotopias are disturbing, probably because they secretly undermine language, because they make it impossible to name this and that, because they shatter or tangle common names, because they destroy syntax in advance, and not only the syntax with which we construct sentences but also that less apparent syntax which causes words and things (next to and also opposite one another) to hold together. This is why Utopias permit fables and discourse: they run with the very grain of language and are part of the fundamental dimension of the fabula; heterotopias (such as those to be found so often in Borges) desiccate speech, stop words in their tracks, contest the very possibility of grammar at its source; they dissolve our myths and sterilize the lyricism of our sentences."[5]

Indeed, Princen's photos and the way they are combined in a book (the format, the binding) undermine the existing order of architecture and planning in the same way as Borges' enumerations undermine philosophy. They do so by showing unexpected activities and places, which nonetheless possess a surprising vitality that makes them hold our attention. They do not even pose the question of what style we ought to build in, for the spaces portrayed are totally styleless. Semiotics is relevant, if at all, only where it relates to the traces left behind by the activities. Perhaps a modern-day Sherlock Holmes could read and explain those traces, but for the rest of us they are plain puzzling. There aren't even enough different coloured Magic Markers to fill in all the different photographed activities on an urban or landscape planning map. These are activities that drive planners to distraction, as demonstrated by the maps meant to show the space to be reserved for leisure activities and nature in the Dutch government's most recent spatial futurology exercise.[6] The coloured squares are scattered with abject randomness and thus uniformly (what else?) across the map of the Netherlands.

Princen's photos nonetheless have nothing to with Borgesian fabulation. The places in the photos actually exist or existed, and the activities do or did take place there. That makes them perhaps all the more disturbing. Quite apart from the fact that Princen's photos function as autonomous works of art or architecture, their place in the architectural discourse could be not unlike that of the American grain silos whose photographs were reproduced in Wasmuth's Monatshefte, the photographs of aeroplanes and cars in Le Corbusier's Vers une Architecture, or the photos of metropolises in the lectures and books of such city builders as Van Eesteren and Hilberseimer. They confront architects, urban planners and landscape designers once more with the evidence of their own myopia – "des yeux qui ne voient pas" as Le Corbusier wrote. Now, however, it is not about the forms and technologies we are blind to, but new forms of human behaviour, organization and spatial use.

Michel Foucault developed the concept of heterotopia further in his famous text which has been influential among architects and urban planners, Of Other Spaces: Utopias and Heterotopias[7]. Whereas the goal of Les Mots et les Choses was using the idea of a heterotopia to break through the ostensible homogeneity of Western culture and "restoring to our silent and apparently immobile soil its rifts, its instability, its flaws", in Of Other Spaces Foucault interprets the metropolis in such a way that we can see this fragmented realm as one of opportunities and freedoms, as one in which *otherness* becomes a real possibility.

Of Other Spaces is about spaces which in a *primitive* society would be privileged, sacred or forbidden, and reserved for those in a state of crisis: adolescents, menstruating women,

6   Dutch Ministry of Housing, Spatial Planning and the Environment (VROM)/Rijksplanologische Dienst, *Ruimte maken, ruimte delen, Vijfde nota ruimtelijke ordening*, The Hague, January 2001.

7   Foucault, Michel. "Of Other Spaces: Utopias and Heterotopias." In *Rethinking Architecture: A Reader in Cultural Theory*, edited by Neil Leach. London; New York: Routledge, 1997.

the elderly etc. Foucault argued that these heterotopias were vanishing from our society although vestiges survived in institutions like boarding schools and military service for young men. They made it possible for the first manifestations of male sexuality to take place *away from home*. The deflowering of young women would similarly take place in an *other* space, in a train or hotel while on a honeymoon trip. Contemporary heterotopias may also be recognized in prisons, old-age homes and mental hospitals – indeed in all functions, also including burial grounds and hospitals, which modern urbanism has banished to the city outskirts. Of Other Spaces also notes the significance of gardens, which, like Borges' Aleph, are capable of juxtaposing the most unlikely of things. The text also refers to amusement parks and tourist villages as concentrations of intense experiences in a single locus. He describes motels as places where men can leave the world and their morals behind them to enjoy undisturbed illicit sex, but he also speaks of places with a specific, exemplary character where the daily rhythm was strictly regulated and planned, in contrast to the chaos prevailing outside, such as Jesuit colonies in Paraguay. "Brothels and colonies, here are two extreme types of heterotopia," writes Foucault. "Think of the ship: it is a floating part of space, a placeless place, that lives by itself, closed in on itself and at the same time poised in the infinite ocean, and yet, from port to port, tack by tack, from brothel to brothel, it goes as far as the colonies, looking for the most precious things hidden in their gardens. The ship is the heterotopia par excellence. In civilizations where it is lacking, dreams dry up, adventure is replaced by espionage, and privateers by the police."[8]

However widely separated Foucault's examples may be in importance and in distance, they coalesce to produce the image of a city: our contemporary metropolis. Des espaces autres is a text that reconciles us with the city – as it does Foucault himself, who previously savaged the metropolis in his writings as a disciplining machine. Suddenly it appears there are sanctuaries in the city. It has been suggested that Foucault was inspired to write Of Other Spaces by his discovery of the gay lifestyle in San Francisco with its clubs and SM dungeons. It was liberation to him. The freedom of movement of the ship where you can sign up, allows one as an individual or as a group to plot one's own course, to put together one's own program of activities and ports of call, to bypass others, and so stage one's own biography. This means it is also an optimistic text, and that is how several generations of architects and planners have interpreted

8   Idem.

it. To them, it was a liberating and perhaps even a visionary text, on that describes a city that has room for pluriformity.

Now, 35 years after Foucault's text, what we once called the city has turned into a huge, sprawling patchwork of heterotopias. Gated Communities spring up alongside Common Interest Developments, shanty towns alongside trailer parks, Megacinemas alongside peepshows, and so on again and again to far over the horizon. This is what Roemer van Toorn calls <u>The Society of the And</u>: an endlessly stuttering of and, and, and... But it is a stuttering which when viewed from a car or a plane looks like an endless sea where the crest of one wave is barely distinguishable from the next.[9] The architect appears in this Deleuzian metropolis at best as a surfer riding the waves – assuming he has the courage, like Rem Koolhaas, to claim such a heroic role for himself. But in any case we know that surfers spend most of their time lying belly down on their boards waiting for the next surfable wave, and then most of them surf only briefly before sinking back into the brine.

In his book <u>After the City</u>, Lars Lerup introduces the term *dross* to characterize the outstretched urban landscape of Houston. Dross is layer of scum that forms on metal during smelting, but is also used in the sense of dregs, of worthless stuff as opposed to valuables or value. Needless to say, in Lerup's vision and in accordance with Guy Debord and Rem Koolhaas, most of the urban landscape is made up of dross. But in this dross it is the *stims* that count. These stims seem to be a contemporary, smaller version of Foucault's heterotopias. Stim is a word Lerup came across in William Gibson's science fiction novels, where they are a kind of virtual reality version of soap series in which people can actually participate. But, as Lerup says, the word *stim* also has connotations like <u>Stimme</u>, voice, and <u>Stimmung</u>, ambience. Lerup uses this word for the unexpected and often improbable places where small groups of people start to meet and in which specific ambiences are created by technological means. The voices of these stims reverberate through the city by means of the communication media.[10] They cause people to move around through the city in a chaotic, almost situationist <u>dérive</u>.

There is a huge difference between Lerup's city and the ship, which Foucault describes at the end of <u>Of Other Spaces</u> as the ultimate heterotopia. City-dwellers do indeed use the heterotopias in the way that Foucault hoped, but the role of the ship has long been taken over by the car and the plane.

9   Van Toorn, Roemer. "The Society of the And (an Introduction)." *Hunch*, no. 1, 1999.

10 Lerup, Lars. "Stim and Dross." In *After the City*. Cambridge, MA: MIT Press, 2000.

11 Houellebecq, Michel. *De wereld als markt en strijd.* Amsterdam: Arbeiderspers, 2011; *Elementaire deeltjes.* Amsterdam: Arbeiderspers, 1999; *Platform.* Amsterdam: Arbeiderspers, 2002; *Die Welt als Supermarkt.* Reinbek Bei Hamburg: Rowohlt, 2001.

That's our way of surfing the world. The car takes us to the shopping mall and to the red light district. We can book an EasyJet flight for 15 Euros to some fabulous location where we can spend a weekend pigging ourselves and shopping for souvenirs and sex. The motel scene Foucault sketches in Of Other Spaces stood for liberation from the oppressive morals of the Sixties, but now it has evolved into spring break tourism with its bounty of self-indulgence.

The city Foucault described in Of Other Spaces, not long before May 1968, has long since turned into, which interprets the world in terms of market and battle, the world of the *Elementary Particles* in which, only temporarily and shame-faced, we can dream of a *Platform*.[11] In other words, it is the world of the author Michel Houellebecq and not that of Michel Foucault in which we now live. It doesn't matter if some or other activity is morally repugnant: there is no longer any metaphysics which could justify such a morality, and that is exactly what makes everything so joyless, uninspired and frigid. Looking at *other spaces* from Houellebecq's view point, isn't it no wonder that he polemically seeks the cause of the world's disintegration not just in capitalism, but above all in the liberation movements of the Sixties and Seventies which Foucault helped inspire.

Apart from being a set of ambiances, places, properties, fragments and fracture lines, today's city has become despite Foucault's attempt at characterization ever more a network of networks. It is not just a stable set of a limited amount of networks for traffic, drinking water and sewage, inhabited by uniform and stable communities, but an almost unlimited set of interfering networks of many different kinds, giving birth to and inhabited by even more different lifestyles and subcultures. Metropolitan culture and the urban way of life influence large parts of the countryside. Each of these lifestyles and subcultures uses the urban landscape in a different way. This certainly changes the use and the character of what we traditionally consider as public space, which is not necessarily the space where everybody meets everyone any longer. But these lifestyles and subcultures also produce bigger or slighter modifications and alterations to the urban landscape. Now, these alterations or modifications do not necessarily need to involve whole quarters or the rise of completely new typologies. The sometimes relatively small size and temporary nature of subcultures makes them look for niches in the urban tissue. More and more heterotopias arise. We can expect them to become increasingly outspoken and specific in the years

12 Foucault, Michel. *Surveiller et punir: Naissance de la prison.* Paris: Gallimard, 1975.
13 cf. De Tocqueville, Alexis. *Democracy in America.* New York: Vintage Books, 1990.

ahead, and at the same time more retiring and temporary, because their very multiplication makes them smaller. They seem subject to the same principle as affected power in Foucault's Surveiller et Punir, which completely atomized.[12]

The new phenomenon of an unprecedented high individual mobility enables people to travel larger distances and to go exactly to those places they want to visit. They know about these places and they know exactly what they want to do there because they have heard about them in the media: either because someone called them on the phone, because they heard about them on the radio, read about them in printed or electronic media, or because they saw them on TV.

These are the places and activities Bas Princen photographs. They may not seem spectacular, they may be ephemeral and the groups involved may not be so big, but on all photographs we see that people are involved or even immersed in them in the most serious way – even if they are having fun. It is as if we experience the next step in the cultural process driven by democratization as described by Tocqueville: it is not just a matter of the massive production of pulp, but now the pulp gets more and more differentiated.[13] The pulp fragments, splinters and finally evaporates, leaving groups of people involved in empty rituals without a temple or tabernacle.

What these people have are gizmos, as Reyner Banham called them in one of his best known books, which he published in 1965 just two years earlier than Foucault's Of Other Spaces. Perhaps the twenty-first century really will turn out to be the era of gizmos, even if Reyner Banham first noted the revolutionary role of the gizmo in twentieth century America. Interestingly, Banham also talks about surfboards, but in his case it is to demonstrate that every historical or ritual £aspect has vanished. Gizmos are point zero of design, and they can as easily be new patents as they can Baudrillardian simulacra. "The man who changed the face of America had a gizmo, a gadget, a gimmick – in his hand, in his back pocket, across the saddle, on his hip, in the trailer, round his neck, on his head, deep in a hardened silo", Banham writes. "From the Franklin Stove, and the Stetson Hat, through the Evinrude outboard to the walkie-talkie, the spray can and the cordless shaver, the most typical American way of improving the human situation has been by means of crafty and usually compact little packages, either papered with patent numbers, or bearing their inventor's name to a grateful posterity. Other nations, such as Japan, may now be setting a crushingly competitive pace in portable gadgetry,

14 Banham, Reyner. "The Great Gizmo." In *A Critic Writes: Essays by Reyner Banham.* Berkeley: University of California Press, 1996.

15 *Surveiller et punir,* see Note 12; Foucault, Michel. *Les Machines à Guérir.* Bruxelles: P. Mardaga, 1979; *Naissance de la clinique: une archéologie du regard médical.* Paris: PUF, 1975.

16 See Note 14.

but their prime market is still the US and other Americanized cultures, while America herself is so prone to clasp other culture's key gadgets to her acquisitive bosom that their original inventors and discoverers are forgotten – Big Kahuna mysticism aside, even the Australians seem to have forgotten that they were the first White Anglo-Saxon Protestants to steal the surfboard from the Polynesians, so thoroughly has surfing been Americanized. So ingrained is the belief in a device like a surfboard as the proper way to make sense of an unorganized situation like a wave, that when Homo Americanus finally sets foot on the moon it will be just as well the gravity is only one sixth of earth's for he is likely to be so hung about with packages, kits, black boxes and waldos that he would just have a job to stand under a heavier g."[14]

Although Of Other Spaces is primarily a philosophical and literary text, it comes across as rather nineteenth-century in comparison to that of Banham. Foucault's *other spaces* consist of walled-in fragments of the city – indeed, of buildings, which elsewhere, in Surveiller et Punir and Les machines à Guérir, he defines as machines because they produce a certain behaviour.[15] The ship that binds places together and makes space fluid is actually a rather clumsy, outdated machine for producing forms of behaviour. Perhaps Foucault needed that crudeness to highlight the fractures in thinking and in the city.

Unlike Foucault's hefty machines, Banham's relatively tiny gizmos ensure that the fractures will be overcome almost without effort. They transform the world into the smooth space that Foucault reserved for Utopia. So it is revealing that Banham chose a quote from Arthur Drexler as the motto for The Great Gizmo: "The purpose of technology is to make the dream a fact … The end is to make the Earth a garden, Paradise; to make the mountain speak."[16] Cars, motorbikes and speedboats are the vehicles which take over the role of the steamship in this *gas-powered pastorale* (Banham).

Gizmos, like Foucault's machines, produce not only the direct effects for which they were made but also behaviours. They are not only solutions to concrete problems and means of conquering barriers. Once a gizmo exists, it is so seductive that the user has to seek problems and barriers in order to use it. It is not a case of the biotope engendering a species; the gizmo goes in search of its ideal biotope. In this world, the *dérive*, walking through the city in an alternative fashion, in search of specific experiences in order to undermine the society of spectacle and the order imposed from above, has long ago been absorbed by capitalism. In <u>Of Other Spaces</u>, Foucault observes (but does not expand on the idea) that, since the sixteenth century the boat was simultaneously both the greatest instrument of economic development and the greatest reserve of imagination. The same applies now to the car, the plane and the communications media. The playful, footloose human of Constant Nieuwenhuys has become a reality – not because we have more leisure time but because we use what leisure we have more intensively.

We spend more and more on our leisure time. Globally speaking, the leisure economy now involves more money than any other sector. It is not only tourism for which people travel great distances in search of authentic, specific experiences, but more local leisure activities (not to mention recreational shopping) add up to a substantial mileage. The leisure industry produces every necessary and imaginable gizmos and gadgets to support these activities. They make it possible to venture into the most inhospitable areas, be they covered with snow, mud, rocks, lianas, sand or water. Because the gizmos are relatively small and barely intervene between the body and the environment, they make it possible to experience the body/environment relation in a more intensive way. Should anything go wrong other gizmos will snap into play to prevent a catastrophe, and the experience is preserved on camera for display to the home front, who must be seduced into following. The Camel Trophy exists both as a direct experience and as a TV programme.

These gizmos have long ceased being merely *functional* objects, insofar as that term might be considered applicable to leisure accessories, but are now predominantly objects that help the possessor to express his or her identity. Consider the huge, diverse ranges of trainers and other sports clothing sold by companies like Nike and Adidas, and now also by serious fashion houses like Yoshi Yamamoto, Dolce & Gabbana and Prada. The people who wear these products do so more often for everyday life activities other than sports. They have become an important part of the individualization process of Western society. They make it possible for people to live out their fantasies, even without the help of virtual reality.

A gizmo is not just a thing in its own right. Gizmos are tied up with much larger organizations and lifestyles (in the sociological sense, i.e. the way an individual organizes his life by means of institutions) than is directly legible from the object. They are linked into networks – which may be anything from networks of sales staff, service departments or filling stations to social networks and communication networks. And it is these last, in particular, that have proliferated so enormously since Foucault, Banham and Lerup wrote their texts. Wireless networks and satellite links make it theoretically possible to plug in anywhere in the world. GPS receivers moreover make it possible to determine your position anywhere in the world. The result is that the organizations behind the gizmos and the behaviour they produce are increasingly invisible to the naked eye. We see only the perplexing consequences, such as people who lurk in corners or walk along the street with a vacant, preoccupied gaze, while they emit loud, animated utterances. Are they just insane or are they talking to someone on a mobile phone?

These are the forms of behaviour the Bas Princen photographs. Perhaps it is no coincidence that he first studied industrial design and then architecture. To illustrate the difference between the forms of behaviour generated by the *old* networks and structures and by the new, it may be worth comparing Bas Princen's photos with those of the Austrian artist Walter Niedermayr.

Walter Niedermayr makes large photographic prints of landscapes that are used for leisure activities. In some cases they are rugged rocky terrain and sometimes snow-laden mountains. People appear only sporadically and sometimes only as tiny figures. In his photos of ski resorts they look lonely, pale and ephemeral against the white background, in a way reminiscent both of nineteenth-century romantic landscape painting and of certain groups of figures by the sculptor Alberto Giacometti. The people in Niedermayr's photos form apparently groups whose origin is unclear. Are they due to chance? Are they a result of local snow conditions on the piste? Are they clusters of friends? Only in an incidental example, such as the ski school in which all the children wear identical jackets, is there clearly evidence of a motivated pattern. In the background or margins of Niedermayr's photos, however, we always notice the infrastructure that facilitates these activities which are taking place in the supposed snowy wilderness: piste markings, ski-lifts, artificial snow, hotels, coaches, trains, lift passes etc. The cover of his book, <u>Civil Operations</u>, reproduces a map of a skiing area which shows pistes, shelters, funicular railways and ski lifts.[17]

17 Niedermayer, Walter. *Walter Niedermayer: Civil Operations*. Wien; Ostfildern-Ruit: Kunsthalle; Hatje Cantz, 2003.

The difference in themes of the photos of Niedermayr and those of Bas Princen may not seem all that great at first sight, but they exist nonetheless. Niedermayr is concerned with classic forms of mass tourism facilitated by major infrastructural interventions, but much though the tourists depend on artificial aids there is always a nature experience involved. In Princen's landscapes, on the other hand, there is scarcely if any trace of the magnificence of nature, and the range of leisure activities is much greater and more diverse. The activities in the photos by Bas Princen not infrequently involve practice runs and training sessions for skills which will seriously be put to the test during the one or two week wilderness holidays that the participants can permit themselves annually. For example, there is a photo of backpackers who have set out a marked route through a golf course and adjoining woodlands to practice for a holiday in the Scottish Highlands. The 4x4 enthusiasts have not bought their off-the-roader vehicles to surmount day-to-day problems (apart perhaps from the speed bumps, kerbs, roundabouts and other measures meant to stop them racing through the urban traffic at top speed); on the contrary, having purchased them, the owners have to hunt for suitable areas of terrain which will present a challenge. Exercises like these sometimes evolve into sports in their own right; such as the form of fly-fishing without water in which the aim is to cast a line as far as possible. The activities in Princen's photos are mostly simulations of sports which themselves originally developed as simulations of hunting, fishing and fighting. The gizmos are simulacra of fishing rods, spears and chariots.

The groups of figures in Princen's photos are much smaller than those in Niedermayr's, which, despite the lack of a visible infrastructure, have a much higher level of organization. They are classic examples of what the Internet guru Howard Rheingold has called Smart Mobs.[18] Smart mobs are new, spontaneous, ephemeral forms of organization that can exist by virtue of the ubiquitous wireless networks made possible by such technologies as WLAN, UMTS, GPRS or the ordinary mobile phone services. The 4x4 clubs have websites telling the enthusiasts where they drive their vehicles, complete with detailed descriptions, quality ratings and GPS coordinates. Similar websites exist for countless other activities. Birdwatchers can receive an SMS tipoff when a rare species has been sighted so that they can rush to the location with telephoto lenses cocked. This explains the flocks of photographers, alarmingly well hung with equipment, mustering around a subject which is completely

18 Rheingold, Howard. *Smart Mobs: The Next Social Revolution.* Cambridge, MA: Perseus, 2002.

19 De Ru, Nanne. "Leisure unLeashed, Morals and Meaning in Dutch Leisure Planning." PhD diss., Berlage Institute, Rotterdam, 2002.

20 Von Borries, Friedrich. "Die Markenstadt: Marketingstrategien im urbanen Raum." PhD diss., University of Karlsruhe, 2004.

21 Von Borries, Friedrich. "Welcome to Corporate-Situationism-Mainstream-Paradise." ARCH+, no. 168, 2004.

invisible in one of Princen's photos. Needless to say, the occurrence is a *stim*, as we now know. The draw is actually a tiny bird, so small that it is indistinguishable in the photo. So small, so specific and so rare has the authentic experience become, and so wholly has it been transformed into a media experience, that we must finally concede that it has practically vaporized and lives on only in the personal logbooks of the participants. Maybe it was one of those logbooks that inspired Borges to his enumeration.

Anyone who supposes this evaporation process also results in the dissolution of architecture and urban design must think again. It is just that it is not responded to by the traditional authorities – except perhaps the City of Rotterdam, which realized that the Maasvlakte was turning into a haven of new forms of leisure activity, and therefore provided the minimal infrastructure needed to turn it into a macho centre.[19] Companies like Nike and Adidas are foremost in taking advantage of leisure activities that have developed bottom up to launch new forms of marketing with urban development implications.[20] By setting up informal football pitches, subtly subsidizing new bars, organizing media events and sponsoring tournaments for alternative sports like xgolf, these companies reprogram the city. Both Nike and Adidas have also found new ways of communicating with their individualized public without even parading themselves as brands, which might otherwise frighten off the underground market. Such companies do so with a sound reason: it is individualization and differentiation that enlarge the market for gizmos and fashion goods. We may react to this disparagingly because they are large, commercial companies; but the reprogramming of the city on a situationist model has achieved an unprecedented enrichment and invigoration of what the city used to be. "Goodbye Baumeister – hello Traummeister", Friedrich von Borries has written. "The widespread retrenchment in aesthetic and technological respects does not relieve architects and planners from the consequences of a fundamental transformation of their field of work. They must accept the different conditions and demands more whole-heartedly, and search the present and future situation for opportunities to create the space for non-determined experiences. They should moreover take their leave of the moral and aesthetic rigorism of the Modern, and devote themselves to becoming the architects of everyday activity for the benefit of experience-consumers. Only then is there a chance of architects being clever enough to develop some or other tactic to facilitate freedoms in the future city."[21]

BLACK HOLES IN MEGALOPOLIS

I'm a believer. The Monkees
Rock my Religion. Dan Graham
The Medium is the Message. Marshall McLuhan

If we look at Houston, especially at the dramatic photographs of architectural debris by Bas Princen taken just after a hurricane, we are tempted to say, well, no, Megalopolis can't be any more than the sum of its fragments. But when we speak about a city and about urbanism, this literal fragmentation is not what we mean. Bas Princen's photos are rather a metaphor or a parable for another kind of fragmentation. Houston may be the ultimate capitalist city in the world, and capitalism is known to cause differences and fragmentation – also spatial fragmentation. One does not even have to be a Marxist to observe these phenomena in Houston in the social and racial segregation and the leapfrogging that makes this city sprawl. There is also ample literature on the fragmentation of the city in general.

There is some consolation of course. We could remind of Christopher Alexander, who already in the nineteen sixties, in A City is not a Tree, explained that the city is not a tree but a network of networks, with special, individual programs taking shape on every point where these networks touch or cross each other.[1] In our network society this should lead to an endless blossoming of special places. The Foucauldian solution would be to celebrate the heterotopia of heterotopias that we could find in this archipelago of fragments. But somehow both seem to easy a solution today, where we have so many collective risks and threats to deal with, inequalities to be resolved and desires to be realized. Lars Lerup has covered both the bright and the dark sides of Houston so brilliantly and seductive in Stim and Dross and other articles and books.[2]

It is our uneasy task to take risk and try to see further. I will do this by focusing on a topic that Lars Lerup has consciously avoided because he finds it too scary. And indeed it is scary, because it touches on aspects that sometimes unavoidably come close to historical examples of mass manipulation that have proven more than dangerous. But even if we try to forget about that, the topic is scary because it is about Megalopolis' equivalent of the universe's black holes in which everything disappears. It is scary, because, as in Edgar Allen Poe's

1   Alexander, Christopher. "A City Is Not a Tree – Parts I and II." *Architectural Forum* 122, no.1 and 2, April and May 1965, 58–62.
2   Lerup, Lars. "Stim and Dross: Rethinking the Metropolis." In *After the City*, 46–63. Cambridge, MA: MIT Press, 2000.

story <u>A Descent into the Maelstrom</u> we have to temporarily give up our resistance to come out of it; in order to understand it we have to become fans or believers. And why not? It is about everyday phenomena that are for the most part rather innocent: it is largely about leisure. But we will see how sports fans and believers can constitute a substantial communal force.

Astrodome

For better or for worse, in all its fragmentation, Houston is also a city that may give us some indications of how in the future megalopolises could become more than the sum of their parts. It may come as a surprise to many, but even if Houston is this endless, quasi-comatose city that for the most part consists of an endless sea of individual houses, shaded by what Lars Lerup has called a *zoohemic canopy* of broccoli-like trees, it is also the birthplace of some spectacular forms of collective life. The success of these new forms of collective life depends on a symbiosis between live and televised audiences. The buildings accommodating this new collective life are basically enormous halls that can accommodate events from baseball to football, from Wrestlemania to rock concerts and from demolition derbies to religious masses and victims of a hurricane. They exist in other megalopolises as well. <u>Palais /</u>, the magazine of the Palais de Tokyo in Paris, published a series of photographs that shows the different appropriations of the Superdome in New Orleans, for example, including the use as a shelter for hurricane Katrina.[3]

The original 1965 Astrodome still is the most striking example of such buildings. For a long time the biggest air-conditioned space in the world, this gigantic multifunctional building is at its versatile best during the Rodeo, changing the arena for calf roping, bronco riding or a country and western gig within minutes. Giant monitors ensure that the audience can see what is happening – even if it is far away, relatively small in size and happens in a few seconds like bull riding – because they enlarge, multiply and repeat the event, producing collective rushes of adrenaline. Media walls deliver all kinds of statistics that make the event even more exceptional. Sometimes they say: *WE WIN*, and we can't do anything else but believe it.

Looking for images of the Astrodome on the Internet, I was struck by what I assume was meant as a poster for the Astrodome. In a grainy black and white it depicts a heap of

3   "Superdome." *Palais /. Palais De Tokyo Magazine,* Summer 2008, 6–16.

190   Reality Bytes – Bart Lootsma

car wrecks in the center of the arena. Two ramps launch cars that crash in full flight, adding new wrecks to the existing pile. The text underneath reads Il Duomo, as if we are dealing with a religious building here.

The Astrodome changed the conception of multifunctional buildings and stadiums all over the world. Even if its role has been taken over by the Reliant stadium next door, the Astrodome, with its round non directional ground plan and movable tribunes defining the playing field, remains a quintessential building.

Lakewood Church

Houston also hosts the two largest television churches in the United States: Lakewood Church, a non-denominational Christian mega-church with an attendance of more than 43,500 per week on one location, and the Second Baptist Church, with an attendance of 23,659 per week on 5 locations, according to the Top 100 Largest Churches on www.sermoncentral.com. Preaching that material and worldly success is a path to immortality – the only possible way to overcome this Original Sin being hard work –, these capitalist churches may not be so different from larger corporations and are taken very seriously in Forbes for their exemplary marketing methods.

Lakewood Church is housed in the Compaq Center, a building that was never meant to be a church but a sports arena. It is the former home of, among others, the NBA's Houston Rockets. The arena has 16,800 seats. The pulpit is more like a theatrical or musical stage, with wide curving stairs to allow for spectacular entries. Three enormous video screens that show Joel Osteen, his wife and the performing bands and choirs in detail to the crowd, surround it. Bible texts that loosely relate to what is spoken about are blended in. The pulpit or stage is flanked by two quasi rock gardens that separate it from the audience. It is in this context that Joel Osteen challenges the members of his parish to discover the champion in themselves.

Lakewood Church makes use of the most modern com-munication media, from television to streaming Internet and addresses a whole range of specific target groups with special programs. It reaches over 90% of American households and 7.000.000 people in 140 countries. The televised collective trance in the church is transferred to the audiences at home. As an act of will, they can buy CDs, DVDs and books from the services. I understand that one of Joel Osteen's books was number one on the bestseller list of The New York Times.

Masses in Lakewood Church are more like rock concerts with large bands and choirs filling the stage-like pulpit. Scripture seems no more than a loose inspiration for Osteen's speeches, which come closer to motivational training than traditional preaching. In Houston, Lakewood Church is in many ways a second chance church that takes up and helps drop outs with programs that in welfare states would be organized under democratic supervision and financed by taxes. The question is how independent or vulnerable the people that Lakewood helps really are when they subscribe to its ideals. Even if Joel Osteen does not want Lakewood Church to be openly politicized, like many other churches in the United States are, this entrepreneurial form of welfare and the message that everybody can be a winner represents the real affirmatively capitalist political message of the church.

Rock my Religion

In his documentary Rock my Religion (1982–1984) and in an essay with the same title from 1985, Dan Graham already pointed out the relationship between American religion and rock music in an attempt, as he said, "to restore historical memory" by showing that history is still present today, even if it may be largely hidden or obscured "by the dominant ideology of newness",[4] In this complex film, consisting of found footage of both Shaker dances and rock concerts, text rolls and a narrating voice, Dan Graham points out the ambivalent relation between capitalism, or a puritan individualism, and communalism, which he sees as an unresolved conflict. "In the 1950s", Graham writes, "a new class emerged, a generation whose task was not to produce but to consume; this was the teenager. Freed from the work ethic so as not to add to post-war unemployment and liberated from the Puritan work ethic, their philosophy was fun. Their religion was rock'n'roll. Rock turned the values of traditional American religion on their head."[5]

Graham describes rock as "the first musical form to be totally commercial and consumer exploitive. It is largely produced by adults specifically to exploit a vast, new adolescent market whose consciousness it

4   Graham, Dan. "Video Related to Architecture." In Dan Graham: Selected Writings and Interviews on Art Works, 1965–1995, edited by Adachiara Zevi, by Dan Graham, 116. Rome: I Libri Di Zerynthia, 1996.
5   Graham, Dan. "Rock My Religion." In Rock My Religion, Writings and Art Projects 1965 – 1990, by Dan Graham, edited by Brian Wallis, 80–95. Cambridge, MA: MIT Press, 1993.

tries to manipulate through radio, print, and television. Rock, modelling itself after Hollywood, often took average teenagers or established non rock or pop music singers and molded them into charismatic rock'n'roll stars with manufactured cults of personality. But, ambiguously built into rock'n'roll is a self-consciousness that it *is* a commercialized form and thus is not to be taken totally seriously by the teenagers who listen to it."[6]

One of Graham's points was to explain how in the 1970ies artists like Patti Smith took this one step further to propose "rock as a new art form that would come to encompass poetry, painting, and sculpture (the avant-garde) – as well as its own form of revolutionary politics. (…) For a time during the seventies, rock culture became the religion of the avant-garde world".[7] Indeed, apart from much of Smith' own work, minimalistic compositions on rock guitars like Glenn Branca's The Ascension from 1981 still witness this. However, in a similar reversal, from the nineteen seventies on, churches tried to win souls back by introducing rock music and rituals in their masses. "Rock performers electrically unleash anarchic energies and provide a hypnotic ritualistic trance basis for the mass audience."[8] Pastors like Joel Osteen try to do the same with an overwhelming success, which is not so surprising as, in a way, the rock'n'roll ritual is *coming home* to a light, even ironical form of religion in which pastors like Joel Osteen may begin their masses with a joke making fun of ambivalence – as it actually has happened.

A Hillsong concert at Lakewood that one can find on Youtube – Hillsong is a Pentecostal mega-church, based in Sydney with extensions in London, Kiev, and other cities, but it's also a kind of rock band that scored a number one hit in Australia and is travelling the world – culminated in a part that comes close to techno music, underpinned with an impressive light show in bright white and blue light involving the complete audience. The excited audience reacts to it by showing the light of their mobile phones, producing a sea of small blue lights. The resemblance of this scene to a part of Dan Graham's film Rock my Religion, in which Puritans, encouraged by what is probably their pastor on a guitar, carry out a wild trance dance, lighting flames as media to show the presence of the devil, is striking.

The difference between the wild Puritans and Lakewood is not so much the difference in scale or between the simple shack and the climatized arena. As Joel Osteen sees it, there is not much difference in the communal functioning of

6 Idem.
7 Dan Graham, *Rock my Religion*, video, 1982–1984.
8 Ramirez, Jessica. "No Politics from This Pulpit." Newsweek Web Exclusive. January 25, 2008. www.newsweek.com/id/103290.

the church in his father's time, when it was in a simple warehouse, as today on a national scale.[9] The difference is the media involved from both the sides of the church and of the audience. Here, the media are definitely the message. "I am a big believer in the media," says Lakewood's pastor Joel Osteen, "That has always been my passion."[10]

Lagos

Lakewood Church may be the biggest television church – or rather: media church – in the United States, but it is not an exception. We find similar churches all over the world – and even bigger ones. In Lagos, Nigeria, a city that really makes us wonder if it is more than the sum of its parts, we find the Winners Church, also a radically capitalist church. "You know every business fortune is built on ideas." The pastor says to his congregation that consists again of thousands of people. "Every living soul is a business because life itself is a business. Jesus gave them talents and said: Do business with this till I come."[11] It is documented on the DVD Lagos Wide & Close, made by Bregtje van der Haak on the occasion of Rem Koolhaas' research in Lagos. Indeed, it is a perverse spectacle to see how during the mass dozens of volunteers collect envelopes with money from extremely poor people, which leave the church in enormous bags stowed into small vans. Koolhaas says about the Winners Church: "it fits in our project in making manifest the incredible scale of the city, the incredible capacity to organize and the incredible power of potential latency in Nigeria. If that can happen, the city can also decide in five years to completely reinvent itself. Of course the sad thing about winners is that there are also losers. I realize people are horrified by it but I think it is a really amazing and plausible thing for there."[12]

Maybe the lesson to be learned here is not in the first place about religion, but about something else. Maybe it is more about hope. And if we are even more down to earth we might say: maybe it is more about the potential power of advertising and marketing. And in general: maybe there is more potential in the media to reorganize the city than we have previously thought.

9   Dooley, Tara. "Spreading Its Word." *The Houston Chronicle*, September 26, 2004, sec. A.

10 *Lagos Wide & Close: An Interactive Journey into an Exploding City*. Directed by Bregtje van der Haak. Amsterdam: Submarine & VPRO, 2005. DVD.

11 Bregtje van der Haak, *Interview with Rem Koolhaas*, idem.

12 Ibidem.

Ruhr City[13]

So, let's go to Europe after this; let's go to the Ruhrstadt. I ask you to imagine a metropolis in the heart of Western Europe with an enviable strategic position. With 3.7 million inhabitants, it is one of the largest conurbations in Europe. It is a city with an excellent road, river, and air infrastructure. Several of the largest German companies are based here. It is the largest Turkish city outside of Turkey: one million Turkish people (whom, strangely, you do not see) are living here. There is an above-average level of education, particularly for Germany and the Ruhrstadt has many universities and colleges. It is a city where more money is spent on culture than in London or Paris, with museums, theaters, cinemas, concert halls, and cultural monuments. It is a real leisure city, where the relationship between areas for recreation and built-up areas is 50:50.

You can ski in the morning – even if only in Mark Girardelli's indoor Veltin's Alpine Centre – and spend the afternoon on a beach. It is a city with several large football stadiums and soccer clubs that have won more trophies than all the other cities in Germany combined. Churches are small and mosques are many but almost invisible. In short – it is a city that has and lacks everything one expects a successful modern city to have and lack.

But at the same time the Ruhrstadt it will never be a *city*: it consists of about twenty individual cities – among them Duisburg, Essen and Dortmund – and it is divided over three regions. The particular way in which in the nineteenth century cities started to grow explosively around and between mines and heavy industry produced a further fragmentation. In fact, more fragmentation is almost unthinkable. Yet it is one incredible unity. When you look at the place as a whole, on satellite images or maps, it looks totally amorphous, as if it is in a state of entropy – you can't distinguish one city from the other on a satellite photograph of the area. It looks like a Jackson Pollock painting. What comes closest to structure are the landscape, the rivers and the roads, the infrastructure, and, interestingly, the highway network.

In fact, the Ruhr region is not successful at all. It is shrinking at the same rate as the cities in the eastern part of Germany. It has a lot to do with the reputation it has. The image that most Europeans, and maybe even Americans,

13   *Ruhr City and Arena auf Schalke* are based on research on the Ruhrstadt under my guidance at the A42. org Masters in Architecture at the Academy of Arts in Nürnberg by Bruno Ebersbach and Philipp Reinfeld respectively in 2003–2004. See also Lootsma, Bart. "Ruhr City – A City That Is, Will Be or Has Been." In *M City: European Cityscapes*, by Marco De Michelis, 194–202. Cologne; Graz: König; Kunsthaus Graz, 2005.

have when you speak about the Ruhrgebiet is of a rural area whose farms have been ruined by a cruel industry, as in the famous photograph by Alfred Renger-Patsch from 1929. Of course, it's supposed to be always winter there. But if you zoom in on the satellite image, you will notice something completely different. You will see architectural fragments that have been carefully designed but lose themselves in the whole. And if you go down there yourself, it actually looks quite attractive, with a lot of green space. Viewed as a whole, it is a much more interesting city, or more attractive city, than you might think.

Arena auf Schalke

So, there is this city that has potential, but that also has this incredibly bad reputation. It is like German soccer, professional soccer, which had this exceptionally bad reputation in the 1980ies. It was violent; if you went to the games, there was always bad weather; etc. But all that changed when small commercial television stations started to do their broadcasting from the stadiums – even though they didn't have the right to the complete matches. They could only show fragments. The new media attention led to a stunning revival of soccer. A series of new and larger stadiums was built all over Europe, many of them with covered or indoor playing fields like their original example: the Astrodome.

One of them is the Arena auf Schalke, one of the most famous stadiums in Germany. You can see it from everywhere in the Ruhrgebiet as it is built on top of a hill, and from the Arena auf Schalke you can look over the complete Ruhr area. It was initially planned to be a kind of covered stadium, very much like the Astrodome, you might say, but they took it one step further, as soccer cannot be played on Astroturf and grass does not grow indoors: at the Arena auf Schalke, you can move the playing field outside. That means, just like the Astrodome, you can use it for all kinds of different events – a rock concert, an opera, a motocross, whatever. And like the Lakewood Church, there's this relationship to television and the media. The monitor in the Arena auf Schalke used to be the biggest television in the world. The whole building is actually a television studio and all bars and restaurants are styled like television studios because you have the interviews before, you have the interviews after, etc., in which the audience is at least an important background. But it is not just that: the audience has to get the feeling that they are part of a media event that its

members would normally only be able to see at home.
And for the audience at home, they are the witnesses that
the event really took place.

The buildings and programs discussed in this article
represent a general tendency: the same has happened with
such desperately different programs as for example
shopping and skiing, producing indoor shopping malls and
skiing. In the process that generates these buildings as black
holes in the city, there are different phases. In the first
phase, there is just the activity with a neglectable audience
that takes place in open air, with hardly any spatial facilities.
In the second phase, audiences become increasingly
important and the scale and spatial facilities increase. In the
third phase, media attention produces an interest to visit
and participate in the events. It also increases income from
advertising and merchandising. In the fourth phase, the
events move indoor to avoid the interference of the weather
and to be able to have a controlled environment suitable for
television recordings. To make an efficient use of the
building, there is a constant strive for multifunctionality. As
the only thing that count are the events, these black holes
turn into relatively uninteresting *black boxes* from the
outside, just striking in their sheer sublime immenseness that
is even more poignant as they usually stand isolated on
parking fields.

Conclusion

If media can reanimate soccer and if media can reanimate
churches, can they also reanimate cities? Can they turn
Megalopolis into more than the sum of its parts? And do we
need a real event to start from or can it also be a vision
or a fantasy? The answer seems to be yes. Heidiland in
Switzerland for example proves that it can also be the latter.
Heidiland is a land people only know from the children's
books by Johanna Spyri, an imagined place. Today, you can
go to Switzerland and there really is a Heidiland, as a tourist
destination. It exists. There was so much demand from
tourists from all over the world that a whole area in
retrospect was actually named Heidiland. It even has an
official exit on the motorway.

It should be possible to use this particular mix of specific
programs, large, black box-like buildings and media to
organize Megalopolis. They are at least the proof that the
power to achieve these massive phenomena is there. It could
make larger changes in other fields and even with other

contents and goals as well, as Rem Koolhaas hinted at in the interview on Winners Church in Lagos. Regarding the many collective risks and threats we face, the inequalities to be resolved and desires to be realized it would be great if that would happen. The problem is, that it is not simply possible to modernly say: "if you have a mess, get a vacuum cleaner", as it is still difficult to figure out if the secret of these mechanisms lays in a kind of pre-modern symbolic capital or has freed itself completely from it and lays somewhere in the future, beyond our reach.

SOMETHING'S MISSING

Something's Missing

Would we recognize Utopia if we saw it? And would we recognize it if we only saw a glimpse of it, a residue or a fragment? Would we recognize it if it was a building or only if it was a drawing for a building? Would we recognize it immediately, or only after it was explained to us? And then: if we did recognize it, would we accept it and embrace it as Utopia or reject it as a Dystopia? After all, Utopia and Dystopia always go hand in hand, just as Utopia and fatalism do. Among historians and theoreticians who have written on the subject of Utopia, there seems to be widespread consensus that Utopias are produced in the darker periods of history. Utopian thinking, as it took its definitive shape in the 16th and 17th century, can be considered as Western society's answer to the dramatic end of the Middle-Ages. Even if Lewis Mumford concludes his book The Story of Utopias with a plea for Eutopia, the good country in which all ambiguities of Utopia have disappeared, his main argument seems to be the evocation of an atmosphere of doom. Without any explanation, we suddenly have to choose between Mumford's Eutopia and Oswald Spengler's Untergang des Abendlandes.[1] After the catastrophes of the Second World War, it is Sigfried Giedion who, following a critical analysis of why the Modern Movement in architecture and urbanism lost the battle to more conservative and even reactionary forces in the 1930s, makes a dramatic plea for an intensive collaboration between modern architects and modern artists. "Artists can more easily exist without the general public than the general public without artists. Why? Because mechanization runs amuck when there is no line of direction and when feeling cannot find a suitable outlet." Even in the few countries where modern architecture had won he finds that *something* is missing in the built environment. "*Something* is an inspired architectural imagination to satisfy the demand for monumentality."[2] According to Giedion, this should be a new monumentality that, in contrast to the classical monumentality that returned in the architecture and urbanism of the 1930s, should be inspired by modern art, which by now had not only matured but was also understood by large sections of the population. "What began as necessary structural abbreviations now emerges as symbols."[3]

Similar lines of thought seem to be the origin of the question posed in Latent Utopias, an exhibition and book by Zaha Hadid and Patrick Schumacher.[4]

1   Achterhuis, Hans. *De erfenis van de utopie.* Amsterdam: Ambo, 1998.

2   Giedion, Sigfried. *Architecture, You and Me: the Diary of a Development.* Cambridge, MA: Harvard University Press, 1958.

3   Ibid.

4   Hadid, Zaha, and Patrik Schumacher. *Latent Utopias: Experiments within Contemporary Architecture.* Wien; New York: Springer, 2002. Published in conjunction with the exhibitions shown at Landesmuseum Joanneum, Graz.

5   Czaja, Wojciech. "Adonis auf Krücken." *Die Presse/Spectrum*, August 3, 2002.

6   See note 1.
7   Lyotard, Jean-François. *La Condition Postmoderne.* Paris: Les Éditions de Minuit, 1997; Fukuyama, Francis. *The End of History and the Last Man.* New York; Toronto: Free Press; Maxwell Macmillan Canada, 1992.

"Every time needs its utopia(s). A society that no longer reflects its development is uncanny, a monstrosity." But somehow it seems that they mean particularly the current time. In a recent interview, Hadid remarks that we are living in *very uninspired times*, in which *the extravagant* has no place any more.[5] However, Giedion's new monumentality was embedded in the Utopias of modern urbanism. How is that today? In the 1940s and 1950s, there may indeed have been a more widespread consensus about the symbolic meaning of modern art. Modern art today takes very different forms, which cannot so easily be characterized as symbols. So how could we imagine the reconnection of architecture, urbanism and Utopia again?

From the first frontispiece of Thomas More's Utopia from 1516 on, Utopias have always been linked with architectural representations, even though they did not always correspond to the text. The first frontispieces of More's Utopia depicted medieval landscapes that were very different from the regular planning described by him. On the other hand, one might say that all architectural projects have Utopian aspects, because they all deal with improvements to life in a particular situation. Some architecture is even called Utopian or visionary because it proposes, wants to trigger, or can only be realized in a completely different society.

The question is however what Utopia we would be talking about and what role architecture could play in the achievement of it. Alan Greenspan, the director of the American Federal Reserve Bank, is for example greatly influenced by the ideas of Ayn Rand as she expressed them in, among others, The Virtue of Selfishness: A New Concept of Egoism and Anthem. As such, these ideas largely influence every citizen on earth already. Indeed, Rand's ideas find their architectural counterpart in her novel The Fountainhead. As the secret word in Anthem is EGO, one might argue that the recent phenomenon of *star architects* is immediately related to Rand's Utopia because it is realized through recent political developments that are largely driven by the United States' monetary politics.[6]

Over the last 25 years or so it has indeed become increasingly difficult to speak about Utopia. Jean-François Lyotard proclaimed the end of the great narratives in his highly influential book La condition postmoderne in 1979 and after the fall of the communist empire Francis Fukuyama even spoke of "The End of History and the Last Man".[7] The New Economy was supposed to put an end to the

8 Tafuri, Manfredo. *Progetto e utopia*. Roma-Bari: Laterza, 1973.

9 Tafuri, Manfredo. "L'Architecture dans le Boudoir. The Language of Criticism and the Criticism of Language." *Oppositions*, no. 3 (1974): 37–62.

10 Lootsma, Bart. "The Diagram Debate or the Schizoid Architect." In *ArchiLab*, edited by Marie-Ange Brayer and Béatrice Simonot. Orléans: Ville d'Orléans, 2001.

11 Howie, Gillian. *Deleuze and Spinoza: Aura of Expressionism*. Basingstoke: Palgrave, 2002.

phenomenon of recessions. As early on as 1973, the architectural theoretician Manfredo Tafuri destroyed the belief that architecture could bring us a new and better society and that all attempts to do so would finally be absorbed by capitalism in his book Progetto e Utopia.[8] Around this year almost all individual groups who produced radical architecture in the 1960s, from Haus-Rucker-Co to Superstudio and from Constant Nieuwenhuys to Archigram, dissolved. In his 1974 essay L'Architecture dans le boudoir, Tafuri furthermore speaks of the defeat of the avant-garde that leaves architects with no choice but to give up all architectural ideology, all dreams about its social functioning and to reduce all Utopian residues to a zero degree and instead concentrate on the play with historical fragments of a language of which the code has been lost – all of this in the service of saving architecture at least.[9] This is indeed what the official architectural debate has been focusing on ever since, notwithstanding the attempts to formulate new cosmologies as well, mainly inspired by philosophical and scientific sources such as those of Gilles Deleuze, chaos theory, complexity, and so on.

Even the rise of new computer technologies was seen and applied more in the light of these cosmologies than in the light of Utopian speculations, which is remarkable given that the rise of new technologies usually triggers whole series of Utopias and dystopias. The only aspect of this line of thought that could be considered Utopian in the Deleuzian tradition is the deconstruction of Bentham's Panopticon in Deleuze's interpretation of Michel Foucault: the striation of the Panopticon, read as a diagram, is then replaced by other diagrams that try to produce smooth surfaces allowing a freer inhabitation after a nomadic model.[10] This model is strongly based on buildings and depends on individual architects and clients, which largely hinders the Utopian potential. But one could also criticize it on another level, as the philosopher Gillian Howie has done recently in her book Deleuze and Spinoza.

In Howie's analysis, it is exactly the inspiration Deleuze takes from nature that is problematic, as it interprets the world from a mystical romantic perspective and thereby brings it under a fatalistic spell. She suggests that it is no coincidence that Deleuze's thinking is so widely received in a particular historical context in which we speak of *the end of man* and at the same time that liberal individualism is booming.[11] Natural and organic metaphors that try to summarize metaphysics as expressed by nature are of course part of the tradition of

12 Kelly, Kevin. *Out of Control: The New Biology of Machines, Social Systems, and the Economic World.* Reading, MA: Addison-Wesley, 1994.

13 Hardt, Michael, and Antonio Negri. *Empire.* Cambridge, MA: Harvard University Press, 2000.

The quotes of Slavoj Žižek and Fredric Jameson appear on the back cover.

liberal individualism and are for example worked out in Adam Smith's theory of the Invisible Hand as it has been revived by authors like Kevin Kelly in his book Out of Control, The New Biology of Machines, Social Systems and the Economic World.[12]

However, suddenly over the last couple of years an almost desperate longing for new Utopias in the sense of ideological constructs that might give direction to the development of society has been more and more widely felt. This explains the largely enthusiastic reception of the book Empire by Antonio Negri and Michel Hardt that Fredric Jameson characterizes admiringly as a "prophetic call for energies to come." Slavoj Žižek even considers it "a rewriting of the Communist Manifesto."[13] Parallel to this, it is striking that almost forgotten architectural and urban Utopias like Constant's New Babylon and Yona Friedman's Ville Spatiale are shown in this year's Documenta in Kassel, while Paolo Soleri was already rehabilitated at the Biennale in Venice in 2000.

I share the desire for new Utopias, but just like the curators of the Documenta and the last Biennale – exhibitions that usually focus on recent and contemporary work – today I don't see them appearing clearly as bold visions that could yet compete with those we know from, for example, the architects of the French revolution, the German Expressionists or the Russian Constructivists. That is: I do not see them as aesthetic models. What I do see, however, is that people set up a climate, lay the foundations and produce the knowledge on which eventually Utopias could blossom. I refer to the overwhelming amount of research that has been done over the last ten years or so. This year's Documenta shows many examples from the art world that try to investigate and question existing realities critically, sometimes even resulting in works that come closer to photojournalism and documentary filmmaking than to art. Research has become a key issue again in the debate about architecture and urbanism as well. Architects and architectural offices like Stefano Boeri and Multiplicity, Rem Koolhaas and OMA/AMO, Raoul Bunschoten and CHORA, Winy Maas and MVRDV; institutions like the Harvard Project on (what used to be called) the City, the Berlage Institute, the Bauhaus in Dessau and ETH Studio Basel; galleries like arc en rêve in Bordeaux and the Triennale in Milan; and travelling exhibitions like Cities on the Move set up ambitious projects that try to understand recent changes in the urban environment. All these focus on the broader social, economic, and cultural context of architectural and urban design instead of on projects, although projects done by the architects carrying out the research are inevitably seen in the light of their research. This already seems an enormous change since a period in which architecture withdrew itself to the *boudoir*. But what about Utopia?

In an essay in the Documenta catalogue, Molly Nesbit gives a possible answer to this question when she refers to a discussion between Ernst Bloch, the philosopher of hope, and Theodor Adorno in 1964. "Adorno declared that there could be no picture of Utopia cast in a positive manner, there could be no positive picture of it at all, nor could any picture be complete. He went far. Bloch would follow him part of the way, then stopped short. He summoned up a sentence from Brecht and said it contained the incentive for Utopia. Brecht had written "Something's missing." "What is this *something*?" Bloch asked. "If it is not allowed to be cast in a picture, then I shall portray it as in the process of being. But one should not be allowed to eliminate it as if it really did not exist so that one could say the following about it: *It's about the sausage.* Therefore, if all is correct, I believe Utopia cannot be removed from the world in spite of everything, and even the technological, that must definitely emerge and will be in the great realm of the Utopian, will only form small sectors. That is a geometrical picture, which does not have any place here, but another picture can be found in the old peasant saying, there is no dance before the meal. People must first fill their stomachs, and then they can dance. The sausage and the dance could be taken as an aphorism for Marxism, which, he explained, is the only precondition for a life lived in freedom, happily, meaningfully. Bloch and Adorno were taking Utopia as the ground upon which to draw the line between life and death," Nesbit continues. "As they tossed the questions back and forth, it is clear enough that the picture and the sausage-dance were secondary to the lines of metaphysics. But what of the picture and its vision? Is the Utopian picture itself to be considered missing, or may we see Utopia in a picture with something missing, a picture that comes with empty pockets?"[14]

Maybe Tafuri started out with the wrong expectations. Maybe if we were to step aside for a moment from the expectation that the Modern Movement's main argument was to change things and try to perceive it as a collection of individuals who in the first place were facing the same or similar problems – the growth of metropolises, the rise of the masses, congestion,

14 Nesbit, Molly. "The Port of Calls." In *Documenta 11 – Platform 5*, edited by Heike Ander, Nadja Rottner, and Museum Fridericianum (Kassel). Ostfildern-Ruit: Hatje Cantz, 2002. Exhibition catalog.

pollution, et cetera – and had to find solutions for them, we could still learn a lot. Of course the solutions created by Le Corbusier, Otto Neurath, Van Eesteren and Van Lohuizen, Hilberseimer and others were produced with very specific political forms of organization in mind – which were by the way very different from each other – but it seems as if, particularly in recent architectural history, only the visionary aspects of their work have been emphasized and criticized. And visionary projects are doomed to fail. This does not dismiss their necessity: indeed, they offer a perspective that can be debated and reflected upon. It is in the nature of their single perspective that they must be compromised in order to take effect.

But maybe if we try to see the projects of the Modern Movement in a different way, not so much as visions but as a means to understand the reality that the architects and urbanists were facing at the time and focus on their research, the tragic failure that has overlain these projects since the 1970s disappears. If we see them as individual moments of synthesis in a collective process of modernization that could never be steered by one person or body, by one ideology or another, they appear differently. Not as words or syllables in a language that could just be repeated over and over again, but as essays, as landscape paintings, photographs, snapshots of a city at a particular moment in time, using the media of architecture: plan, section, elevation, and perspective. What we would be interested in them is not the projective, visionary aspect of them, but the analytical side: the "sausage", as Bloch would call it, the raw material from which they were made and that the visions processed. We would be looking for cities that are hidden within these *visionary* cities or that are even covered up by them. It is, for example, no coincidence that Le Corbusier's City for 3,000,000 inhabitants has exactly the same population size as Paris did at that time. Similarly, Van Eesteren's and Van Lohuizen's calculations and designs for the general extension plan for Amsterdam were based on an extrapolation and reshuffling of the data they found in that city. Maybe this analysis could help us in research today, not only by taking their methods literally as happens now, but by analyzing the analysis critically and comparing it to the problems we face today, which are so different from, and sometimes even contradictory to, the problems that people faced one hundred years ago. This is necessary, because while the early modernists dealt with cities that were closed entities, with a clear distinction from each other and from the countryside, today we are dealing with urbanized regions that are globally interconnected and interdependent in complex relationships. If the early modernist visions were intended for nation states, today's nation states are in a process of dissolving. While the solutions of the modernists were intended as a solution for the masses, today we will somehow have to deal with the process of individualization.[15] These issues are not just important to set up a coherent research program that would define Utopia implicitly as *something missing*, but they are also crucial in understanding why it is so difficult to construct an explicit contemporary Utopia. Remember that Thomas More's original Utopia was an island and that most Utopian visions depict a closed system or entity. Another reason why it is such an enormous task is because, as Ulrich Beck writes, "any attempt to come up with a new concept that would provide social cohesion must depart from acknowledging that individualism, diversity, and scepticism are deeply rooted in Western society."[16] If we agree that new Utopian models would have to find their departure in the given reality, that they would have to offer at least a general idea of a political organization, that they would have to deal with the forces of globalization and respect individualization, we can suddenly distinguish two contemporary architectural, or rather urbanistic Utopias. One is a series of projects or <u>machines</u> developed by Winy Maas and MVRDV, the other the work of Raoul Bunschoten and CHORA. Maas' Utopias follow in the tradition of Utopias that, in answer to scarcity, believe they can calculate the tension in society between needs and resources. We find this already in More's Utopia, in which the inhabitants are consciously aware that the pleasures they enjoy do not get in the way of greater common interests. We also see the continuation of this tradition in Bentham's Panopticon, which he saw as a machine that would function completely independent of the motives of the people involved but produce behaviour *automatically*.[17]

MVRDV's <u>Datatown</u> pushes the urban projects of Le Corbusier, early Hilberseimer and notably Van Eesteren and Van Lohuizen one step further to the scale of a nation state.[18] It is a series of theoretical exercises on an autarchic city state, <u>Datatown</u>, measuring 400 by 400 kilometers and with 241 million inhabitants. Datatown would thus be the densest place on earth. This density would force the inhabitants to come up with collective decisions about their behaviour and the way they organize their country spatially to avoid ecological catastrophes. Datatown shows how collective behaviour has an effect on the spatial organization of a country or city. Hence it makes use of existing

15 Lootsma, Bart, and Mariëtte van. Stralen. *Research for Research*. Rotterdam: Berlage Institute, 2001.
16 Beck, Ulrich. "Je eigen leven leiden in een op hol geslagen wereld." ARCHIS, No. 2, 2001.
17 See note 1.
18 MVRDV. *Metacity/Datatown*. Rotterdam: 010 Publishers, 1999.

statistical data. The effects of these statistical data about collective decisions are translated into *stuff* – buildings, streets, cities and landscape – that are projected as three-dimensional simulations on four sides of a cube. The visitor to this cube can experience the city and how it changes with changes in collective behaviour. So he can see the effect on the city when all its inhabitants decide to become vegetarians, when they deal with waste in a particular way, when all energy is produced by the wind, etcetera. In each case, several options are shown. The idea is of course that visitors to the cube are helped to bring out their vote on or in the national government. Datatown presupposes a representational democracy as we know it in the Western world in the most classical way. The major weakness of the project is of course that it can only operate if we accept that nations are indeed autonomous units, whereas we know that the concept of the nation state is in crisis and so the concept of a representational democracy is in crisis as well. The other weakness lies in the use of statistical data applied in the same classical way as the early modernists and notably Van Eesteren and Van Lohuizen would use it. This means that the model presupposes not only a society that largely consists of masses, but in turning this into a design method it also presupposes that everything is distributed equally based on a political consensus. It presupposes in other words a social democracy or a welfare state. In more recent and even more Utopian *machines* developed at the Berlage Institute in Rotterdam, such as the <u>Region Mixer</u>, Maas takes the whole world as his territory, dealing with flows of migration, food, and energy production. Again, the ideal would be a more or less equal distribution of resources, income, and people. Basically a piece of software, The <u>Region Mixer</u> has therefore an *equalizer function* like those we know on a stereo. Of course, this model again presupposes some kind of very global representational democratic body, like a more powerful version of the United Nations, to operate it. Apart from this, it is interesting that when Maas treats the whole world as if it were a modernist city, he comes up against the same problems of externalization as the modernists. Where in the completely planned version of the Netherlands Van Eesteren and Van Lohuizen ultimately needed an artificial piece of land in the sea, the Maasvlakte, as a kind of safety valve to accommodate all undesired and unforeseen functions, here Maas comes up with a satellite-like piece of land for food production that would circle around the earth. It will be developed in collaboration with NASA.

Bunschoten's Utopia starts out from very different premises. As his point of departure, he takes Spinoza's concept of politics, as it has also been revived recently by Gilles Deleuze and notably Antonio Negri.[19] In Negri's interpretation, Spinoza refuses to see the political community as an order that is imposed on individual desires from outside or in the form of a social contract. Even different forms of representational democratic systems are considered as residues of the single transcendent power of the monarch. Instead, society is the quasi-mechanical (non-dialectic) result of interactions between individual forces that, by uniting themselves, form a collective power. As in nature, political relationships are nothing but the structures that the collective productive power appropriates and renews by unfolding itself.[20] For Spinoza, these relationships and structures are always *right*, without attributing any moral consequences or opinions to them.

In his work, Bunschoten traces the seeds of this productive power in reality by looking for individual initiatives and, by introducing game structures, he suggests or simulates possible liaisons between them to suggest the production of larger spatial organizations. To trace these initiatives Bunschoten developed a method in which beans are thrown on a map of a city and individual participants then go to the location to discover the forces that are at play there. They record these forces in the form of small narratives and develop possible scenarios for their further development in combination with others in a potentially endless process of folding and unfolding. The beans are of course a metaphor for the potential germination of these forces into a new organic whole. Bunschoten's most recent projects take the form of websites on which a myriad of those germinations can be found and followed. Rather than relying on traditional governmental planning organizations, he takes these individual initiatives or prefers NGOs or *spontaneous* organizations as caretakers of larger projects.[21]

If we agree that the end of Utopian thinking is largely connected to what Lyotard calls the end of the grand narrations, it is interesting to see that Bunschoten introduces

19 De Spinoza, Benedictus. "Tractatus Politicus (in Opera Posthuma, Jan Riewertz, Amsterdam, 1677)." In *Hoofdstukken uit de politieke verhandeling*, edited by W. N. A. Klever. Meppel: Boom, 1985; Deleuze, Gilles. *Expressionism in Philosophy: Spinoza.* New York: Zone Books, 1992; Negri, Antonio. *The Savage Anomaly: The Power of Spinoza's Metaphysics and Politics.* Minneapolis: University of Minnesota Press, 1991; See also note 11.

20 A. Matheron in his introduction to the French translation of Antonio Negri's *The Savage Anomaly* in the introduction by W.N.A. Klever to *Hoofdstukken uit de politieke verhandeling*, see note 19.

21 Binet, Hélène, Raoul Bunschoten, Takuro Hoshino, and CHORA. *Urban Flotsam: Stirring the City.* Rotterdam: 010 Publishers, 2001.

new forms of narration, which we also see developing on the Internet and in new media. In this concept, the different case studies as we saw them at the last Documenta, in Stefano Boeri's research as he develops it with his group Multiplicity and the research I did at the Berlage Institute, which now appears so desperately fragmentary and often so frustratingly analytical and merely critical, this research in which there is always *something missing*, could potentially be connected to produce a new force. Could this become a new form of Utopian architecture? But then what about the architect who traditionally finds his legitimization in exactly the kind of grand narratives Lyotard has dismissed?

In his introduction to the French translation of Antonio Negri's book on Spinoza, The Savage Anomaly, A. Materon writes that he completely agrees with Negri, whereby he says that here we find the antipodes of the trinity Hobbes-Rousseau-Hegel: "And I recognize with him the immense revolutionary significance and the extraordinary actuality of this doctrine: the right, that is the power and nothing else; the right that the holders of political power possess, that is the power of the crowd and nothing else: that is the collective power that the crowd allows them to have and allows them again but that they can also withdraw from their disposition. When the people revolt, it has the right to do so by definition and, ipso facto, by definition the right of the sovereign disappears."[22] A revolution or uprising is therefore legitimized when it succeeds. We could say the same about Bunschoten's architectural Utopia and we know therefore that that will take a while as for now the powers of the state – even if they are disintegrating – and the powers of capital – even if they soften up – are still quite dominant. Here I would like again to recall Gillian Howie's difficulties with the actuality of Deleuze's thinking and his interpretation of Spinoza.[23] In terms of Utopian thinking, relying on a metaphysical reading of nature is problematic because, as Colin Bird writes in The Myth of Liberal Individualism: "I can believe that the state is really an organism and yet deny that it has any moral significance whatsoever. In fact that a jellyfish is *organic* does not elevate it to a moral status equivalent or beyond that of human beings. Similarly, I can deny that collectivities or states are in any sense organic or anthropomorphic and yet claim that they have a greater claim on our moral attention than mere human individuals."[24]

22 See note 20.
23 See note 11.
24 Bird, Colin. *The Myth of Liberal Individualism.* Cambridge; New York: Cambridge University Press, 1999.

THE PARADOXES
OF CONTEMPORARY
POPULISM

The Paradoxes Of Contemporary Populism

The rise of populism in Europe goes hand in hand with the Crisis of the welfare state and representative democracy. Therefore it is no wonder that architecture, although maybe not in the sense of exceptional architectural masterpieces but as housing and urbanism, is one of the main issues for populist politicians. The issue is primarily about financing, ownership, and shifting large flows of money from the government to the private sector. Populist arguments are largely about these issues too. They are about the possibility to own and invest in one's own house and about the freedom the owner may have to shape it to fit his of her individual needs and desires. Therefore, this issue is not so much about architectural style, as it is about the freedom to live the way one wants and to design his or her own property. This is central to populist arguments. But the rhetoric of post-modernism may in some cases be helpful for populist politicians and in the end the results of populist politics may be largely postmodern or historicised in a confused way. Populists and postmodernists may not necessarily share the same enemy but they at least share a common symbol of an enemy: the large pre- and post-war modernist housing estates. For populists this symbol represents the State, for postmodernists it represents Modernism in its most alienated form.

Processes leading to the privatisation and deregulation of the housing market are not new. They started already in the 1970s in Thatcherist England and were sped up in the 1990s and the first years of this century under the politics of the Third Way in the Netherlands, Great Britain, Germany and Austria, and under the pressure of budgetary conditions for European countries to participate in the Euro. In a relatively short period of time compared to the period it took to build up systems of public housing, this has already led to considerable shifts in the financing of the built-up environment. As the building industry is responsible for a large part of a nation's economy, these shifts led to shifts in power as well and paved the way for new forms of populist politics. This is perhaps not so different from the way Silvio Berlusconi's political success was largely enabled by his control over the media industry in Italy. Real estate firms largely financed the late Dutch populist Pim Fortuyn and his political parties.

Together with health care and education, providing public housing has been at the core of the welfare state from the beginning. Over the last century, in most European countries, in order to deal with housing shortage – caused by large-scale migration from the countryside to the industrialised cities, war and the post-Second World War baby boom – and its consequences – speculation, unhygienic living conditions and an uncontrollable growth of several metropolises – different systems of housing corporations were built up that develop, build and today manage enormous estates of affordable housing. These corporations are financed by rents, state-guaranteed loans and subsidies and employ large numbers of people. Today, the housing stocks and land by themselves represent a considerable amount of capital.

After periods of great success in the 1920s, 1930s, 1950s and 1960s, from the early 1970s on there is a growing dissatisfaction with the housing these corporations provide. Particularly in the reconstruction period after the Second World War and the economic and technological growth of that period, housing production became largely industrialised and standardised to be able to cope with the massive demand – which it did extremely successfully. The monotony, anonymity, and mono-functionality of these quarters became appreciated less and less. In the same period, the nineteenth-century quarters and city centres had been neglected or torn down. Housing corporations and architects came up with new concepts of housing, which succeeded each other rapidly. However, they could not do whatever they wanted because important parts of the system are also complex laws, rules, norms and regulations that form the conditional framework for subsidies and further financing. These notably limit the amount of square metres and typologies in relation to price. Most of this legal and financial framework was developed in the 1930s and 1950s, in a period in which Western societies were still defined by class distinctions. Public housing was developed for the masses that, in a representative democracy, would serve their interests. Representative democracy and industrial production, by their nature, are both very suitable for handling issues that relate to large quantities and statistical data. Within the enclosed space of the nation-state, prognoses based on population surveys were still reliable. For example, the predictions about the growth of a city like Amsterdam from 1929, stating that the city would have between 800.000 and 1.2 million inhabitants in the year 2000, were quickly reacted upon and enabled the city to work with the famous Algemeen Uitbreidingsplan by Van Eesteren and Van Lohuizen until recently with only minor interpretational changes.

1   Beck, Ulrich. "Je eigen leven leiden in een op hol geslagen wereld." *ARCHIS*, No. 2, 2001.

Today, such predictions would be almost impossible as cities are globally related in such complex ways that local surveys, even in combination with comparisons to other cites, would never be enough. On top of that, from the 1960s on, a process of individualisation developed in Western welfare states. Paradoxically, individualisation is also largely a consequence of the success of the welfare states. While individualisation may have first appeared as something to fight for, today we realise more and more that it is something that is forced upon us – be it by the soft seductive strategies of the media industry and politicians or by the economic and political forces that create migration. Paradoxically, the basis of individualisation is formed by both the eternal desires for the dream world of freedom and the fear of poverty, starvation and war. It is produced by prosperity and high levels of education that make people able to choose and to decide for themselves, just as much as by the economic deprivation that tears people away from their traditional bonds, families and communities.[1] All of this challenges the way the welfare state traditionally takes care of housing and urbanism. People, with all their individual biographies and desires, demand individual solutions for their lives.

2   For this definition of populism see Wikipedia. https://en.wikipedia.org.
3   Bos, Wouter. "Een beetje populisme mag." *De Groene*, no. 8, 2005.

Now, if we take populism as "a rhetorical style that holds that the common person is oppressed by the *elite* in society, which only exists to serve its own interests, and therefore, the instruments of the State need to be grasped from this self-serving elite and instead used for the benefit and advancement of the people as a whole" and if we see populists as reaching out "to ordinary people, talking about their economic and social concerns", appealing "to their common sense", then it is obvious that the systems and organisations that were developed to provide public housing are ideal targets for populists from both the left and the right and any direction or route in between.[2] And indeed, almost all political parties are guilty of it. It has, in reaction to the success of the populists, even become normal and acceptable. Or, as the new leader of the former social democratic party in the Netherlands recently wrote in the left-wing intellectual weekly De Groene: "A little bit of populism is allowed".[3] As if the PvdA (Partij van de Arbeid) had not been a party wholesaling in grandstanding already for years, paving the way for the more radical populism of Pim Fortuyn.

The most worrying and unfortunately predominant form of populism in Europe today is not a grass-roots phenomenon. It

4   Frank, Thomas. "The Rise of Market Populism: America's New Secular Religion." The Nation. October 30, 2000. www.thenation.com.

5   Fukuyama, Francis. *The End of History and the Last Man.* New York; Toronto: Free Press; Maxwell Macmillan Canada, 1992.

is a specific form of what Thomas Frank calls Market Populism.[4] Frank describes the 1990s as an era of "many and spectacular avant-gardes, of loud and highly visible youth cultures, of emphatic multiculturalism, of extreme sports, extreme diets and extreme investing". But even if we "marvelled at the infinite variety of the Internet and celebrated our ethnic diversity" we have probably hardly ever seen such an amount of intellectual consensus about the role of businesses in society. Even the leaders of the left parties accommodated themselves to free market faith and the New Economy. Frank analyses how politicians throughout the political spectrum started to believe that markets are a populist system, which is more democratic than democratically elected governments. "With their mechanisms of supply and demand, poll and focus group, superstore and Internet, markets manage to express the popular will more articulately and meaningfully than do mere elections. By their very nature markets confer democratic legitimacy, markets bring down the pompous and the snooty, markets look out for the interests of the little guy, markets give us what we want."

"Many of the individual components of the market-populist consensus have been part of the cultural-economic wallpaper for years", Frank writes. "Hollywood and Madison Avenue have always insisted that their job is simply to mirror the public's wishes, and movies and ad campaigns succeed or fail depending on how accurately they conform to public tastes. Similarly, spokesmen for the New York Stock exchange have long argued that stock prices reflect popular enthusiasm, that public trading of stocks is a basic component of democracy. And ever since Randolph Hearst, newspaper tycoons have imagined themselves defenders of the common man." Still it remains surprising how populism, originally a rebellion against the corporate order and a political tongue reserved by definition for the non-rich and non-powerful, has now become the tongue of the wealthy.

Frank explains this by saying that the generation of '68 in the United States, the generation that is in power today, was not interested in class struggle, but in the first place despised the *wisdom and values* of the American middle class. Therefore the Republicans could often harvest electoral gain from within the working class by appealing to these values, like patriotism and the family. This echoes what Francis Fukuyama writes in his introduction to The End of History and the Last Man, in which he argues that capitalist democracy is the end phase of society.[5] Fukuyama emphasises the importance of *thymos*, the feeling of self-respect, and relates it to religion, nationalism, the whole complex of ethical values and norms of a people and the way people feel united in small communities. This may be true for the United States in the more radical forms we have learned to know over the last couple of years, whereby we should not forget that the United States never was a welfare state. In the United States, Jeffersonian philanthropy and charity, sometimes carried out by large organisations, have always taken up large parts of the tasks of the welfare institutions that in Europe were created by self-organisation, revolution or by means of a representative democratic process. Most recently, it is the new phenomenon of the *capitalist churches*, television churches like the Houston based Lakewood Church, that on one hand provide many welfare-like services, and on the other have an enormous effect with a populist version of Baptist religion preaching that "everyone can be a winner".[6] Taken seriously in Forbes and sometimes reaching 95 percent of the American Households, these churches have become an influential factor in American politics. In Europe we do not see these kind of desperate and radical developments yet. We must admit that it is true however that in Europe the generation of '68 was also less interested in class struggle than it originally may have seemed. On the other hand, until the 1990s, the influence of left-wing parties, the fact that much badly paid work was done by immigrants and production was being moved to countries with low wages made the middle class so dominant that the class struggle seemed over. Still, also in Europe we see a reflection on cultural and family values that is increasing in reaction to massive immigration in some cities, particularly after 9/11.

In this context, it cannot be coincidental that Pim Fortuyn's *unvollendete*, posthumous autobiography bears the title Autobiografie van een Babyboomer (Autobiography of a Baby Boomer).[7] One of his other books De Verweesde Samenleving (The Orphaned Society) is an "emotional plea for more attention, love and respect for the crucial norms and values in our culture", by which he means the "Jewish-Christian Humanist Culture" and "human scale as touchstone for the public domain".[8] (Silvio Berlusconi finances the publication of Fortuyn's books in Italian.) The real reason for the revival of rebirth of all these values, however, is not necessarily to be found in the values themselves. The reason has more to do with the way in which they are connected to the values of new successful entrepreneurs that support their populist protégés or front men with money that enables them to market and advertise themselves in ways other politicians could only dream about.

6   Lakewoodchurch.com. https://www.lakewoodchurch.com/.

7   Fortuyn, Pim. *Autobiografie van een babyboomer.* Uithoorn; Rotterdam: Karakter; Speakers Academy, 2002.

8   Fortuyn, Pim. *De verweesde samenleving.* Uithoorn; Rotterdam: Karakter; Speakers Academy, 2002.

These are the paradoxes of market populism: its critique of the presumed dominant elite of the welfare state is not in the service of the people but of a different, new elite that is the product of the successful welfare state itself and the way this success was dealt with in Third Way politics.

Pim Fortuyn was the ultimate post-modern politician: a gay former Marxist academic who became entrepreneur and after that a *politician without a party*, as he writes in his auto-biography.[9] He was post-modern, complete with the self-irony that goes along with it: he dressed in suits that until recently were only worn by actors in Brechtian or children's theatre that have to play gangsters or capitalists. His chauffeur drove him in a Daimler stretched limousine. He lived in a house with a butler downstairs, two little dogs on the bench, a collection of post-modern paintings and sculptures (many of them representing himself) and a flag with the (re-invented) family herald in front of the door. He was made big by the commercial media, whom he showed his house and talked about the most intimate details of his love life – including his visits to darkrooms – in a way that reminds one of reality shows like Big Brother and Pop Idol, that can turn *normal* people into stars overnight. His most important medium was the Sunday morning television program Business Class, a talk show hosted by the wealthy real estate broker Harry Mens on the Dutch commercial TV station RTL 5. It is a program in which politicians, business-men and – women appear next to captains of industry or those who buy time in the commercial breaks. As a regular party-independent columnist, Fortuyn could criticise every-thing and everyone and build up his image and popularity long before he decided to accept the role as party leader of Leefbaar Nederland (Liveable Netherlands). Local political parties that had become successful in the years before and now decided to go national originally formed Leefbaar Nederland. It was Harry Mens who, at Fortuyn's request, asked his friends in the real estate business to put money into the party during beggars' banquets.

However, Fortuyn's political career for Leefbaar Nederland was short-lived. During the election campaign of 2002 he was thrown out, because he proposed to strike the article in the constitution that forbids discrimination. As we learn from a reconstruction in NRC Handelsblad his financers immediately and shamelessly asked for their money back from Leefbaar Nederland and – again with their money – Fortuyn founded his own party. When Fortuyn was assassinated just before the 2002 elections, four out of five financers of

9   See note 7.

10 Chorus, Jutta, and Menno de Galan. "Bouwwereld tilde LPF van de grond." NRC Handelsblad (Rotterdam), July 27, 2002, Saturday Supplement (Zaterdags Bijvoegsel) sec, p. 19.

the LPF (Lijst Pim Fortuyn) came from the real estate business. But also candidates for a seat in the Dutch parliament tried to pay for a place on the list. After his death a long mud fight started, in which the financers tried to gain absolute control over the party that had become a major force in the parliament and even became part of the government. They claimed that *shareholders* always have the final say in a company. When that failed again they asked their money back and even tried to have the party declared bankrupt – which was refused by the court. In the end, the members of parliament tried to continue independent from the party. The shocking picture that appears from NRC Handelsblad, a quality right-wing liberal newspaper in the Netherlands, is that of a small group of nouveau riche men who tried to buy their political representation.[10] How did this become possible?

In the 1990s the Netherlands, like most European welfare states, joined the international trend in which the government withdrew. The unification of Europe had an important part to play in this, because the creation of a free market without frontiers took precedence. This obliged the Dutch government to abolish, privatise or adapt many (semi-) governmental bodies, subsidy regulations and laws. For architecture and urbanism, the most important moment in this process was the abolition of subsidies for social housing in 1994. The debts of the housing corporations were remitted all at once and since then they have had to operate as independent concerns without governmental support. The corporations may have lost their subsidies; more important seems to be that the government has lost an important planning instrument. With the enormous amount of house building taking place, it had been until then a reasonably controllable and certain factor in the creation or national recommendations for town and country planning, regional plans and urbanisation plans. The government was able to make clear decisions about where house building was allowed and where not. But the government also lost control over the architectural and urban quality of the new quarters themselves. In the Vierde Nota Ruimtelijke Ordening Extra (VINEX, Fourth Recommendation for Town and Country Planning), the exact locations for house building were still indicated, but, in anticipation of the transition to a free market system, constructors, investors and speculators began to buy up the land at these locations. They often do this in an extremely strategic way, following for example the zebra model, in which they buy strips of land from farmers in certain areas, leaving other strips clear. For the local authorities it turns out to be much more expensive, too expensive in most cases, to buy this land and thus they are forced to negotiate with the owners about its development. The real consequences of this situation became clear much too late. It means that the authorities, even before making real plans, have to make agreements and contracts with the parties in the market, in which many procedures and details are agreed upon. The new quarters are then developed by new *ad hoc concerns*, in which the local authorities have no more weight than one of the other parties. Often the urban plan is still developed by or commissioned by the municipality, but it is subjected to many amendments in the process. The creator of the plan is appointed as supervisor and is responsible for the quality of the project. However, he hardly gets any support from the authorities, in the sense that the authorities *arrange* things, and if he fails it is almost impossible to penalise him. Besides, the government, as opposed to some time ago, cannot make a list of architects that it would favour for their specific cultural quality, because within EEC legislation, the architect is an entrepreneur like any other and competes freely with his architect-entrepreneur colleagues. As this competition is a based upon economic principles, cultural qualities hardly play a role any longer and besides the architect's fees are steadily going down. The offices which are superior in quality give up and concentrate on specific, better paid projects and most of the house building is increasingly going to third, fourth or fifth rate offices.

Present day government follows a policy in which individual house ownership is encouraged. For this purpose, plans that are being realised at the moment have to make room for individual parcels where individual principals can build houses of their own creation. In imitation of Carel Weeber, this is called Wild Living (Het Wilde Wonen), although in practice it is, of course, far from *wild*. These individuals may have a lot of money but they have, to put it mildly, very common taste. They generally build so-called *boerderettes*: houses vaguely reminiscent of farms, sometimes following the Dutch example, often cheered up by influences from French country-houses, English cottages and Heidi-houses. Here the principals also prefer architects of a lower standard, because otherwise they are too expensive; or they do not work with any architect at all, but, for example, directly with contractors or firms offering catalogue houses. For the higher quality architecture offices, the creation of an individual house is an unremunerative task, except maybe for the Moebiushuis of UN-Studio or the Dutch House of OMA, which is only accepted as a friendly favour or because of the special wishes of the client. In addition to all this, municipal supervision on architectural quality is being reduced. Every city and village in the Netherlands has a commission that advises the mayor and the councillors about the architectural and urban quality of all construction requests. Cities and villages now have to formulate a policy so that the aesthetic control criteria of the commission become *objective* – whatever this means. Besides, owners may shortly be able to carry out fairly large alterations to their houses without previous permission and may build fences, garden houses, carports and garages.

One-family houses require a lot more space and the open Dutch landscape is being spoilt in many places by the newest developments. It is sometimes called <u>white mildew</u> because of the predominantly light colour of the brick used.

Some politicians, such as Adri Duyvestein of the Partij van de Arbeid (PvdA, Labour Party), attempted to break the power of the housing corporations and the big construction firms to create a more varied living environment, more adapted to the individual wishes of the house buyers. In short: they tried to move from an economy of supply to an economy of demand. But obviously the different entities in the market adapted to the developments within a short space of time. Big investors and housing corporations based on the new enterprise mould, but also supermarket chains such as Albert Heijn and employment agencies such as Randstad, will determine the organisation of the Netherlands in the coming years since the authorities lack ideas. Entire quarters and shopping centres are put on the market as a *product*. Great interest has been shown in the American <u>New Urbanism</u> and thematic quarters have sprung up like mushrooms: living near a golf course, living near the water, living in a marina, with the retro-architecture that goes with it. Sometimes they are designed by architects like Rob Krier, but more often improvised by local architects. For shopping centres Krier, Charles Vandenhove, Jon Jerde, Robert Stern and Sjoerd Soeters are the favourites again, as Dutch architects generally are not able or do not want to create this historicising architecture with an acceptable degree of quality.

While other countries are full of admiration for what the generation of Dutch architects that I portrayed in my book <u>SuperDutch</u>[11] achieved, this has changed in the Netherlands during the last few years. There simply seems to be

11 Lootsma, Bart. *Superdutch – New Architecture in the Netherlands.* New York, NY; London: Princeton Architectural Press; Thames and Hudson, 2000.

architectural fatigue. In the first place, the interest within the Netherlands in the SuperDutch generation's work has decreased. Since the magazine ARCHIS has lost its leading role in the Netherlands to the commercial magazine de Architect and was narrowly saved from abolition, it takes a completely indifferent position and is hardly interested in architecture. Forum and Widerhall disappeared from the scene, while the extremely serious and academic OASE took their place. But in the daily press, the biggest change was perceptible since the middle of the nineties. And however much the professional world might be impressed with the great number of publications about Dutch architecture, these pale in significance compared to the publications in daily newspapers, which evidently have a greater influence. This is particularly true of the NRC Handelsblad, a rightwing liberal paper, which is conducting a real crusade, led by the critic Bernard Hulsman, against what he calls the *modernistic architecture* of the SuperDutch generation. In his articles, he has already verbally destroyed some projects several times, such as the Erasmusbridge by Ben van Berkel, the Schouwburgplein by Adriaan Geuze and the KunstHAL by OMA, sometimes years after their realization. On the other hand, Hulsman continually makes a plea inspired by Charles Jencks, for the post-modern architecture of the early eighties and architects such as Michael Graves, Robert Stern, Rob Krier, Sjoerd Soeters and others. In 1997 Hulsman also offered Carel Weeber the opportunity to defend his Wilde Wonen (Wild Living) in a page-long article – while he completely passed over the fact that Adriaan Geuze and West 8 and MVRDV had al ready developed much more interesting concepts before. Weeber's Wild Living was no more than a light version of West 8's plan *Wilderness* for AIR Alexander from 1993 and MVRDV's Light Urbanism from 1995. The latter two projects had a much more ecological background, because they imagined individual houses on very large plots, providing a continuity of green space. This aspect disappeared completely in Weeber's plan, which he had created for the constructor ERA Bouw, in favour of a vague plea for the liberty of house buyers and against the architect. According to Weeber, the role of the architect would go to be industrial designer, who creates standard parts that should be for sale in construction markets. This was a remarkable plea, if we consider that Weeber was still the president of the Bond voor Nederlandse Architecten (Confederacy of Dutch Architects) at that time. If we look at the developments in Dutch architecture and urbanism, we can only conclude that everyone is at Hulsman's beck and call. At the moment he is by far the most influential critic within the Netherlands. Precisely in Hulsman's writings Post-Modernist and Populist rhetoric blend into a mix with consequences that can hardly be overseen.

In no time individual home ownership has become the basis of Dutch architecture and planning and neo-historicism rules. At the same time, a superficial look on the new quarters reveals very quickly that the real issue in this case is not about in what style to build at all.

Research at the Berlage Institute in 2000–2001 learned that the consequence of all this is that within a few years a small number of major producers of catalogue houses dominate the market. In other words: again we have an economy of supply that is only slightly concealed in a retro-style guise. Inside we may find completely modern interiors (mostly coming from Ikea) and outside the gardens – that also have become a major industry – maybe modern or Japanese or whatever styles the lifestyle magazines propose in that year.

The Fifth Memorandum on Spatial Planning that was in the making, and that already in itself was the weakest ever produced, was abandoned and replaced by an even weaker one. The market has been given an even more important role. In the bigger cities, a more varied offer of housing will be realised to reintroduce the middle class and higher incomes, to come to "a more balanced distribution of groups of inhabitants" and to "improve the quality of the housing stock". Housing corporations are forced to sell their rental flats faster. Where the less wealthy groups of inhabitants have to go, many of them immigrants of course, nobody knows. Today, for the first time in thirty years, the Netherlands is facing a housing shortage.

For the first time ever in the Netherlands, the consequences of segregation, culminating particularly under Moroccan and Antillian youth, become clearly apparent. The murderer of filmmaker Theo van Gogh, a radical populist columnist in the footsteps of Fortuyn, is a Moroccan who originally was involved in all kinds of social work but was disappointed in his opportunities in the end and became easily seduced by Islamist terrorist scouts.

Here we see that an apparently simple and innocent measure like the abolishment of subsidies for public housing in no time leads to new concentrations of money and power. There is no question that the largest part of these new concentrations is legal. But the enormous growth of these concentrations, on one hand, and the ideologically determined reduction of rules and control, on the other, also led to new forms of organized crime. It is not just the Russian mafia that launders its money by investing in real estate in cities like London and Amsterdam. Also local criminals have discovered the potential of the real estate market. This goes far beyond money laundering. Criminals blackmail real estate tycoons to move, sell and resell real estate for prices that may not exactly be their market value. This however is very difficult to verify by the authorities, not in the least because of the complex networks of firms that is involved. Over the last couple of years, a whole series of executions of criminals and real estate brokers shocked the Dutch society. Some of the criminals and businessmen are currently under trial. The murder of one real estate broker, Willem Endstra, known as the bank of the underworld, in 2004, who talked to the police before he died, triggered a whole series of confessions and arrests. Willem Holleeder, a notorious criminal who became known as one of members of the gang who kidnapped Freddy Heineken and his driver in 1983, is currently under trial for among others, this murder. The trial was postponed after Holleeder had to undergo heart surgery. Therefore, it is not yet clear to what extent he is the Godfather of organized crime in the Netherlands. But that is not the only complicating factor for the police. The new organized crime does not seem to have a hierarchical structure anymore but its protagonists work in constantly changing, irregular networks, in which upper- and underworld are often hard to distinguish.

Exactly those new concentrations of money and power, both legal and illegal, financed and supported Fortuyn. Just like post-modern architecture defines the new developments in the market using quasi-historical images, it was Fortuyn who, as a post-modern politician, appealed to his audience, The People with well-known images. And just as we have learned to believe over the last decades that an architectural language has nothing to do with ideology, it was the former Marxist Fortuyn who was proud of his ideological emptiness.

And even if today the Lijst Pim Fortuyn practically no longer exists, many parties have taken up parts of its programme and populist strategies. This is not surprising of the traditional right-wing parties, but the former Dutch Social Democrats, the Partij van de Arbeid, have also left all traces of their original ideology behind in their latest manifesto – without being able to offer anything new yet. After some years of quarrelling, in 2006, the LPF did not gain enough votes to return in the Dutch parliament. Winners of the elections were a new right wing party focussing on immigration politics and the Socialist Party that originated in the Maoist parties from the 1970s and 80s.

From a country that had a leading role in introducing Third Way politics in the Purple Governments in the 1990s and seemed economically and culturally exceptionally healthy to such a degree that all other European countries and even Bill Clinton were looking at it with great interest, in a few years' time the Netherlands again has gained a leading role, but now as an example that others certainly do not want to follow. The side effects of Third Way politics, particularly in the field of architecture and urbanism, can hardly be overseen.

Even if it is clear that welfare states and western European democracies have to change, it has become clear that populist criticism is not enough and that new perspectives soon have to be developed. The populism as introduced by Pim Fortuyn in the Netherlands that is now followed by others had a devastating effect, not just on architecture but on the Dutch state as a whole.

THE COMPUTER AS CAMERA AND PROJECTOR

Within a relatively short space of time the computer has come to be an accepted feature of architecture, both in the design process and when it comes to the everyday operation of buildings and the city. Yet we are constantly aware that the consequences of the computer's introduction into architecture will eventually be much more far-reaching than is presently the case. From the very beginning, architects, artists, media designers and theorists have nonetheless speculated about these implications. It is after all a theme that invites extensive speculation and experiment and this has led to a spate of publications, installations, symposia, built experiments, and exhibitions. Among the latter is the series of exhibitions collectively entitled Transarchitectures. Transarchitectures 01 was held in 1997 and according to Marcus Novak, participating architect and one of the pioneers of virtual architecture, it was the first exhibition devoted specifically to this subject. With the passage of time and the increase in the number of exhibitors it is now clear that the individual architects, on closer inspection, have such radically divergent interests and use or develop such radically different software that, unlike a few years ago perhaps, it is no longer possible to lump them all together under the one heading. There is a growing danger that the general public will interpret the whole thing as "architects lost in cyberspace" – to misquote the title of the celebrated issue of Architectural Design which included the article by Marcus Novak from which Transarchitectures takes its name.[1] Novak goes so far in his article as to identify cyberspace in glowing terms as the last hope for a radical continuation of modernism: "Cyberspace as a whole, and networked virtual environments in particular, allow us not only to theorize about potential architectures informed by the best of current thought, but to actually construct such spaces for human inhabitation in a completely new kind of public realm. This does not only imply a lack of constraint, but rather a substitution of one kind of rigor for another. When bricks become pixels, the tectonics of architecture become informational. City planning becomes data structure design, construction costs become computational costs, accessibility becomes transmissibility, proximity is measured in numbers of required links and available bandwidth. Everything changes, but architecture remains."[2] This recital recalls the short story by science fiction writer William Gibson in which a woman who has experimented endlessly with facelifts and wafer-thin exoskeletons in quest of eternal youth, finally submits to sampling in cyberspace – from where she phones

1 Novak, Marcos. "Transmitting Architecture." Architectural Design Profile, no. 118 – Architects in Cyberspace (1995).
2 Ibid.

3   Gibson, William. "Wintermarkt." In *Biotech*, by NOX 2. 1992. (Originally published as "The Winter Market," in *Burning Chrome*, London, 1988)

4   Spuybroek, Lars. "The Motorization of Reality." *ARCHIS*, November 1998. (Also published in *A+U* no. 349)

the shaken narrator. After all, he reasons, she may wander through cyberspace forever more, but doesn't that mean that she is in fact dead?[3]

In an interview Paul Virilio warns us that there is no reason for euphoria yet because virtual transarchitecture is still in its infancy. He also reminds us of the architect's task to build the real space and to allow the actual space of the program and the latent virtual space to coexist inside it. The only buildings that can perhaps be said to approach this ideal today are the H2O Pavilion by NOX and Kas Oosterhuis and NOX's V2 Lab.

In the same interview, Virilio points to the need to devise a new perspective – literally, in the sense of a method for structuring perception and designing – that takes account of the integration of real and virtual space. This would in his view bring about a revolution comparable to the one launched by the discovery or invention of perspective during the Renaissance and he argues rightly that the great Renaissance architects Alberti and Brunelleschi were equally great painters and theorists: "The perspective of real space of the Quattrocentro doesn't only organize paintings, but the city, politics."

Instead of trying to guarantee the eternal life of an existing architecture in a different medium, our strategy today should be the contamination of that architecture with other media and disciplines in order to produce a new and more robust mongrel breed. In an article The motorization of reality, Lars Spuybroek sees the computer, by analogy with the wooden perspective machines of the Renaissance, as "a tool for structuring visibility."[4]

It is a machine that, depending on the software used, can register reality in the form of video images or other data input, but that is equally capable of simulating, controlling, projecting, and broadcasting reality. The computer is an instrument for visualizing things that cannot be seen with a traditional camera or the naked eye, or for visualizing things in a different way. Tamás Waliczky and Art + Com are examples for using the computer to visualize the aspect of time in visual perception. Steve Mann uses a head-mounted camera with a permanent online link to a web site to explore the invisible limits of the security systems that are continually monitoring us: where and when is observation associated with power? Who has the right to observe where and when and who not? In 10-dencies, Knowbotic Research uses the computer as a machine for visualizing invisible force fields in the city in order to make them available for collective actions which can then be elaborated in a network environment.

But the computer is also a projection instrument. Projection can also be understood as the realization of an architectural project developed entirely in accordance with the logic of the computer. Greg Lynn's project for an industrially produced house is an example of this. It makes use of the rules defined for computer-controlled production robots (like the ones used in the automotive industry) which permit extensive variations in the item under production provided certain basic conditions, a kind of DNA, are met. In light of this, Lynn's design can be seen as a series of embryos for CAD/CAM-produced assembly-line houses.

Interactivity is the next stage. Here the computer becomes a machine that converts observations – input – directly into projections by means of special software. This makes it possible to design and build spaces that react directly to the behavior of the visitors who enter them. The rods in Christian Möller's Audio Grove installation convert physical contact into sound and light effects. And in its Chamberworks installation, Ocean makes use of an interactive sound and light system that registers the movements of visitors inside a complex spatial installation. But this interactivity can also play a role during the design phase, as in Greg Lynn's earlier designs like the H2 house in Schwechat near Vienna, or in Ocean's design for the physical part of Chamberworks. By firing particles inside a computer-simulated model of reality, Ocean generated a pattern of lines that was then used to model the installation.

Perhaps as we peer at the totality of presentations, we shall catch a glimpse of a future architecture. But let us above all look at them open-eyed and critically: where do these machines fail? Where do the accidents occur? Surely the essence of machines is that they break down? To quote media artist Bill Viola: "Yet try as I might, I cannot image the moment of my death."[5]

5   Viola, Bill. "The Visionary Landscape of Perception." In *Reasons for Knocking at an Empty House: Writings 1973–1994*, edited by Robert Violette. London: Thames and Hudson, 1995.

THE DIAGRAM DEBATE

OR THE SCHIZOID ARCHITECT

The Diagram Debate

Or the Schizoid Architect

1 Bijlsma, Like, Wouter Deen, and Udo Garritzmann. "Editorial." OASE, no. 48 (1998).

2 Deleuze, Gilles, and Félix Guattari. Capitalisme et schizophrénie 1 : L'Anti-Œdipe. Paris: Les Éditions de Minuit, 1972.

Over the past few years, the diagram has occupied an essential place in the debates touching on architectural design. In their introduction to a special issue of the architecture review OASE devoted to the diagram,[1] like Bijlsma, Wouter Deen and Udo Garritzman write, "The diagram is a graphic representation of the evolution of a phenomenon. There are lines, a structure and a form; it works by reduction, abstraction and representation. As a medium, the diagram serves a dual function: It is a form of notation, analytical and reflexive, which sums up; but it is also a model for thinking, synthesizing and productive, which engenders." The way architects make use of the diagram sometimes favours the former role, sometimes the latter. Most often, the diagram constitutes a practical solution that enables one to express simply an overall complexity within the framework of communicating with the client, the members of the firm, or the general public. Ideally, the diagram serves as a conceptual tool through which things evolve, eventually reappearing transformed.

It is in the fundamental works of philosophers like Michel Foucault, Félix Guattari and Gilles Deleuze that one should seek the theoretical reason for the use of diagrams in design work in architecture. In the first chapter of Capital and Schizophrenia,[2] a text that architects have more or less forgotten or suppressed, Deleuze and Guattari write, "Capital is indeed the body without organs of the capitalist, or rather of the capitalist being. But as such, it is not only the fluid and petrified substance of money, for it will give to the sterility of money the form whereby money produces money. It produces surplus value, just as the body without organs reproduces itself, puts forth shoots, and branches out to the farthest corners of the universe." At the time (the year 1972), Deleuze and Guattari could not go too far. At most, they could sketch out a parallel between desiring production and social production: "...the forms of social production, like those of desiring production, involve an unengendered non-productive attitude, an element of anti-production coupled with the process, a full body that functions as a socius. This socius may be the body of the earth, that of the tyrant, or capital. This is the body that Marx is referring to when he says that it is not the product of labour, but rather appears as its natural or divine presupposition. In fact, it does not restrict itself merely to opposing productive forces in and of themselves. It falls back on ("il se rabat sur") all production, constituting a surface over which the forces and agents of production are distributed, thereby appropriating for itself all surplus production and arrogating to itself both the whole and parts of the process, which now seems to emanate from it as a quasi cause. Forces and agents come to represent a miraculous form of its own power: they appear to be *miraculated* (miraculés) by it. In a word, the socius as a full body forms a surface where all production is recorded, whereupon the entire process appears to emanate from this recording surface."[3]

Nowadays, to establish a relationship between desiring and social production no longer poses a problem: the computer takes care of it. As a sophisticated tool, the computer not only influences every particular aspect of social life, but above all it establishes a multitude of new relationships. Everything is indeed converted into a flow of data, an infinite interpolation of 0 and 1, which can be apparently exchanged and manipulated without difficulty. This flow of data has assumed the role of capital and even more than that. We live today in a *space of flows*, to borrow Manuel Castells' expression,[4] within infinite networks, in which machines, men, desires and merchandise are linked to, and converted into, one another. It is a space that gives rise to altogether new relationships of power, symbolized by the new financial centres and cities that are springing up at exotic and improbable sites even today, Shenzhen, Singapore, Kuala Lumpur or Hani Rashid's virtual stock market. It is a space in which there is not even an immediate link between money and gold reserves. Everything simply merges in a series of metamorphoses whose beginning and end are impossible to situate. It is here that society produces its own delirium: "Everywhere *it* is machines – real ones, not figurative ones: machines driving other machines, machines being driven by other machines, with all the necessary couplings and connections".[5] Nevertheless, this situation does not resemble the stammering and stuttering Society of the And described by Roemer van Toorn.[6] What energy has not been spent, over the years, so that these couplings and connections take place in fluidity and silence? Since the old telephone exchanges, with their plugs and loud switches, and Hollerith's crackling perforated card machines, to the supple software programs of computers, immense progress has been accomplished. Nowadays everything has become process and the world is adapting. Data are indeed the bodies without organs of the second modernity.

3   Ibid.
4   Castells, Manuel. *The Rise of the Network Society.* Malden, MA; Oxford: Blackwell Publishers, 1996.

5   See note 2.
6   Van Toorn, Roemer. "The Society of the And (an Introduction)." *Hunch*, No. 1, 1999.

7   Spuybroek, Lars. "Machining Architecture." In *The Weight of the Image: Teaching Digital Design Techniques in Architecture*, by Lars Spuybroek and Bob Lang (Arup). Rotterdam: NAi Publishers, 2001.

For architecture and the software that has been developed for architectural design, the consequences of this evolution are obviously important. In a text recently published in conjunction with a NAi workshop,[7] Lars Spuybroek (NOX) writes, "Maya is the most integrative tool available today. Students can combine typical data analysis from programs like Excel (Microsoft Office) with image manipulations from stills or films from Adobe PhotoShop or Premiere and the amazing surface modelling tools in Maya. The drill [the students were given to do in the course of the workshop] emphasized time-based tools like Inverse Kinematics (skeletons with bones and joints, generally used to animate bodies such as running dinosaurs), Particle Dynamics (generally used to simulate snowstorms, fire and smoke, or flocks of birds) and Soft Body Dynamics (used for complex material behaviour like fabric in the wind, rubber or jelly-like geometry interacting with other surfaces or force fields such as gravity, turbulence and vortex). One cannot overestimate the effect of this type of software on the minds of architecture students." Spuybroek is nevertheless one of the few to understand that these effects are the effects of machines, not metaphors, as Deleuze and Guattari write. "An organ-machine is plugged into an energy-source-machine: the one produces a flow that the other interrupts. … Hence we are all handymen: each with its little machines. For every organ-machine, an energy-machine: all the time, flows and interruptions. Judge Schreber has sunbeams in his ass. *A solar anus*. And rest assured that it works: Judge Schreber feels something, produces something, and is capable of explaining the process theoretically."[8] It is in this sense that we can almost consider the famous schizo as the prototype of contemporary architecture.

Diagram

Yet if we interpret everything in terms of machines and the effects of machines, if everything flows and merges, how are we going to get a grip? Here the diagram plays a fundamental role. Deleuze borrows the concept from Michel Foucault, who employs the word in Surveiller et punir (1975) with respect to panopticism. Foucault observed that the panoptical prison had a function that went beyond that of the building itself and the penitentiary institution, exercising an influence over all of society. Stressing the function of these machines, which produced various behaviours, he discovered this coercive action in workshops, barracks, schools and hospitals, all of which are constructions whose form and function were governed by the principle of the

8   See note 2.

panoptical prison. According to Foucault, the diagram "is a functioning, abstracted from any obstacle ... or friction [and which] must be detached from any specific use".[9] The diagram is a kind of map that merges with the entire social field or, in any case, with a *particular human multiplicity*. Deleuze thus describes the diagram as an abstract machine. "It is defined by its informal functions and matter and in terms of form makes no distinction between content and expression, a discursive formation and a non-discursive formation. It is a machine that is almost blind and mute, even though it makes others see and speak."[10]

Little wonder then if diagrams have conquered over the past few years an increasingly important place in architecture and town-planning debates, for these disciplines themselves have taken on more and more the appearance of a process and the (built) results influence processes. This evolution is also fostered by the fact that in Foucault's work, the diagram presents a very clear architectural and machinelike dimension from the outset. The analyses of the Downtown Athletic Club that Rem Koolhaas puts forward in Delirious New York,[11] as well as his examination of Arnhem's panoptical prison, appear to be directly inspired by Foucault.

Naturally, most architects make use of diagrams in order to obtain exactly the opposite effect of Foucault's panopticon, or the *striated* space that Deleuze and Guattari describe in Mille Plateaux[12] as "the space instituted by the State apparatus". The two philosophers contrast that space with the nomadic, smooth space that should offer greater liberty to those living in or using it. In recent years then, architects have used all available means to render the space of their buildings and towns as *smooth* as possible, or at least to suggest that. The building is nothing more than a space that develops in a continuous, folding slope and which ideally is seamlessly joined to the ground. If the OMA design for the Villette park is the oldest and still the most visible example of this idea, the Jussieu library, and the open floor in OMA villas that organizes the space between the various individual living rooms, also enter this category because they impose no particular behaviour on the inhabitants. Here the rolling floor is a significant ornament, a form of architectural metaphor, a part for the whole.

9 Deleuze, Gilles. *Foucault*. Paris: Éditions de Minuit, 1986.

10 See note 9.

11 Koolhaas, Rem. "The Downtown Athletic Club." In *Delirious New York*. London: Academy Editions, 1978; Koolhaas, Rem, and Bruce Mau. S, M, L, XL.

12 Deleuze and Guattari. *Capitalisme et schizophrénie 2 : Mille plateaux*. 1980.

13 Hollier, Denis. "Bloody Sundays." In *Against Architecture: The Writings of Georges Bataille.* Cambridge, MA: MIT Press, 1992.

14 Giddens, Anthony. "Living in a Post-Traditional Society." In *Reflexive Modernization: Politics, Tradition and Aesthetics in the Modern Social Order,* by Ulrich Beck, Anthony Giddens, and Scott Lash. Cambridge (UK): Polity, 1994.

Of course, it remains to be determined whether the freedom that architects imagine they are offering with this concept is a genuine freedom. In his preface to the English translation of his study La Prise de la Concorde,[13] Denis Hollier points out, in reaction to the theories of Bernard Tschumi and Jacques Derrida, that the liberty in question is a fictive one, because architectural spaces are, by definition, a part of the social system. The earliest texts by Tschumi were partly based on Hollier's work. To avoid any misunderstanding, the English translation is therefore entitled Against Architecture. Nevertheless, Hollier's critique has broader significance and is not only a response to Tschumi.

Datascapes

In the schema developed by Bijlsma and his associates, the MVRDV Datascapes tend more to analysis and representation. They are visualizations of laws, rules, norms and statistical probabilities, and as such they constitute representations of what the sociologist Anthony Giddens calls abstract systems,[14] that is, bureaucratic systems where the trust in the system as well as the people, institutions and machines that represent it, lies in one's confidence in a certain specialized expertise. In reality, these Datascapes show that the space around us is virtually shot through from the outset with the dominant forces of society. In a single design, there are several abstract systems at work. These systems nevertheless indicate the maximum limits within which the architect can produce his designs. Once the different Datascapes at work have been brought to light, the design becomes the subject of a negotiation in which the architect plays the part of an intermediary and director. Even if the density of legislative and regulatory norms exercises a powerful influence over the design, it is not true that it springs automatically from the accumulation and interference of different Datascapes. To borrow Deleuze and Guattari's expression, Datascapes are not abstract machines, but rather bodies without organs onto which, in principle, each idea can be projected. Similarly, there are instances in which the authorities and assimilated powers impose an invisible discipline on a space. In the final design, MVRDV exhibits the greatest possible number of Datascapes, which are not necessarily in agreement; when all is said and done, the approach is more of a refined form of deconstruction than a unifying technique, in which the design apparently takes shape in the margins.

Apparently, that is, because MVRDV conserves a secret diagram somewhere that really generates the designs. And if the margins are considered a locus of freedom, Hollier's critique is applicable once again.

In the installation Metacity/Datatown, Datascapes seem to function as machines that generate architectural designs for cities. Metacity/Datatown shows how transformations of collective behaviours lead to a transformation of the constructed landscape. The growth in population density of this imaginary city, moreover, remains an important instrument because it reduces the margins. But clearly it is also a form of rhetoric since it refers to a disturbing future scenario in which the population increases so much that it is *necessary* to take rigorous steps. And the inhabitants of the Netherlands, a country that is heavily populated, fear this scenario of the future more than any other place on the globe.

Consequently, Metacity/Datatown is above all a didactic tool that forces us, viewers and potential inhabitants of the city, to make political choices. These choices may eventually lead to models that have nothing in common with the models presented in the installation. In this regard, like MVRDV's earlier designs, Metacity/Datatown is first and foremost a reflexive design, as Ulrich Beck and Anthony Giddens understand the term, namely, a democratic design that explicitly grants the socius an active role by confronting him with social risks in the form of future scenarios.

The project 3-D City, which Winy Maas realized with the Berlage Institut, explores the limits within which a highly dense and compact situation is possible in a series of large architectural models that examine specific commissions for the city. In this commission, however, MVRDV's secret program is becoming increasingly clear. Suddenly, the piece is no longer a mere didactic design that forces viewers to choose. Indeed, Winy Maas openly describes it as an attempt to create a utopian city in order to anticipate the problems posed by both the increase in the world's population and the protection of the environment. The EXPO-pavilion in Hannover also revealed this change since the building was designed in such a way that it passed for an isolated fragment of a large city that remained to be constructed. In this regard, it was a prototype, recalling the experiments carried out by the Japanese metabolists in the 1960s.

From the start of the presentation of Datascapes, Winy Maas consciously established a comparison with some of the famous spectacular designs in the history of architecture. At that point, the work once again amounted to a rhetorical process aiming to show that it was not absolutely necessary to draw first on imagination and individual creativity in order to realize spectacular designs. In no way was daily reality an obstacle to creativity; on the contrary, daily reality could prove sufficiently spectacular if one opened one's eyes to it.

In 3-D City, however, the intention from the start is to create a spectacular city mixing images of Fritz Lang's Metropolis, Archizoom's Superstudio, Archigram's Fifth Element and the cities of science fiction and Hilberseimer, without Maas's seeming to worry about the intentions concealed by these images or the public's reaction. A certain ambiguity thus continues to weigh on the question of whether the 3-D City design constitutes a (makeshift) pragmatic solution for a spectacular problem, a radical extrapolation from an existing situation altogether in keeping with Superstudio's Twelve Ideal Cities, which contains the essential critical message of a utopia to be realized with pragmatic means. A large number of ideas and values associated with this utopia remained unspoken, not to mention the paranoia of what would happen if we refuse to explore 3-D City. MVRDV's secret diagram appears increasingly like an indeterminate utopian city having an unprecedented density. But what kind of behaviour is this machine going to produce? The exploration of the physics of the constructed environment, which MVRDV inaugurated with Datascapes, seems to turn into an exploration of what Alfred Jarry called *pataphysics*, that is, the disturbing, surrealist physics of the possible. And this is precisely the physics of the schizophrenic that serves as a basis for Michel Carrouge's bachelor machines and the desiring machines of Deleuze and Guattari. As I see it, it would be preferable to undertake a critical evaluation of the *physics* that Datascapes temporarily provide. We might perhaps deduce the values that would be useful in the next stage. Admittedly, the debate has only just started because most architects and critics unduly persist in viewing the Datascapes design only as one of the many mini-theories that today's architects put by in order to justify their work. In that context, the 3-D City design may be a necessary, though risky, provocation, since exploration of Datascapes is in danger of getting lost in an increasingly strong demand for quantities and intensities.

15 Van Berkel, Ben, and Caroline Bos. "Diagram Work."
Any, no. 23, 1998.

The architect's dream

Ben van Berkel, Caroline Bos and UN-Studio, on the other
hand, seem to take the opposite approach. In their editorial
published in the special issue the review Any devoted to the
diagram,[15] they explicitly describe the diagram as a "loophole
in global information space that allows for endlessly expansive,
unpredictable, and liberating pathways for architecture:
The end of the grand narrative does not mean that architects
no longer dream their own dreams, different from anyone
else's". As they affirm in Mille Plateaux, Deleuze and
Guattari demanded of their books, concepts and diagrams
that they help to maintain a rhizomatic relationship with
(parts of) reality. In other words, they had to use their roots
in order to forcibly draw from the world their nutrients.
With Van Berkel & Bos, this relationship is radically reversed.
Like the architect's dream, the diagram is projected onto the
world. Readers will note that implicitly the ideal of freedom
expressed here does not concern inhabitants/users but
rather the architect. Obviously, this is a polemical stand
taken against the architecture of Rem Koolhaas, MVRVD,
Christiaanse, Neutelings, West 8 and many others, which Van
Berkel & Bos consider as pragmatic architecture. In reality,
the situation is more complex of course. Certain UN-Studio's
designs, for example, are based on extremely detailed
statistical and quantitative analyses; in other instances,
ideas are integrated in an extraordinarily refined, precise
manner. Nevertheless, unlike the *pragmatic*, UN-Studio
favours a formal, aesthetic and metaphorical treatment of
analyses: literally even, as when Van Berkel & Bos put a
portrait of the Manimal on the cover of their book Move. This
computer-generated image, in which human faces and animal
heads merge as in a dream, replaces the symbolic figure
of a man drawn in a square and a circle, once imagined by
Leonardo da Vinci. Whereas Da Vinci's diagram is the symbol
of humanism and the central place that man, in this view,
occupies at the heart of the world and the cosmos,
this Manimal is the symbol of a *posthumanism* in which all
possibilities merge with one another. Yet in Van Berkel &
Bos's designs, as in the work of numerous contemporary
American architects, this posthumanism does not in any way
change the position and role of the architect. Just as the
architects of the Renaissance, in the eyes of art historians,
seem to have first of all expressed symbolically a view of the
world through their constructions, Van Berkel & Bos appear
to retain such a privileged role for the architect. However,
if everything merges, if there is no longer either a beginning
or an end to discover, the architect's role is necessarily

affected: how is one to lend henceforth symbolic form to reality here on earth and, by doing so, resolve and reconcile breaks, oppositions and conflicts? To fill that role, the architect must turn to a higher order, which remains hidden to most mortals but which he can make visible, be it with his arse, like President Schreber attracting heavenly rays in Deleuze and Guattari's work.[16]

To that end, Van Berkel & Bos (along with many others) use diagrams that are notably borrowed from genetic technology, chaos theory, complexity theory, string theory, etc. How this theoretical physics is integrated in the design is hardly different from the way in which metaphysics was symbolically translated in past architectural designs, if we are to believe the classic interpretation proposed by historians of art and architecture. The desire to express in architecture the fundamental outlook of a period is naturally a respectable conception of the discipline. Apart from that, popes and priests are not enough for metaphysics, it also demands architects and artists. Moreover, chaos theory, complexity theory and string theory are extraordinarily interesting, and are studied in depth and scientifically grounded. Nevertheless, these theories have yet to teach us anything about the way we behave (or ought to behave) as individuals in everyday life. At most, chaos theory can explain the behaviour of a large-scale population by analogy with equivalent populations. On the other hand, we still do not know at what size those populations ought to maintain themselves. On the purely scientific level, these theories offer no manuals for specific situations. It is improbable that they can, for example, suggest what behaviour one should adopt when an architectural design faces irreconcilable interests. The other way around, these theories offer critics no indication of how they should judge designs. If it is true, for example, as Sanford Kwinter pointed out during a lecture at the Berlage Institut,[17] that the entire world, indeed the entire cosmos, is vibrating and that these vibrations determine everything, according to string theory, then by definition any construction obeys this determination, whether it is a building by Rem Koolhaas (as Kwinter, in this instance, would like rather surprisingly), Ben van Berkel, Daniel Liebeskind, Rob Krier or some talented unknown.

Of course we are fooling ourselves if we imagine that a certain type of architecture or town-planning whose forms are in motion can offer greater freedom, and thus contribute to preventing conflicts, the idea being that these forms adapt more naturally to certain flows. If this is the

16   See note 2.

17   Kwinter, Sanford. Lecture, Berlage Institut, Amsterdam.

18 Bird, Colin. *The Myth of Liberal Individualism.* New York: Cambridge University Press, 1999.

way we must interpret these designs, as certain architects inspired by Kevin Kelly, for example, believe we must, one ends up constructing a theory that in reality recalls the liberal individualism of F. A. Hayek, based upon a belief in a *spontaneous order*, an *invisible hand*, more than the Deleuzian critique of capitalism. As the political scientist Colin Bird has remarked, "I can believe that the state really is an organism and yet deny that it has any moral significance whatsoever. The mere fact that a jellyfish is *organic* does not elevate it to a moral status equivalent [to] or beyond that attributed to human beings."[18]

It is no accident if the work of UN-Studio proves a success when it comes to resolving complex questions of infrastructure, organizing, for example, Castells' *space of flows* in the case of the Arnhem railroad station. Here the different forms of infrastructure and the movements are statistical data in a way. Indeed, it is not difficult to translate the flow of passengers into a flow of data. Theoretically, freedom is at stake here, on the individual level, since different possibilities are available for changing trains, but these possibilities are not realized at the site and, moreover, most can be ignored by the mass of people, in terms of the design. The Arnhem station is a machine that looks like the motor of a Ferrari equipped with shiny smooth manifolds. The way the diagram of the Klein Bottle forms in this design a formal lead that runs throughout it once again presents a meaning that is especially symbolic and magic, so transcending the original situation that one can almost speak of an inversion. The concept of transportation flows suddenly seems like the specific expression of a superior order which exercises its power over all the other parts of the design.

Involuntary (de)construction

Greg Lynn has explained on many occasions how the design for the Korean Presbyterian Church in New York was generated by means of diagrams. How in the computer different *meta blobs* interacted according to their zones of assigned gravitational force. How they grew and melted together into new forms until they achieved a state of equilibrium. How these meta blobs stood for different programs, single rooms that merged into one big room with a single surface that incorporated the entire program. How the clients loved this, because they could actually manipulate the forms themselves, making things bigger and smaller without destroying the coherence of the overall concept. Then he introduced a different strategy. A series of tubes was put on the roof of an existing building that we hadn't seen before, the ancient Knickerbocker Laundry. The tubes grew and developed into a rib-like structure with an inner and an outer skin. Tubes were added for access and circulation. In this phase, the smoothness of the blobs was already partly replaced by a certain degree of segmentation, but everything still seemed to be melded together. After that, there must have been a third phase in which the project was adapted to the building methods of the contractor. Constructions appeared and an industrial facade was introduced. In this phase, the project lost its initial smoothness. Today, it looks almost like a deconstruction of a blob.

What at first seemed to withdraw from language became language again; the diagrams were re-appropriated by language. Today, all the materials suddenly tell a multitude of stories, about what they are, how they are made, how they are put together and how they relate to other materials. What appeared initially as a coherent form informed by all kinds of complex systems, suddenly became a complexity again. And it goes further than that because this is a church-factory, a religion plant, which hosts services for 2,500 people. It simultaneously accommodates multiple non-sectarian programs in 80 classrooms, a 600-seat wedding chapel, various assembly spaces, a choir rehearsal space, a cafeteria and a day care centre. Imagine all these people here, individuals coming from different places around New York, carrying memories from Korea, moving around, doing things in different constellations, like a giant ant farm.

Now, in itself this is not a problem, because as the building stands there it is in some ways maybe even more convincing than if it had been a smooth blob: that would have made a much more disturbing, science fiction-like effect. It would have appeared as if aliens or at least something from *out there* had just landed. Of course, Greg Lynn himself likes these references and he has referred to B-movie blobs on many occasions with a certain perverse pleasure. Because however much disgust and queasiness they may inspire in movie audiences, they also seem to possess a higher form of intelligence. "The term *blob* connotes a thing which is neither singular nor multiple but an intelligence that behaves as if it were singular and networked, but in its form can become virtually infinitely multiplied and distributed."[19] This is an interesting metaphor for a building, because a building is never just one thing and is always caught up in a constantly changing, complex web of relationships and stories. That is what makes architecture so fascinating.

19 Lynn, Greg. "Blob Tectonics, or Why Tectonics Is Square and Typology Is Groovy." In *Folds, Bodies & Blobs: Collected Essays*. Bruxelles: La Lettre Volée, 1998.

This process of change doesn't even stop when the building is realized, but continues forever. After it is realized, it is appropriated by the people who use it, for example. I remember a lecture by Peter Eisenman from a long time ago in which he talked about one of his early houses. When it was realized and the clients came for their first visit, the wife exclaimed, "But I thought we were going to get a Heidi-house!" They first moved into the basement and from day one changed the house and slowly inhabited it until they felt it was their own. Eisenman appreciated that, as he had consciously built in the house a certain resistance. In a way, how the engineers and builders dealt with the original schemes for the Korean church and adapted them to construction methods that they felt familiar with is probably not so different from Eisenman's anecdote, except that it happened even before the realization.

Lynn, however, has always criticized such an approach, or at least he has criticized a deconstructivist architecture that lives on such conflicts and exploits them in geometrical conflicts. Instead of that, he proposes an architecture that is malleable, fluid and supple, to accommodate and integrate all these conflicting forces in a new whole. "Complexity involves the fusion of multiple and different systems into an assemblage that behaves as a singularity while remaining irreducible to any single simple organization."[20]

The building becomes part of a larger ecology and changes with that, which is made possible in the design phase by the latest animation software. In the end, a form is chosen that is static,– however static like a sailing boat, which has a form that allows it to perform well in many different situations. It incorporates all these situations and the final form is mediated between them. In the case of a boat, one could make it more comfortable or faster by changing the parameters, and in the same way one could change the building according to the client's wishes.

But of course, the basic question is what different parameters are selected to play a role in the original ecology? How complex is this ecology really? Who makes the selection of the forces and on what grounds? And, last but not least, couldn't it be that geometrical conflicts in the form of fractures and ruptures are essential to certain ecologies?

In the case of the <u>Korean Presbyterian Church</u>, the ecology still seems to be quite simple. That is not so strange, as it was one of Lynn's first experiments with this way of working.

20 Lynn, Greg. "Possible Geometries." See note 19.

21 Lootsma, Bart. "Eindelijk Echt Ambidexter." *De Architect*, March 1991; see also Lootsma, Bart. "Diagrams in Costumes." *A+U*, no. 342, March 1999.

In the first phase of the design process, a software was chosen that allowed one to locate different parts of the programme, let's say the different chapels, the altar and the choir, into *meta blobs*, which grew together. Now their sizes and relationships could be altered, while they remain related and the overall design coherent. Then the original building was introduced and the model roughly adapted to that roughly, because they still appear as separate entities. In later, similar attempts to introduce a new organization into an existing building, like NOX's design for the V2 Lab in Rotterdam from 1998, the relationship between the new and the existing form seems already more fluent and integrated. However, it is exactly this limited initial ecology that makes Lynn's finally realized building appear as a deconstruction of the original diagrams. These are almost completely hidden in the final construction and detailing. In that sense, in the completed Korean Presbyterian Church, Lynn comes close to the loosely layered way Ben van Berkel and Caroline Bos use diagrams in their designs as *interactive instruments*: as a kind of mission statement in the management of whole projects rather than something that should be realized literally. In an old piece on Van Berkel's work, I spoke of them with a reference to a text on the oeuvre of the Italian painter Francesco Clemente, which Van Berkel always admired, as a kind of *diagrams in costumes*.[21] The dream of the architect is buried in the whole – that is at one and the same time much more interesting than just that dream.

However, Lynn seems to be more ambitious than that. Much more than Van Berkel, whose work is produced in an innovative yet traditional practice that deals with real commissions, his work springs far more from a tradition of academic and theoretical research and should be evaluated as such. In all his projects, Lynn chooses his own parameters to work with. In the House Prototype in Long Island, they are the topography, the wind and the noise from the nearby road, for example, and in the H2 House for Vienna, it is the light from the sun and the cars from the nearby highway. He also selects a particular software and recently, in his Embryologic Housing project, he opted for a production method as a starting point. As almost scientific experiments in a controlled environment, these projects are incredibly valuable and already influential among a broad group of architects. However, the question is whether that is the sole reason Lynn allows for only a selected number of parameters in his projects. It could also be that his desire to produce a coherence in the design in the first place gets in the way of realizing this coherence in the final building, because the real

22 Deleuze and Guattari. *L'Anti-Œdipe*. See note 2.
23 Lynn, Greg. "It's out There... The Formal Limits of the American Avant-Garde." *Architectural Design Profile*, no. 133 – Hypersurface Architecture (guest-edited by Stephen Perella) (1998).
24 Spuybroek, Lars. "Machining Architecture." See note 7.

ecology in which that finds itself is much more complex than Lynn's selection of forces that play a role in it. "Any object supposes the continuity of a flow, any flow, the fragmentation of the object", write Deleuze and Guattari.[22] Fearing the fragmentation of the object in the reality of everyday life, architecture withdraws into a body without organs. Michael Speaks could be right when he says that Lynn, like his mentor Peter Eisenman, is still too much interested in the metaphysics of architecture.[23]

Machine effects

Unlike MVRDV, whose work makes use of the diagram above all as a integrating form of notation, a formal abstraction of a given complex reality, and Van Berkel & Bos and Greg Lynn, for whom the diagram is a chosen form that generates and structures the design, Lars Spuybroek is alone in conceiving the diagram as a complete machine. "The diagram is a very clearly lined network of relationships, but it is completely vague in its formal expression", writes Spuybroek in Machining Architecture. "Diagrams love pulp, and they only recognize materials at their most heated and their weakest stages. The diagram is basically a conceptual input/output device which swallows matter and, while restructuring, also ejects matter. In that sense, every informational plane is always an interface between material states... The diagram ... is an engine, a motor: it doesn't want to impose itself on matter, but to engage in a process of continuous formation; it operates at the backside of the image, on its blind side. Diagrams are the informational nodes and codes of the world; they are stabilizing contractions in material flows – first they channel and then they relax. They are faces in a landscape, singular perceptions connecting streams of actions. They are lenses, mirroring a movement: first a contraction of matter-energy onto an organizing surface, then an expansion into many new other structures."[24]

Contraction is the phase during which information is collected, selected, converted and graphically organized in a virtual machine. It is a process in which a three-dimensional network is converted into a two-dimensional surface. Spuybroek describes it as a movement towards quality, order and organization. Then there occurs a process of expansion in which the machine, the diagram, is put into the material, spreads throughout and gives it a shape. This is a development that enables one to shift from a two-dimensional surface to a three-dimensional structure. Spuybroek describes this as a movement towards quality, materials and structure.

Up to this point, there is nothing in this approach specifically involving a computer. In principle, an expressionist method of working, described by Vassily Kandinsky, for instance, as the chain Emotion-Gefühl-Werk-Gefühl-Emotion, is equally suitable.[25] A process of contraction (Einfühlung) and expansion (Expression), which is endlessly repeated, is also at work here. In that case, individual people are themselves the machine. This process, however, can only be active in that it is a process that is transmittable to others, as if there existed an agreement about the nature of human beings, and all men corresponded to a humanist ideal. This is problematic if we accept that individuals are part of flow networks, in which they must endlessly make choices, and that these choices continuously modify the position, identity and therefore nature of these individuals. The process then becomes altogether subjective. In the architecture of UN-Studio and Greg Lynn, that subjectivity is not resolved because they choose diagrams that exist outside the process to generate their designs. Spuybroek's intention then is to free as much as possible the design process of the architect as well as the individual person by constructing an abstract machine that also lies outside himself and which is linked to the world rhizomatically.

As Spuybroek sees it, the computer is only a machine that reinforces communication between different diagrams. It is a diagram in and of itself, and the specific computer programmes are also diagrams in and of themselves. For Spuybroek, there is no difficulty in describing as material computers the dynamic models borrowed from Antonio Gaudí and Frei Otto, which he uses in certain designs to determine his buildings' form of construction. These are material diagrams because a change in one area influences the form of the overall project. The design process comprises then, in the end, a chain of different diagrams forming a design machine since they are coupled to one another and are continuously converted into one another. For this reason, Spuybroek believes that schools that teach computer-aided design should offer as well instruction in computer-aided conceptualization and computer-aided manufacturing.[26] Even if the computer is an expression of a tendency to make everything smoother, more fluid, Spuybroek shows that there still exist couplings and connections that harbour within them possibilities of choice. The *space of flows* is not a fatality: We can still manipulate it in our own way.

25 Cf. Whyte, Ian Boyd. *Bruno Taut and the Architecture of Activism*. Cambridge (UK): Cambridge University Press, 1982.

26 Spuybroek, Lars. See note 7.

27 Spuybroek, Lars. "Off-the-Road-5 Speed." Edited by Ali Rahim. *Architectural Design (Contemporary Process in Architecture)* 70, no. 3 (June 2000); Pélenc, Arielle. "Wetgrid. Lars Spuybroek on His Exhibition Design 'Vision Machine.'" *ARCHIS*, August 2000.

Since then, NOX has developed this way of working in a series of designs and completed projects that include Off-the-Road-5 Speed, a housing design for Eindhoven in which the five speeds refer to as many diagrams; Wetgrid, an idea for the exhibition Vision Machine held at the Musée de Nantes, or the D-Tower of Doetinchem.[27] The D-Tower design assumed a form that is, in the end, both real and virtual, for, apart from being a real object, the tower itself is also a new diagram which continuously transforms the population of Doetinchem's input to an Internet site.

What is interesting yet problematic in NOX's way of working is that the result (the design and buildings that arise from that) is almost impossible to represent. It is interesting because these designs normally permit a large amount of interactivity with the future inhabitants and users of the building, or because they may play on the modification of subsidiary constraints until a relatively advanced stage; it is also problematic because the design proves difficult to present to a client, for example, who requests that the final form is visualized before the last stage of the process. Thus, up to this point Spuybroek has relied on clients who have been able to reflect at the high level of abstraction of the design process and interpret diagrams on their own. If we wish to consider the computer as a true tool in design rather than a mere implement, if we want to know to what extent we are manipulated in the *space of flows*, it is unavoidable that we resign ourselves to this method. But then again, if Schreber was able to theorize about himself, there is no reason why we cannot as well.

MULTIPLE EXPOSURE

ON ARCHITECTURE, ARTIFICIAL LIGHT AND MEDIA

Multiple Exposure

On Architecture, Artificial Light and Media

Bright lights in big cities have fascinated architects from the start. Erich Mendelsohn published several photographs of New York's Broadway in <u>Amerika: Bilderbuch eines Architekten</u> in 1928 and was completely flabbergasted by them, in particular by a multiple exposure by night, taken by Knud Lønberg-Holm, because it even enhanced the spectacle.

"Unheimlich." He writes: "The contours of the houses have been blurred. But in our consciousness they still rise, run after each other, overrun themselves. That is the madness of the flame writings, the rocket fire of moving light advertisements, diving up and down, disappearing and breaking out over the thousands of cars and the light swirl of the people. Still unorganized, because exaggerated, but already full of fantastic beauty, that will be accomplished one day."[1] On the following pages, Mendelsohn printed a photograph of Broadway by day, showing a chaotic collection of bleak neon signs and their scaffoldings against the backdrop of grey buildings, with the text: "The mysterious, drunk, loses the spectacle of the night. Is only unharnessed, wild, overscreams itself. Grandiose madness of the world-fair: Collars, sugar, Orpheum, tooth brushes, tobacco and 'Vote Charles E. Gehring.'"[2]

Mendelsohn understood the relationship between architecture and light, both natural and artificial light, very well. With the arrival of electric lighting, architecture became gradually more alienated from Le Corbusier's "masterly, correct and magnificent play of masses brought together in light."[3] In the American city, sunlight revealed the actual chaos that many European architects – including Mendelsohn – criticized. At night however, this chaos could be tricked out, camouflaged and replaced by a fantasy world.

Inversion and Immersion

The role of artificial light in architecture is defined by two principles: inversion and immersion. The principle of inversion is obvious: light appears in the dark and neon signs stand out against a dark background. What remains are just the signs and architecture disappears. This kind of light is something we look at in the first place, from a distance.

1   Mendelsohn, Erich. *Amerika: Bilderbuch Eines Architekten*. Berlin: Rudolf Mosse, 1926.

2   Idem.
3   Le Corbusier. *Ausblick Auf Eine Architektur*. Gütersloh; Berlin: Bertelsman, 1969.

The signs look completely different by day. Than we just see the improvised chaos that was constructed to make them shine at night.

There have been many attempts to integrate lighting in architecture. Usually, architects look for solutions that underline the volumes and contours of their buildings. Mendelsohn's own Schocken department stores in Stuttgart (1926–1928) and Chemnitz (1927–1930) are good examples of this strategy. In Stuttgart, the rhythmic alignment of windows and the bold typeface that forms the name Schocken produce a strong graphic image at night. In Chemnitz, Mendelsohn uses the effect of inversion in the purest possible way: the ribbons of windows appear in dark contrast to white stucco ribbons by day; at night they produce the opposite effect, when the ribbon windows are brightly lit, leaving the parapets dark in contrast.

The principle of immersion is very different. It was only toward 1890 that the introduction of electricity made it possible to create a second daytime. Bright lights were placed at regular intervals along the surf line of Coney Island, "so that now the sea can be enjoyed on a truly metropolitan shift-system, giving those unable to reach the water in daytime a man-made twelve-hour extension. What is unique in Coney Island – and this syndrome of the Irresistible Synthetic prefigures later events in Manhattan – is that this false daytime is not regarded as second rate. Its very artificiality becomes an attraction: 'Electric Bathing.'"[4] Whereby the question is what was considered more important: bathing in the sea or bathing in electric light.

Immersion is in many ways the effect of a virtual space that, because of its enhanced presence, seems to draw us in and makes us almost forget about reality. Immersion is of course a principle that underlies many literary, theatrical, and cultural phenomena in general, which draw us in and take us away on a trip. However, for some reasons, particularly moving patterns and projections of light seem to be particularly fascinating, whether as fireworks or as moving images. Light always has a further reaching effect: it holds the promise of surrounding us and often does, be it as omnipresent daylight or as ambient light.

Inversion and immersion come together in the computer, in large video screens and in media facades that can wrap whole buildings. The image on the computer, originally a cathode ray tube and today an LCD flat screen, is drawn by

4   Koolhaas, Rem. *Delirious New York*. London: Academy Editions, 1978.

light on or against a dark background. The same is true for the large plasma screens and OLED and LED media facades that increasingly define our living environment. All architecture, real or virtual, is therefore drawn by light in some way, and both are communicated through the Internet. This increasingly causes a blurring of the borders between the real and the virtual on all levels.

Cineac

An early modernist building that plays with both inversion and immersion in an intelligent way is the Cineac in Amsterdam by Johannes Duiker and Bernard Bijvoet from 1934. It was a small cinema with a continuous program that tried to be the moving equivalent of popular weekly magazines during which people could come in and leave any time they wished. The daily newspaper Handelsblad – today NRC Handelsblad – owned the building. In an article that appeared in the Newspaper Handelsblad in 1934 entitled 'Modern Theatre Building,' Duiker emphasized the role of the building as a machine, offering the audience a perfect climate and acoustics not to be disturbed from the movie experience, which is immersive by nature. 'The general public has requirements but does not reflect and knows less about a theatre than about an airplane. One knows somehow that a plane made of bricks cannot fly. But the public is not interested whether or not a theatre is made of bricks for it doesn't understand the consequences.'[5] The Cineac was not an attack –in Duiker's words – 'on romantic instincts by means of sultry architecture' like the famous art deco Tuschinsky Theatre across the street. 'The Cineac theatre offers a business-like publicity, doubtless sober but at the same time unsettling because of authentic realities taken from life.'[6] Duiker writes. Indeed, the building is a key example of the Dutch variant of 'Neue Sachlichkeit' or New Sobriety.

Neon billboards reading 'CINEAC' and their scaffoldings are integrated in the architecture of the building and logically extend the steel structure. Intriguing is the space on the first floor, where the projectors are situated. The public can see these projectors from the street and it can even see them better at night, when the space is lit.

'By stripping away the architectural facade to reveal the "machine as medium," the literal technology to that produces the illusion is exposed, both demystifying it and making it accessible to the average person,' Dan Graham wrote in his

5   Duiker, Jan. "Modern Theatre Building (from E. J. Jelles, C. A. Alberts, Duiker 1890–1935)." Forum (reprint), no. 5 and 6, January 1972. Also Architectura & Amicitia, Amsterdam, 1976, p. 80.
6   Idem.

7 Graham, Dan. "Theatre, Cinema, Power." In *Rock My Religion, 1965–1990*, edited by Brian Wallis, 170–89. Cambridge, Mass.: MIT Press, 1993.

8 Idem.

article Theatre, Cinema, Power.[7] Comparing the CINEAC to the Totaltheater project of Walter Gropius and Erwin Piscator from 1927, Graham writes: "Beyond its reduction of social function to social metaphor, a further difficulty with Duiker's project is that, like many Bauhaus projects, it involved a one-way perspective whereby the outside spectator looks objectively (like a scientist) at the machine to analyze its effects. In actuality, in the cinema – as in real life in the city – all looks are two way and intersubjective. In the film itself, the characters look at one another, or one character may look at another who is momentarily out of frame, or else that character is looked at. Similarly, the spectator is vaguely aware of the presence of other spectators mimicking his or her own looks at the screen and at other viewers. The psychological circuit of intersubjective looks and identifications is echoed in the architectural form (interior and exterior). It is difficult to separate the optics of the architecture (including the film apparatus) from the psychological identifications constructed by the film images."[8]

These observations were the inspiration for Graham's own theatre projects, like Cinema, from 1981. In this project, which clearly refers to the Cineac, Graham proposes a theatre with facades clad in mirroring glass, in which the audience is separated from the street just by a transparent glass wall, to demystify the complex relationship between audience and passersby, between theatre and real life, depending on the light conditions inside and outside. If it is dark inside, the audience cannot just watch the film, but simultaneously the passersby – who at that moment cannot see what happens inside. If the inside is lit, passersby might be seduced to join the people inside, who are now visible to them.

Dusk: the Seduction of the Interior

This element of seduction is characteristic for many architectural photographs that are shot at dusk, while at the same time the buildings are brightly lit from inside. The brief moment at dusk enables the photographer to show inside and outside of the building simultaneously, because light intensity inside and outside is more or less the same. One can say this allows demonstrating the transparency and structure of buildings. But it does more. In a colour photograph we immediately associate the warm, yellowish light coming from the inside of the building with warmth, cosiness and homeliness contrasting with the bluish light and the upcoming cold and darkness of the night outside. Thus, it makes the house or building more desirable to us. We want to be inside and merge with the building. This is an effect that even works in black and white photographs, as several photographs of Case Study Houses by Julius Shulman demonstrate. In his famous photographs of the Stahl House by Pierre Koenig in Los Angeles, we see cool, modern, rich, and happy people in a glass box, hovering over and overlooking the Los Angeles grid. We cannot hear what their conversation is about. Excluded, peeping in from the outside, we would like to join them and be part of this elegant social event. Shulman's photograph of the Chuey Residence in Los Angeles by Richard Neutra plays this game of inversions even further, using the mirroring of the pool and lamps inside and outside to produce an effect as if there is an artificial moon in the pool and a sun in and the house.

Ecstacity

Dutch urbanist and chairman of the CIAM Cornelis van Eesteren used the same Lønberg-Holm photograph Mendelsohn was so fascinated by in slide shows in the 1920s to convince his audiences that the functional city was not necessarily boring. The illuminated advertising signs in New York were in his view 'one of the elements that help prevent the functional city from turning rigid.'[9]

So, even if architects are usually control freaks and very aware that they could not define the content of what would be shown, it was exactly the wild, uncontrollable nature of the phenomenon that appealed to them. It could bring their buildings and cities alive. This idea was formulated most poignantly by Sigfried Giedion, Fernand Léger and José Luis Sert in their influential 1943 manifesto 9 Points on a New Monumentality.[10] According to this manifesto, architects and artists together should design city centres in which these spectacles could take place to bring back a sense of communality.

Indeed, public spaces with a concentration of media facades do tend to attract a crowd. Just think of Piccadilly Circus in London or Times Square in New York. However, the attitude towards media facades from the side of local politicians seems more reserved today than ever – apart from the 'usual suspects' like Las Vegas, Times Square and some quarters in Japanese cities like Tokyo, Osaka and Fukuoka.

9. Van Eesteren, Cornelis. Het idee van de functionele stad: ein lezing met lichtbeelden 1928/ The Idea of the Functional City: a lecture with slides 1928. Rotterdam: NAi Publishers, 1997.

10. Giedion, Sigfried, José Luis Sert, and Fernand Léger. "Nine Points on Monumentality." In Architecture, You and Me: The Diary of a Development, by Sigfried Giedion, 48–52. Cambridge, MA: Harvard University Press, 1958.

11 Coates, Nigel. *Guide to Ecstacity.* London: Laurence King, 2003.

Cities try to ban media facades, not just in Zurich, where the local alderman says 'he does not want to live in a slot machine' but also in Sao Paolo, where the mayor recently banned all billboards. At the same time architects, artists and media designers seem more excited than ever to rethink the opportunities media facades offer.

The new developments that enable whole buildings to turn into computer or video screens are a decisive step in a process that will finally turn the city into what Nigel Coates calls <u>ECSTACITY</u>, a city half-real and half-imaginary that builds upon the existing city and is totally immersive by nature.[11] Of course, the city has always been an immersive experience, as we undergo it bodily and with all our senses. What is new though is the way real and virtual space merge. It is not just newer and bigger screens that will accomplish that. Equally or even more important will be things like pervasive computing, wireless communication networks, GPS and its next improved European version, Galileo, that will also work inside of buildings. The current developments in *big* or *pervasive games*, computer games that play in the real world, may even be more spectacular than those in the field of big screens. They hint at completely new ways of social, spatial and creative organization in the city.

Dazzle Painting

To understand what media facades do to architecture, we might return to the beginning of the 20th century, when architects and artists were defining a new artistic and architectural vocabulary together. Modern art was one of the driving forces behind the complete rethinking of architecture. Several painters decided, often after first collaborating with architects, to become architects themselves.

Theo van Doesburg, artist, writer, and architect, founder of De Stijl, was aware that his art was far ahead of architecture. Impatient, he hoped that his colour schemes for stained glass windows, tiles, woodwork, and increasingly larger surfaces would 'deconstructivate' (dekonstruktiveren in Dutch) – to freely translate his own vocabulary at the time – the rather simple volumetric constructions he was dealing with into 'counter-constructions.' Dutch architects like J. J. P. Oud and Cornelis van Eesteren initially liked that, until Van Doesburg, who considered an architectural education as an obstacle to come to a pure architectural image, inevitably lost all connection to reality and gravity, insisting on the superiority of his artistic vision. In many

12 Le Corbusier. "Architecture and the Arts."
In *Le Corbusier, Architect, Painter, Writer*, edited by
Stamo Papadaki, 141–45. New York: Macmillan, 1948.
(originally published in *Transition*, no. 25, Autumn 1936)

13 Idem.
14 Colomina, Beatriz. "The Split Wall: Domestic
Voyeurism." In *Sexuality & Space*, edited by Beatriz
Colomina. New York: Princeton Architectural Press, 1992.

ways, his colour concepts for different buildings reminded of the practice of *dazzle painting* as it had been developed during the First World War to make large ships unrecognizable for enemy submarines by painting them in abstract geometric patterns in contrasting colours.

Inscription of Plastic Thoughts

Le Corbusier, even though he had a parallel career as a painter, had a very different opinion than Van Doesburg. For a long time he kept the two careers not just separate, as an architect he would even keep quiet that he was painting for a long time. Le Corbusier was quite aware what colour could do to architecture.

At least until the late 1930s, Le Corbusier remained opposed to wall paintings and murals. Architecture in itself should be a plastic event. 'Today we are saturated with images (…) we are swamped with images through cinema as well as through the magazine or the daily newspaper. Is not, then, a great part of the work formerly reserved for painting accomplished?'[12]

According to Le Corbusier unemployed artists – in the nineteen thirties several European countries founded programs that tried to provide unemployed artists with work decorating buildings – should look for work in film or photography. As such, they might find a place in architecture, such as with the 'mur à photomontages' that Le Corbusier had installed in the Pavillon Suisse in Paris in 1932.

Paintings, art, should be kept out of sight until the moment one really wanted to immerse in them and meditate. Then one could get them out of a closet. Polychrome walls could support architecture's plasticity but the only places suitable to invite an artist would be walls that were there for other than strictly architectural reasons. Artists could blow them up. 'I can also, if the place is suitable, have recourse to a painter, ask him to inscribe his plastic thought in the spot, and with one stroke open all the doors to the depth of a dream, just there where the actual depths did not exist.'[13] Therefore Beatriz Colomina is absolutely right when she wrote about Le Corbusier's first murals in the beautiful house of Jean Badovici and Eileen Gray in Cap Martin as a kind of rape.[14]

Only after the Second World War, under the influence of the manifesto '9 Points on a New Monumentality' as written

15 See Lootsma, Bart. "Le Corbusier Synthèse des arts. Kunst unter den Flügeln der Architektur." txt.architekturtheorie.eu. November 22, 2009. http://txt.architekturtheorie.eu/?p=1331.

16 Le Corbusier. *Vers une Architecture (Towards a new architecture)*. Paris: Les Éditions G. Crès, 1923.

by Giedeon, Léger and Sert, Le Corbusier joined the younger architects in the CIAM and started striving for a Synthesis of the Arts. Then he painted a large mural instead of the original 'mur à photomontages' in the Pavillon Suisse, that had been destroyed during the war. The emptiness of the centre of Chandigarh was exactly there to enable mass spectacles as desired in the manifesto of the three long time members of the CIAM. They would be surrounded by sculpturally interesting and spectacularly lit facades.[15]

Through the Roof

With colour, light, and also coloured light became increasingly important in Le Corbusier's post-war work – far beyond beyond the famous quote that defines architecture as "the masterly, correct and magnificent play of masses brought together in light." This quote just explains that "Our eyes are made to see forms in light; light and shade reveal these forms; cubes, cones, spheres, cylinders or pyramids are the great primary forms which light reveals to advantage; the image of these is distinct and tangible within us without ambiguity. It is for this reason that these are beautiful forms, the most beautiful forms."[16]

Parallel to the introduction of murals and freer, more sculptural forms in his architecture, Le Corbusier started experimenting with different sources and qualities of light, both natural and artificial, to introduce particular aesthetic effects. The play with natural light one can witness particularly in his sacred buildings, like the chapel and the church in the convent of La Tourette (1953–1960), the chapel in Ronchamp (1953–1955) and the St. Pierre church in Firminy (1954–2006). First, Le Corbusier starts to use the different qualities and character of light during the day more consciously than ever. The movement of the sun during the day becomes one of Le Corbusier's favourite diagrams, which he has drawn over and over again and which he has incorporated in many art works. The effect of this movement can be most clearly appreciated in the church of La Tourette, in which the sun projects a sharp line in the austere space, which moves during the day with the movement of the sun. But Le Corbusier also used the differences between the bluish morning light at dawn and the reddish evening light just before sunset, the pale northern light, and the lively, moving light that comes in from the south, not just to produce a play with light and shadow on objects, but to charge the space atmospherically with light as if it were a material in itself. In his sacred buildings, the light hardly ever comes in directly (unless again as an effect), but is either first reflected via a coloured surface or filtered through stained glass windows.

When composers sometimes write pieces to study or demonstrate all different qualities of an instrument, the chapel of Notre Dame du Haut in Ronchamp is a piece that shows us probably everything one can do with natural light in architecture. To fully appreciate what Le Corbusier has done here, it is necessary to visit the building for a whole day, from the earliest morning to the evening. The sculpture of Notre Dame du Haut that lends the chapel its name and meaning is placed in a window, which is the only window to let in eastern light in the morning. Two chapels are dedicated to morning and evening prayers. The first scoops up just the bluish morning light, which falls on grey concrete. The second catches just the warm light of the setting sun, which is enhanced by painting the interior red. The south side of the chapel is even more spectacular, with the immediate confrontation of a chapel lit by just indirect, unmovably cold northern light with a thick wall animated by the constantly changing southern light of the sun falling through a multitude of relatively small stained glass windows in often coloured niches. Through slits around the large revolving door, sometimes rays of sun penetrate in the space of the chapel unfiltered.

The rich, fancyfull, and profound use of light in the chapel in Ronchamp was exactly the reason why Louis Kalff, a legendary light architect himself and in the nineteen fifties general art director of Philips, invited le Corbusier to design the Philips pavilion for the Expo 1958 in Brussels. The idea was that Le Corbusier would enscenate a spectacle in a pavilion that would have been designed by Gerrit Rietveld, one of the architects of the Dutch pavilion, which hosted Philips. In the end, a tree of products by Philips would appear. As Philips feared that competitors would present colour television or other innovations, they decided just to focus on products related to lighting. Le Corbusier accepted, but could not completely agree with this concept. He clearly told Kalff that he considered the commission, leaving the construction of the pavilion to his collaborator, the engineer and composer Iannis Xenakis, as 'entirely an interior job.'[17] "For this I require a fee, and not for a building that ought to cost very little money and that ought to be more of a hollow structure, made of poured concrete, utterly lacking in 'architectonic' radiance, as they say."[18]

17 See Lootsma, Bart. "Entirely an Interior Job, The Philips Pavilion by Le Corbusier, Varèse and Xenakis." *Rassegna*, no. 81 (December 2005).
18 Idem.

This Poème Électronique, which le Corbusier developed
in collaboration with the avant-garde composer and pioneer
in the field of electronic music Edgard Varèse, thus became
one of the first computerized multimedia environments,
using not only all Philips Lighting products, from simple bulbs
to ultraviolet light, and from fluorescent light to theatre
spots and projectors, the Philips studio for electronic music
and, last but not least an early computer developed
from the silent telephone centrals Philips had developed.
The latter was needed to steer and synchronize all the
different light sources with the film, the accompanying film
projections and the sound, which moved through 480 loudspeakers. Le Corbusier focused completely on the
composition projections of images and lights, turning it
into a mix between an architectural polychromy and a moving
'mur à photomontages' – all produced with artificial
light and projections however, the sources of which remained
hidden for the audience. These 'ambiances,' for which
Le Corbusier wrote a precise 'minutage' would produce all
kinds of effects underlaying the black and white film
projections. They would bathe the audience in coloured light.
They were not completely abstract, however. Many of
them simulated atmospheric light conditions and thus, the
Poème Électronique, which told the story of mankind,
would begin with bands of colour simulating the aurora at
daybreak. How close the original idea of the Philips pavilion
was to Ronchamp show the glass plates Le Corbusier
painted or had painted to be used in theatre projectors.
They were painted with the same technique as the stained
glass windows in Ronchamp's southern wall. They were
not used in the end, as the thin colours would not have worked
with the strong lights in the projectors, to be replaced by
other effects.

Le Corbusier acted towards Philips as if he was not at all
interested in the outward appearance of the pavilion designed by Xenakis, even if it was a revolutionary construction.
For Le Corbusier, the pavilion was primarily intended as an
interior experience that would totally immerse the visitors,
and would make them forget about the formal aspects
of architecture. "It should appear as though you are about to
enter a slaughter house. Then once inside, bang, a blow to
the head and you're gone."[19]

According to Le Corbusier, imagery, murals, large projections
tend to blow up architecture, make it disappear, and inscribe
artificial dreams and depths in places where these would
otherwise not be found. Or even if these depths were to be

19 Bibeb. "Interview met Gerrit Rietveld." Vrij Nederland, April 19, 1958.

found, Le Corbusier realizes that these artistic media are much more powerful than architecture in creating space. He pleaded for the development of jeux électroniques, electronic games that could be installed in architecture. For the Carpenter Center in Boston, for example, a sound piece was developed that would accompany visitors acoustically walking up and down the ramp cutting through the building.

The changes caused by media walls go much further than the deconstruction caused by mural painting. If a painting can blow up a wall than we go literally through the roof with these new media. A good example is the roof designed by Jon Jerde above Freemont Street in Las Vegas on which different, specially edited videos can be played. Many of them use exactly the effect of explosions to immerse us in the belief that there is a completely different space behind it and make the audience go literally 'through the roof.' When the Expo in Brussels was over, because of its construction out of pre-stressed concrete, the Philips Pavilion had to be blown up with explosives. It was an ending that was rather symbolically charged, because of the Poème Électronique reaching its climax with nuclear explosions in the middle and ends with a high whistling sound that seems to foreshadow such a dramatic end, and because of Le Corbusiers ideas about what media would do to architecture in general.

Total Immersion

Total immersion into an imaginary world is the ultimate dream of the media industry. Michael Heim defines immersion as 'A key feature of Virtual Reality systems. The virtual environment submerges the user in the sights and sounds and tactility specific to that environment. Immersion creates the sense of being present in a virtual world, a sense that goes beyond input and output. Immersion clearly has psychological components, but it involves sensory input in ways that surpass purely mental imagination.'[20] Beyond mere sight and sound, interactivity is a crucial aspect of immersion. 'How presence and immersion coalesce remains an open question in VR research.'[21] Total immersion in virtual reality environments for entertainment without this coalescence and its possible alienating effects and risks has been the theme of major blockbuster science fiction movies like Total Recall, The Game and Vanilla Sky.

One might even argue that total immersion is the secret desire of our culture as a whole. Architecture has always

20 Heim, Michael. *Virtual Realism.* New York; Oxford: Oxford University Press, 1998.
21 Idem.

22 Banham, Reyner. *The Architecture of the Well-tempered Environment.* Chicago: University of Chicago. 1969.

23 Lally, Sean, and Jessica Young, eds. *Softspace.* London; New York: Routledge, 2007 .

played its part in this longing, not just producing, well-tempered environments,' as Reyner Banham called them, but in trying to create specific ambiances that go way beyond just air conditioning and functional lighting, adding odours and sounds, invisibly manipulating all our senses.[22] In the book Softspace, editors Sean Lally and Jessica Young explore how because of newly available digital tools these 'once elusive conditionings of space are now opening entirely new possibilities for our understanding, creation and experience of architecture.' This would allow a shift in architecture 'From the Representation of Form to a Simulation of Space.'[23] The architecture pills by Hans Hollein and Archigram's Ron Herron from the late nineteen sixties show how deep this desire to immerse into synthetic or synthetically enhanced environments – even if they would just exist in the mind – goes.

Total immersion in a virtual reality was never really achieved. The simulation of 3D, helmets, goggles, gloves, interactivity, and a CAVE may help but what really helps us to believe that we are part of the event is the bigness of the screen and the extent to which we are surrounded with it. We all know the difference between watching a movie on television or in the cinema or an IMAX theatre. By borrowing a 'real' environment like the city, that is immersive by nature, total immersion could come very close. Big screens on the scale of buildings, for example in the form of thousands of LED's covering their facades, could play a further role in the virtual manipulation of space.

Hybridization

The interest in introducing bigger and bigger screens in the city seems to come from the media and advertising industry first. Disney is probably the best example. The company is the driving force behind the renovation and reanimation of Times Square in New York. Disney has a merchandising store there as well as several musical theatres, a theme restaurant and the ABC television studio. On a video screen, Disney presents its television program. At the same time, they have a studio with glass walls that enables them to record the Good Morning America show with the multimedia facades in the background. Real, mediated and imaginary worlds meet here in such a way that the virtual world becomes a part of reality – and is than broadcasted again as such. Not even Dan Graham could have imagined this kind of complex and ambivalent relationships between audience and spectacle when he came with his project for a cinema, in

24 De Jong, Alex, and Marc Schuilenburg. *Mediapolis: Popular Culture and the City.* Rotterdam: 010 Publishers, 2006.
25 Rheingold, Howard. *Smart Mobs: The next Social Revolution.* Cambridge, MA: Perseus, 2003.

which the projection screen would be made from two-way mirrored glass. In comparison to what really goes on, this art project, which intended to be critical about Miesian modern architecture, appears bleak today. Michael Sorkin may have seen the city as a series of variations on a theme park, but he could never have imagined it as a dark ride so enormous that it becomes the real thing. Today it is the entertainment industry that achieves that the city becomes 'a bastard environment in itself in which everything is continually being transformed and medialized. The physical environment is a hybrid location in which various spatialities merge with one another. In short, the city itself has become a mesmerizing mass medium,' Alex de Jong and Marc Schuilenburg write in Mediapolis.[24]

Hybridization is certainly the most important characteristic of the current wave of medialization of architecture and urbanization of media. The consequences of this hybridization can hardly be overestimated, as they will cause more than just esthetical effects. New forms of social and spatial organization and new, collective forms of creativity will emerge from it that will change our lives and architecture profoundly. Howard Rheingold's book Smart Mobs probably only gives a slight hint of that.[25]

The Building as a Studio

When we focus on this hybridization process in buildings, media screens are just one side of the coin. The other is that buildings, particularly large complexes like shopping malls, sports facilities and American and African television churches, tend to become more and more introverted. Inside they offer spectacles in regularly changing, carefully orchestrated, completely artificial ambiances that are than broadcasted to the outside world. The building turns into a TV studio and television and increasingly other, more interactive Internet-based media are the very basis for its existence. Not just as a studio: their presence in the media attracts crowds that want to witness the real event. Therefore these buildings grow in size so spectacularly, that the event itself can almost only be seen on huge monitors that enlarge what goes on, show slow motions of important scenes and, in the break, images of the audience itself.

The Astrodome in Houston, built in 1965, was probably the original type of such a building, built as a multifunctional coliseum that can house different events quickly after each other: from American Football to Baseball, from pop concerts

26 Koolhaas, Rem. "The Generic City." In S, M, L, XL, by Rem Koolhaas and Bruce Mau, edited by Jennifer Sigler. Rotterdam: 010 Publishers, 1995.

to the yearly Rodeo and Monster Truck races. The famous Astroturf allowed for it that no grass lawn was needed. The financing of European soccer stadiums since the 1990s is unthinkable without this concept. Because until now soccer depends more on natural grass, all kinds of different concepts have been developed to move the field out of the building. The Arena auf Schalke in Gelsenkirchen in Germany not only hosts soccer matches, but also operas, Nordic skiing, pop concerts, wind surfing, and motor cross events.

Architecturally, in terms of an esthetical experience in itself, these buildings and complexes are not very interesting. They are basically big halls and boxes and everything focuses on the different events taking place, that are carefully lit with powerful lights. Under the influence of new technologies, notably LED, these lights become smaller and produce less heat. 'Generic City is like a Hollywood studio lot. A new identity is created every Monday morning.'[26] The events are watched at home on increasingly big flat television screens and beamer projections, that start to dominate the room until they will finally become a room-filling moving wallpaper.

The Architecture of Happiness

This is what it is about: we find ourselves in a dull room, in a dull building, in dull surroundings, doing dull things (work, school) and dream of a world somewhere else: more grand, outdoors, preferably in the nature. Architecture can't compensate for the expulsion from Paradise – a phantasm at least offers consolation.

For a book called The Architecture of Happiness, The Secret Art of Furnishing Your Life, the picture of a woman with long blond hair sitting in a flowered armchair with her back turned at the furthermore empty room, neglecting the view from the window but totally immersed in an Alpine landscape with mountains, pastures, forests, a lake, and flowers on a photographic wallpaper instead, could not have been more well-chosen. Author Alain de Botton actually meant something rather different. Lovingly, the woman even touches the wall, as if she would just want to check the temperature of the water of the lake before stepping into it – or maybe her feet point at the peak of the mountain, where she would like to fly to. Against De Botton's recommendations, she completely forgets about her own home. This photograph and the Independent's recommendation printed on it that the book is 'Engaging and intelligent (...) full of splendid ideas, happily and beautifully expressed' probably says more

27 De Botton, Alain. *The Architecture of Happiness: The Secret Art of Furnishing Your Life*. London: Penguin Books, 2006.

about the secret desires of our culture than De Botton's (sympathetic) mildly therapeutic moralism.[27]

Immersion is not necessarily all about positive thinking and relaxing though. Microsoft already patented an <u>immersive display experience</u>, covering all the walls in a room and offering new gaming experiences, like situations in which you "may turn around and observe an enemy sneaking up from behind" while playing a game. The essence of this development is that all kinds of technologies – but particularly those that use light – produce simulated environments that can be completely different from the real space they are created in or the object they are projected upon.

Decorated Ducks

The work of the Austrian architects collective Splitterwerk is a meditation on immersion in artificial paradises, be it in the form of camouflage – buildings that blend into their surroundings – or in the form of carefully designed wallpapers that perfectly cover a room from wall to wall and floor to ceiling, including all details, and mesmerizing interfering patterns, making it almost immaterial. <u>Texture mapping</u> and <u>pixelization</u> achieve this blend between camouflage and mesmerizing patterns. The image or wallpaper can be perfectly customized to a space, with all its details.

Even if Splitterwerk does not work with media facades but only with static images, their work hints at a series of implications these media facades have for architecture. Basically, there is hardly a relationship any longer between the outer appearance and atmosphere of a building, the building itself, as a structure that we traditionally expect to offer a classical self-contained esthetical experience, its function or program, and the inner appearance and atmosphere. And, apart from the structure, all of these can change any time. Architecture is no longer a decorated shed, neither a duck nor does it has to cry out it is a monument, as Robert Venturi and Denise Scott Brown thought. According to Splitterwerk it can become a *giant decorated tree frog* if it wants to, or broccoli or a strawberry or something completely different next week, a pineapple for example, like it was a gherkin last week. And basically, this isn't even a new idea: it dates back to at least the earliest work of Hans Hollein from the early nineteen sixties, in which we see photomontages of giant train carriages, cars or even an aircraft carrier in landscapes where they would normally not occur. Hollein did not think about a function for these 'buildings' other than offering a cultic space.

If there is anything visionary about the Kunsthaus in Graz by Peter Cook, a building which strange shape is completely wrapped in a media facade designed by realities United, it is not the realization of Archigram ideas from the nineteen sixties, it is exactly the discrepancies between the form and the continuously changing program, between the form and the surrounding city, between the program and the appearance of the skin that, with the help of Realities United, can be programmed in many different ways. Maybe it is not a tree frog, broccoli or gherkin, but it is referred to as the *friendly alien*. In a next step, augmented reality will in principle enable every one of us to project the information we would like to see on our environment by means of glasses or goggles, thus personalizing the environment more and more.

The Depth of Dreams

Now that form and content almost become arbitrary in architecture, the more important question becomes what content the new media buildings will communicate. What kinds of depths and dreams can media walls really introduce in our buildings and cities – apart from simple messages, advertising, news, and the stock exchange? OLED and LED technologies have made media facades significantly cheaper in the last couple of years. Not just the lights themselves and their installation have become significantly cheaper but also their energy consumption was reduced drastically in comparison to the technology used in Jon Jerde's Freemont Street. Because they are lightweight, low-voltage and demand only thin cables, they can be installed relatively easily on existing buildings. By placing differently coloured lights in small clusters, these facades can be programmed and played as if they were giant television – or computer screens.

In comparison to murals and photographic wallpapering, media facades offer the opportunity of an even more immersive experience, not just by their size and the blinking lights, but also because of the introduction of movement and immediate or delayed interactivity with the audience. Movement always catches our eye and keeps us alert. Therefore it plays an important role in the process of immersion. Through interactivity, people get involved in more than just consuming ways of appreciating a work.

Of course, people can also simply be mesmerized by mysteriously fascinating projects that seem to lead a life of their own. There will always be the secret belief that large media installations can communicate higher truths. We see that already in Hollywood blockbusters like Poltergeist, in which the ghost first communicates with the little girl through television, and L. A. Story, in which Steve Martin gets counselling from a billboard along the highway.

Toyo Ito's Tower of Winds in Yokohama has been attributed similar properties. Basically the decoration of the light shaft of an underground shopping mall, this filigree structure is equipped with thousands of small light bulbs that, steered by sensors that pick up the speed of the wind, light and noise, produce ever-changing patterns. These patterns are experienced as the expression of the moods of the tower. Pierre Huyghe's animated video Les Grands Ensembles (1994/2001) of two everyday small apartment towers from the nineteen sixties or seventies suggest that they may have a life of their own as well – even if it may go unnoticed by the inhabitants. The way their lives come together in these towers suddenly seems orchestrated, however. Huyghe's video starts out from an everyday situation. People get up, put lights on, shower and take breakfast or go to sleep, brush their teeth and put lights out. The darkness and snow outside enhance the feeling of alienation but then suddenly a new form of communication on another level appears and finally even produces electronic dance music. Jorge Luis Borges once wrote an essay about the euphoria that comes up when learning a forgotten language by speaking it aloud. Here there is the suggestion that we might get equally euphoric learning a new language – or at least dream of it.

Interesting about the projects for media facades by Realities United, like the one for the Kunsthaus Graz and the more recent one for a building on Potsdamer Platz in Berlin, is that they show that a low resolution of their facades, that openly show the technology behind it, easily excludes this kind of commercial interest and opens the playing field for artists to program the facade. Still, the investments for such a facade are high, the artists are selected, they are the sole creators and the format is fixed. This does not really exhaust the opportunities to offer an immersive experience – but maybe that is exactly the critical angle of the projects.

Immersion and critique

Of course, there are also more critical approaches to the
way media integrate in architecture and in the city. The
artists of Graffiti Research Lab analyze the dominance of the
commercial introduction of screens and media facades in the
city in comparison to graffiti, which is usually considered and
treated as illegal. In Light Criticism they do the reverse and
mount boards with cut out critical texts over monitors at
Manhattan subway entrances. At the same time, they took
the actual technology of producing media facades into their
own hands, developing a special kind of low-tech LEDs with
tiny batteries and magnets attached to them, the so-called
light throwies. They can be thrown on any surface made
out of metal, producing the effect of light emitting plankton
in the city. In other cases they simply take a video projector
and project images on buildings. Regularly, they involve
their audience in the production of images, thereby creating
a kind of basic identification with and thereby immersion in it
as a kind of bottom up procedure in contrast to most
commercial media.

Blinkenlights is a series of improvised media facades designed
and realized by the hacker collective Chaos Computer Club.
They appear somewhere between the technological
sophistication of Realities United and the anarchistic inter-
activism of Graffiti Research Project. The first was realized
in Berlin on September 11, 2001, and the second on the
Bibliothèque de France in 2002. Both use rather low-tech
lights behind the glass façades of the buildings they were
installed in. Because of their size and low resolution, they
can be seen and read from afar. The images and animations
could be programmed by anyone with a mobile phone.

NOX' D Tower combines a sophisticated architectural form
(a kind of decorated duck drumstick) with a carefully
orchestrated and moderated interactive participation of the
population. Artist Q. S. Serafijn designed a website that
involves a selected part of the population of Doetinchem
answering a questionnaire. The results of this questionnaire
can be seen on a website at home and in the tower, as the
general result of the analysis of the data delivered by the
inhabitants of Doetinchem makes the tower change in colour,
showing the collective moods of the population.

How exciting the recent developments in media facades may
be, it is clear that until now none of these architectural or art
installations and neither high resolution screens installed for

commercial purposes achieves the level of immersion into another world that for example a Hollywood movie can achieve – with the exception maybe of the example of Jon Jerde in Freemont Street. Most architects, and the artists even more, seem eager to keep some kind of distance and the question is why that is. Sometimes it is because of a lack of means; sometimes it is because they want to keep a critical distance to the phenomenon. They may immerse an audience socially and creatively to a certain extent when they invite it to program the projections with their mobile phones or over the Internet but on the level of esthetical immersion they seem just as worried as the makers of The Game, Total Recall and Vanilla Sky that this mysterious mechanism that allows us to immerse in an esthetical experience while we are at the same time aware that we find ourselves in a real space might be suspended – maybe even for an indefinite time. The question will of course always remain who wants to immerse us in what and why? What powers and interests are behind them?

Two perspectives

Finally, I would like to show you two perspectives about how media facades could work in the near future: one more pessimistic, one more optimistic and showing the possible broader consequences of the extension of public space into electronic networks.

In the opening scenes of the movie Children of Men by Alfonso Cuarón from 2006 we see people in a coffee shop gazing at a television screen in on which the latest news is broadcasted. The inhabitants of London in 2027 seem more interested in the media hype on the screen than in what really goes on outside in the street. There, even the facade-sized video screens on the buildings remain in the background, showing the memories of children as a kind of guilty subconscious. Then there is a bomb blast. In the following scenes we learn that the television news is a better excuse to take a day off from work than having been just next to this real blast. This is the classic critique of the broadcasted spectacle that alienates us from immediate experiences and, in fact, from life itself. Because in Children of Men, no more children are being born and the shocking news was that the youngest living person on earth has just been killed.

The 2007 Cokreation advertising clip from Coca-Cola is much more optimistic and shows aspects of the hybridization of architecture, urbanism, media and media networks that relate more to the digital and networked nature of the new media facades. A man passes by a shop window with televisions and video cameras and discovers that he is filmed. As a reaction he starts to perform and sing the Kinks song Lola while watching himself on the televisions. Apparently, this amuses the shop assistant, who streams the video to the Internet. All kinds of different musicians all over the world discover it and join spontaneously in a global jam session. At the end of the video, our character walks around a corner and sees himself performing Lola with supporting music on a giant video screen, with a crowd watching and cheering. Here, the television and media screens are not just flat, one-dimensional spaces with an authoritarian one-dimensional broadcasted content but the interactive access to another world. Architectural and public, urban spaces have suddenly and occasionally become connected with a vast digitally networked space. In this network a spontaneously formed community collectively develops an idea, which in the end is shown on a big multimedia screen in the city. This hybridization creates new forms of creativity in which, in the words of Brian Eno, the creative genius of the past is replaced by a creative scenius, a creative multitude that collaborates in unpredictable, rhizomatic ways.[28]

28 Brian Eno, as quoted by De Jong and Schuilenburg, see note 24.

EN ROUTE TO A NEW TECTONICS

With some hesitation, a trend is being recognized in which all senses of the recipient are engaged through electronics and multimedia. Oddly, the history of architecture shows only two completed projects in which architects expressly employed such technologies: the Philips Pavilion by Le Corbusier, Xenakis, and Varèse, and the H2O-Pavilion by NOX and Kas Oosterhuis. A comparison of the two reveals an increasingly interactive relationship between technology and public.

Imagine an architecture that speaks to all the senses, one that "has more, an architecture that bleeds, that exhausts, that turns and even breaks, an architecture that illuminates, that pricks, that tears and rips when stretched," an architecture that is "gorge-like, or that is fiery, smooth, hard, cornered, brutal, round, delicate, colourful, obscene, excited, dreamy, approaching, distancing, wet, dry, heart-beating";[1] an architecture that affects us physically, draws us into itself, allows us to fuse with it, and even represents the ultimate hallucination. The yearning for such an architecture may be as old as architecture itself, but especially in our century, this yearning appears to have become stronger, while the expansion of technical possibilities has made its fulfilment seem ever closer. Think of the Expressionists with their extensive use of coloured glass, allowing the light of sun, moon, and stars to penetrate deep into the interior of the architecture.[2] Think of Theo van Doesburg's Aubette, where coloured walls, film production, and dance music created a new, artificial atmosphere in which no visitor could remain unmoved. And think of the experiments by such diverse talents as Konstantin Melnikov or Samuel Roxy Rothafel of Radio City Music Hall in New York, who wanted to produce an accelerated experience of day and night in his buildings by blowing additional ozone into the air. It is an architecture of the kind realized by Coop Himmelblau in the 1960s, with Wings of Flame, Hard Space, and Soft Space, as well as a series of helmets, glasses, boxes, and inflatable constructions. The 1960s was also the period of Haus-Rucker-Co's experiments with similar multimedia environments, experiments which culminated in Hans Hollein's manifesto Everything is Architecture and his (provisional) all-surpassing architecture pill.[3]

Strangely, this secret longing (secret because it is pursued only surreptitiously, for commercial purposes like shopping malls and theme parks, or for underground happenings like

1 Himmelblau, Coop. "Architektur Muß Brennen/ Architecture Must Blaze." In *ARCHITEKTUR IST JETZT: Projekte, (Un)bauten, Aktionen, Statements, Zeichn., Texte, 1968–1983.* Stuttgart: Gerd Hatje, 1983.

2 See also Scheerbart, Paul. *Glasarchitektur,* Berlin, 1914. München: K.G. Renner, 1986.
3 Hollein, Hans. "Alles ist Architektur." *Bau,* no. 1/2, 1968.

275   En Route to a New Tectonics

4   Conversation between Le Corbusier and L.C.Kalff, Philips General Art Director, on February 25, 1956.

5   Letter from Le Corbusier to Kalff, September 1956.

6   See also Lootsma, Bart. "Eine Ode von Philips an den Fortschritt, die Entwurfsgeschichte des Philipspavillons." Special Issue, *Wonen/TABK*, 1984; Lootsma, Bart. "Le Poeme Electronique Le Corbusier Xenakis Varese." In *Le Corbusier, Aspekte des Spätwerks 1945–1965*, edited by Andreas Vowinckel and Thomas Kesseler. Karlsruhe-Berlin: Ernst, Wilhelm & Sohn, 1986.

techno parties) manifested itself convincingly only twice in the history of architecture: in Le Corbusier's <u>Poème Électronique</u> in his pavilion for the Philips Company at the World Exposition in Brussels in 1958, and in the <u>H2O Pavilion</u>, commissioned by the Dutch Rijkswaterstaat and opened last year on the former dock peninsula Neeltje Jans in Seeland. Both are buildings that speak to all the senses – in the case of the <u>H2O Pavilion</u>, to the point of proprioception. Le Corbusier described his pavilion, whose construction he left entirely to his colleague Iannis Xenakis, as "entirely an interior job."[4] "For this I require a fee, and not for a building that ought to cost very little money and that ought to be more of a hollow structure, made of poured concrete, utterly lacking in *architectonic* radiance, as they say."[5] But at the last minute, when nothing more could really be changed, Le Corbusier experimented with the appearance of the structure in a loose sketch showing the Tunisian pavilion in the background – the simulation of a traditional Arabic city with domes and minarets, against which the Philips Pavilion stood out like a Bedouin tent.[6]

Similarly, Lars Spuybroek of NOX, one of the two architects of the H2O Pavilion, doesn't like people to refer to his design as a building. He himself prefers to speak of a *rolled-up plaza*, largely integrated into the landscape. Both buildings are ingenious constructions of bent surfaces – suggesting that the ultimate architecture is not so much an interior as a fold in infinite space. Only in this way can everything be connected with everything else, culminating in an intense experience that is best compared to a series of hot and cold baths, as in a spa or a Turkish bath. In the H2O Pavilion, this is almost literally the case. Visitors move over slanted and uneven floors, and are confronted in the freshwater section with actual water in all forms of aggregation: ice, cold water, flowing to boiling water, and steam. In addition, there are numerous interactive computer simulations of waves, light, sounds, and the like, in the form of projections supplementing this animation. The manner in which these things occur makes it impossible to determine where the building in the traditional sense ends and other aspects influencing the experience of the space begin. Everything is inseparably connected to everything else and to the public. "The liquid in architecture not only means generating the geometry of the fluid and the turbulent, it also means dissolving all that is solid and crystalline in architecture," writes Spuybroek. "The fluid merging of action and form which is called 'interaction' because

7 NOX (Lars Spuybroek). without title, *Quaderns*, no. 218, 1998.
8 Oosterhuis, Kas. *Quaderns*, ibid.
9 Oosterhuis, Kas. Unpublished article for AA Files.

the point of action lies between object and subject, starts out from the orthogonal basis of perception with the horizontality of the floor perpendicular to the verticality of the window. By merging floor and wall, by merging floor and screen, surface and interface, we will leave the mechanistic view of the body for a more plastic, liquid, and haptic version where action and vision are synthesized."[7]
In the freshwater section by Kas Oosterhuis, visitors are caught by veritable floods and in fact appear to be moving through an artificial underwater world. Nonetheless, "We no longer think of the *artificial* and the *natural* in antithetical terms," writes Oosterhuis. "We regard the omnipresent artificial world, the global synthetic system, as one immense complex organism."[8] The organism of the pavilion not only reacts in numerous ways to programmed algorithms, but also to the public and the environment. A weather station, for example, constantly registers wind speed and water level around the pavilion and transmits this data to a computer, which uses it to calculate the *emotive factor* of the pavilion. This emotive factor, in turn, affects the computers that control the light and sound in the pavilion. The pavilion is marked by the continual play of real and virtual environments, the one passing seamlessly into the other, the building expanding into virtual space.[9]

10 Bibeb. "Interview met Gerrit Rietveld." *Vrij Nederland*, April 19, 1958.
11 See note 6.
12 From the different scenarios, sketches and drawings Le Corbusier made for the visual component of the Poème, we can be fairly accurately reconstruct intention and realization. Two timetables exact to the second, among which a stencilled and then hand-colored book.

In his first sketches for the Philips Pavilion, Le Corbusier, too, was thinking primarily of something organic; the ground plan drawings more precisely resemble a stomach. But Le Corbusier had another reference in mind as well, a more mechanical one, when we remember how he praised the organization of slaughterhouses and factories: "It should appear as though you are about to enter a slaughter house. Then once inside, wham, a blow to the head and you're gone."[10] While the program, as it was finally developed by Le Corbusier and the composer Edgard Varèse, did not in fact function in this sudden and violent way, visitors to the pavilion were nonetheless startled and irritated, probably not least of all because at the last minute, the Philips technicians made unauthorized changes in the program, resulting in a failure of synchronization between the different apparatuses.[11]

The prospect of developing a spectacle of light and sound was the main reason why Le Corbusier accepted the commission for the Philips Pavilion.[12] The visual component consisted of three elements:

13 Petit, Jean. *Le Poème Électronique. Le Corbusier.* Bruxelles: Centrale Graphique, 1958..

14 Cf. von Moos, Stanislaus. "Le Corbusier as a Painter." *Oppositions* 19/20, 1980.
15 See note 6 and Lootsma, Bart. "Kunst onder vleugels van architectuur." *ARCHIS*, no. 12 (1987).
16 Basch, Victor. "L'Esthétique nouvelle et la science de l'art. Lettre au directeur de l'Esprit Nouveau." *Esprit Nouveau* 1, 1920.

image projections, a program for light and colour projections, and two plastic figures, a female nude and a geometric body, symbols of matter and spirit.

The entire Poème lasted 480 seconds and consisted of seven image sequences. Each sequence had its own projections of coloured light, an *ambience* that served to intensify or counterpoint the effect of the pictures and bring structure to the stream of images. "Ambiences that surround the 500 viewers, penetrating them with psycho-physiological sensations: the red, the black, the yellow, the green, the blue, the white. The possibility of evoking feelings, sunrise, raging fire, storm, indescribable illumination."[13] In Varèse's music, silence was to prevail for a moment at the exact middle of the Poème, while the space filled with a hard white light. Accordingly, though today the film is shown with the music, it is incomplete without the coloured *ambiences*. The image sequences consisted primarily of black-and-white photos with a strong sign-like character, following one another in rapid succession and alternating with short strips of black-and-white film. Together, the images told the story of humanity using art from all parts of the world, technological accomplishments, and war scenes (nuclear explosions in the fifth sequence), culminating in a series of images showing people in poverty, numerous babies, and examples from the architecture of Le Corbusier as an opening to the future. The relation between image and colour projections were to resemble Le Corbusier's last paintings, in which the drawing, as the basis for the work, together with the colour function as an independent system of forms obeying its own laws and interacting with the lines.[14]

Le Corbusier did in fact conceive the Poème as a giant, moving wall painting.[15] The independent handling of the figural and non-figural aspects of painting goes back to one of the fathers of experimental aesthetics, Victor Basch. According to Basch, the aesthetic experience should also be separated into its elementary parts; colour, form, rhythm, and tone should each be analyzed individually.[16] Naturally, he was also persuaded of the converse, that works of art could be created through the use of *scientific* data. The theories of Victor Basch exerted a great influence on Le Corbusier and Ozenfant. Under the title Discipline of the Arts and Sight, the latter wrote: "We do not know exactly how it works (but what do we know exactly?). Yet it is evident, that

17 Ozenfant, Amédée. *Foundations of Modern Art.* London: John Rodker, 1931. (London: John Rodker, 1952)

18 Ibidem.

independent of each comprehensible treatment or evaluation, forms and colours are intense enough to influence our primary feelings." Using a series of examples, he goes on to show how colour produces reactions in humans and animals that are intense enough to influence behaviour, as for example in the bullfight. Or again: "In the Lyon light factory, the laboratories where photographic plates were produced were lit with ruby red lights, with the result that the workers were constantly in a state of arousal, and became importunate. As for the female workers, they began having more children, as many as possible. Horrible! A calming green replaced the red and suddenly their birthing rate dropped to around average."[17]

Le Corbusier probably did not expect such spectacular results from his Poème. His Philips Pavilion was intended to be a concentrated conditioning machine. The machine's mechanism was based to a not inconsiderable extent on the composition of just this sort of program of colour baths. Hadn't Ozenfant written that people are machines requiring care and "special instructions for use"?[18] The music by Varèse, a mixture of electronic sounds, recorded noises, and shreds of music produced in a studio specially equipped for this purpose in Eindhoven, likewise bathed the public in sound. For this purpose, over 300 loudspeakers were mounted on the walls of the Philips Pavilion. The spatial orchestration of the sound was probably the most revolutionary aspect of the pavilion. Not only could any fragment of music be played from any corner of the building, the sound could also wander along so-called routes du son. Thus the call "Oh, God" came from above the entrance, a fluttering sound – the technicians called them birdies – ran around horizontally in a circle, while at the end a whistling tone shot up to the roof of the pavilion. In addition to the loudspeakers and the ten 120-watt amplifiers, two tape players were also required to control the sound, one with three sound tracks and the other with fifteen, as well as an impressive battery of relay boxes and telephone switchboards, a precursor of the computer. All the equipment was installed in duplicate, in case of malfunction. Overall, this apparatus gave the service room the appearance of a command central for the first Sputnik launch. The plan was for visitors, after enjoying the spectacle, to stream past this room into the open, the view through a window revealing that this magical occurrence had only been possible thanks to Philips technology. To be sure, what was not revealed was the fact that the central interlock machine, intended to synchronize all the apparatuses, had not been installed, so that the version in which one

19 Vivier, Odile. *Varèse*. Paris: Seuil, 1983.
20 Ibidem.
21 Cf. note 6. As a student in Eindhoven, I came across the most important part of the archives of the Philips Pavilion in 1982. Johan Janssen, a former employee of Kalff, who was involved nearing completion for the realization of the light program, has saved and kept this archive material from the dumpster.

22 Cf. note 6.

experienced the Poème Électronique was actually pure chance. This fact did not, incidentally, make much of a difference for Varèse's music. In her monograph on the composer, Odile Vivier points out that Varèse establishes a relation marked by *dissociation* in order to gain from the material "a power..., deriving from the contrast, a dynamic confrontation of the poles of tension, the visible and the audible rhythms."[19] Indeed, as Varèse confessed to "Mon cher Corbu" – by whose scenario he did not allow himself to be overly constrained – "I was unable [in the middle of the Poème] to achieve the tranquility. It has become the loudest moment of the piece."[20]

Now, as we approach the end of the 20th century, the significance of the Philips Pavilion can be accurately assessed, and not merely because the archives and documents long thought to be lost have become accessible.[21] The Poème Électronique appears to have given birth to an architecture whose central concern is the evocation of atmosphere. The new electronic media, whose effects are simultaneously optic, haptic, and acoustic, thereby constitute an enrichment and enlargement of classical tectonics. It is as if a new chapter were being added to Gottfried Semper's metabolism thesis. Xenakis grasped this even more clearly than Le Corbusier and Varèse. He had already made a name for himself as a composer while still working in Le Corbusier's office. At the Philips Pavilion, however, he was active for a long time only as an architect; its exterior appearance may safely be considered his work.[22] Finally, in recognition of his own abilities, he also received the opportunity to compose a piece for the pavilion, to be played during the breaks when one group was leaving the pavilion and another entering. In Concrète PH – a play on words alluding to musique concrète and the building material concrete, to Philips, and the scale for measuring acidity – the sound of smouldering wood coals was broadcast throughout the pavilion. This slightly singing and crackling noise must have given the visitor the feeling that the extraordinarily elegantly constructed, but only 5-centimeter-thick shell of pre-stressed concrete was beginning to burst, thereby engaging all five of the visitors' senses. To this extent, Concrète PH is most nearly a precursor to the ice wall in the H2O Pavilion. Working on the Philips Pavilion, Le Corbusier considered how he could incorporate the jeux électroniques, (as he dubbed his invented art form) into buildings, it was Xenakis who

23 See also Xenakis, Iannis, and Olivier Revault D'Allonnes. *Xenakis: Les Polytopes*. Paris: Balland, 1975.
24 As early as 1984 the synchronization of the individual elements of the Poème Électronique could be realized using a simple PC instead of the space-devouring machines that were originally intended, as we noted doing a reconstruction in cooperation with the ASKO Ensemble in Eindhoven, Amsterdam, Groningen, The Hague, Utrecht and Hilversum.
25 McLuhan, Marshall. *Understanding Media: The Extensions of Man*. New York: McGraw-Hill, 1964.
26 See Lootsma, Bart. "Metaforen en metamorfosen. Drie decennia weense architectuur." *ARCHIS*, no. 2, 1991.
27 Virilio, Paul. *L'inertie polaire*. Paris: Bourgois, 1990.
28 Spuybroek, Lars. "Motorische Geometrie." In *Technomorphica*, Rotterdam: V2 Organisatie, 1997.

independently continued the tradition of the Poème Électronique in his polytopes, spectacles of sound and light with architectural and even urbanistic implications – or conversely, architectural and urbanistic projects with musical and visual implications.[23]

In the new tectonics, installation technique plays a fundamental role in the broadest sense of the word, but the electronic coordination of effects even more so. The tremendous development that computer technology has undergone in the meantime defines the great difference between the two pavilions.[24] The H20 Pavilion is not only a conditioning machine, which in truth treats people like robots, but also gives rise to a complex, dynamic, reciprocal relation between man and technology, building and environment. The architects' activity in the H2O Pavilion evokes memories of the expectations expressed by Marshall McLuhan with regard to the experimental multimedia environment, namely that it could train us to deal with media bombardment.[25] It was this theory which also inspired Coop Himmelblau, Haus-Rucker-Co, and Hans Hollein.[26] NOX attempts to go a step further and give an answer to Paul Virilio as well, whose book L'Inertie Polaire paints a grim picture of humanity seduced by technology, falling into a condition of a motionlessness bordering on invalidity.[27] Thus in his essay Motor Geometry, Lars Spuybroek nearly reverses the relation between man and environment by comparing the process of learning to deal with technology with someone who, after the loss of proprioception – the perception conveyed by one's own body – must learn to walk again with a prosthesis. In his opinion, such learning processes make the fusion with technology possible, such as is already the case with the car. "If you take the haptic extension of the body seriously, then this means, that everything begins in the body and never quits... There is no exterior anymore, there is no more world in which actions occur, rather, the body creates itself through action, by continually acting, organising, re-organising, to *stay in form*."[28] On the other hand, for precisely the same reason, Lars Spuybroek adventurously tilted the floor of the H2O Pavilion to make it difficult for visitors to hold themselves upright, so that they find themselves in a difficult position, both literally and metaphorically.

BODYSNATCHERS

Bodysnatchers

The aesthetics of the turn of this century, which were based on primitive mechanics and a geometric ideal of beauty, have gradually given way to an aesthetics of ergonomics and aerodynamics. This becomes obvious when we place an early, small camera such as the 1925 Leica A side by side with a recent camera such as the 1992 Canon EOS. The stress on ergonomics gives rise to biomorphic appliances that faithfully follow the forms of the human body. A thin membrane and the human skin separate the internal technology from our inner organism. Microswitchers transmit the impulses of our consciousness directly. We no longer need to trouble ourselves with tedious affairs like focussing and diaphragm adjustment. Unfathomable, miniaturized electronics have largely replaced comprehensible mechanics, just as injection moulded plastics have superseded assemblies of standardized components.

A similar contrast emerges when we place a modern car like the 1992 Mazda Xedos 6 alongside a Voisin built in 1925. As Rudy Kousbroek writes, "The visible changes are largely superficial, starting, literally, with the paintwork. In the days when cars still had starting handles and telephones had something similar, vehicles were painted fire red, canary yellow, aquamarine blue, bottle green or snow white. The significance of these colours, compared to today's pastel tints, is real. Primary colours suggest a distinction between the object and its colour, between the paint and the painted. Pastel colours, on the other hand, give an impression that they are part of the material in its own right, indistinguishable from it. The object is the colour, as it is with chocolate or toilet soap. Under a layer of primary colours, the object remains autonomous. Cross sections of a car from 1925 show a metal shell surrounded by a layer of paint, with a machine inside it: cylinders of naked steel, crankshafts, connecting rods etc. Beneath the pastel colours of the modern car, however, there is no autonomous concept. A vague colour is the colour of the vague. The internals, the mechanics, merge into the upholstery. If we are to take a cross section of a modern car (and an ordinary table knife would go through it like butter), we would find a homogeneous, mushy material, of an identical colour to the exterior, as stodgy and undifferentiated as dough.

Kousbroek clearly does not like modern cars. He harbours an old fashioned ideal of beauty: but that is not to say his observations cut no ice. Cars are becoming more and more indeterminate in shape. The point Kousbroek misses, however, is that the way he describes the car, from the point of view of an objective outsider with the eye of an engineer, is totally different from the way we actually experience cars. We get in and drive. The car is ideally an extension of the body, a prosthesis we prefer to wear as imperceptibly as possible, one which mates up with the body in the most direct possible way. In the case of Formula 1 racing cars, that is literally true: the seat is made of expanded polyurethane foam, moulded accurately to the body shape of the driver who constantly wears his car like a pair of shrink to fit jeans. In expensive saloon cars, the seat adapts electronically under microcomputer control to the driver's physique. The body expands from the driving seat outwards, on the same principles as those by which an artificial limb is incorporated into the wearer's proprioception. It would appear that cars have always been a clandestine kind of phantom limb.

To the driver, the car is not only a means of expanding into the world, but simultaneously a protection against the outside world. This too has implications for the shape. Like nearly all contemporary saloons, the Mazda Xedos 6 was designed with the sole aim of achieving the lowest possible air resistance. Not only does this yield a low fuel consumption combined with a high top speed, but it minimizes the wind noise audible in the interior. Disturbing influences from outside, such as uneven road surfaces, collisions, sunlight or the inquisitive glances of other road users, are eliminated to the greatest possible extent. The Xedos has a monocoque chassis of sandwich-laminated steel sheeting, which staves off external noise and vibrations produced by driving and by the engine. The interior air conditioning is as perfect as an incubator. A commercial for the Mazda Xedos 6 shows an exhausted driver deliberately crashing his vehicle, so as to inflate the airbag, into the comfort of which he then sinks and sleeps. The attentive viewer will notice that he sucks his thumb. To sum up, the car becomes a womb on wheels; and, not surprisingly, that is what it is beginning to look like. Mercedes, too, has an advertisement which plays on the almost maternal security of airbags. The photo depicts a little boy riding in a toddler seat on the back of a bicycle. Before him, scarcely concealed by a fluttering summer dress, are the enormous, soft buttocks of his mother. The oceanic sense of security to which this advertisement appeals is something the Dutch understand perfectly: there has even been a novel and a popular song about it.

Kousbroek writes of the increasing seamlessness of the car: "Today's car was not thought up. It is part of a new psychology which has grown, under the influence of the poetic vision of the society in which we live, out of technology: the psychology of the incomprehensible. Our technical society pictures technology in the same way as aboriginal man pictures nature." He concurs in this respect with what Roland Barthes wrote in his famous essay on the Citroën DS.

Not only did Barthes compare the seamless coachwork of the DS with the seamless robe of Christ and with the skin of a space ship, but he saw it as a precursor, a step in direction of a new, friendlier Nature. Barthes also describes how, when the car was first unveiled at a vehicle exhibition, the DS (Déesse, or Goddess) was hailed by an enthusiastic public who were not just content to gaze it but wished to stroke it intensively and lovingly, and to sit in it, in short: to merge with it. "Seated at the steering wheel, the occupant behaves as though driving with the whole of his body. Here, the object is totally prostituted, appropriated; within fifteen minutes, having descended from the heaven of Metropolis, the Déesse is defiled."

THE ARCHITECT AS A MID-FIELD STRATEGIST

TOWARDS A NEW UNDERSTANDING IN THE GREATER SCHEME OF THINGS

The Architect as a Mid-field Strategist

Towards a new understanding in the greater scheme of things

There was a time in which big soccer players such as Günther Netzer and Willem van Hanegem were called the architects of the center field. They not only plyed exquisite balls that had immediate results, they were also able to read the game and to structure it, to increase or slow down the speed, and to direct their co-players with an incisive gaze, an off-hand movement of the body or a dribble. In today's soccer the Spielmacher or playmakers (why is the German word so often used?) of this caliber are, for all intents and purposes, extinct – even Zinédine Zidane does not play with such a dominant presence and consistency as Netzer and Van Hanegem did. The really big teams today all have several players who, depending on the situation, can play a more dominant role for a while, only to then not stand out in the next match, to play in a completely different position or to even be relegated to the bench. Even David Beckham does not play all the time. But almost all of them can read a match. Perhaps the top trainers have assumed the role of the architect of the Eleven – at least when they have time for this. Most of them are only passing through in the club and can speak of real luck if they are able to complete two years of their contract. At the same time we notice that today's soccer is faster, trickier, tactically more advanced and more international than it was in the days of Netzer or Van Hanegem – not to mention the many medical, legal, commercial, political and media-related aspects that are new, making soccer more fascinating than ever before. It should come as no surprise if there are soon master's study programs, in which you can study to become a soccer trainer, physical trainer, running trainer, physiotherapist, orthopedist, commercial director, security advisor or PR-staff member. What am I saying? All of these already exist. Now that the strikers and defenders are increasingly getting special training sessions with old stagers in the field (how do you make best use of your elbows?), the only thing missing is a master of art for center-field architect. If Adidas and Nike would invest in training an old-fashioned number 10, in soccer players who can do everything and dominate everything? I don't think so. Even Ronaldo was not more than a plaything in the hands of Nike and was completely burned out in no time at all. Sometimes, at important games with a lot of TV viewers, he was once again briefly squashed for what he's worth to get a few points. In the final analysis, his value as a poster child was more important than his performance on the soccer field, as the president of Real Madrid showed when he took over the injured strikers for an exorbitant fee. Three individual exceptional acts could be repeated endlessly in video clips. And in actual fact on its webpage Nike backs the individualist street soccer more strongly than team sport, with the clever, coolly dressed figures with caps presenting their technical tricks.

It is strange that today it's not so easy to define what an architect really is. The architect used to be an individual with an important social role who was respected and revered and who seemed to control everything in the city – only think of Otto Wagner or Hendrik Petrus Berlage. If we believe the accounts of architectural history, then in the days of Le Corbusier and Oscar Niemeyer a chalk-drawn sketch on the board was enough to set entire nations in motion. This time is certainly over – if it ever actually existed. This is part of a more general, social process. Even when getting a medical diagnosis we now seek a second opinion. Apart from that, being an architect is a profession that has become fragmented in specialties – design, detailing, writing texts for competitions, constructive design, design related to building physics, architectural theory and so on – and yet architects still busy themselves with all manner of things. They design buildings, city districts, towns, they reflect on political and organizational issues, design websites, design maps, furniture, tableware, clothing, artworks and cars. They develop corporate strategies or projects together with different investors and communities and listen to ideas and objections. They order information and put together manuals for airplanes, they write, organize exhibitions and much more. Sometimes they make a little sketch. And this seems good. Architecture has never been so fascinating and never before have architects attracted so much media attention.

And yet ever since the introduction of the bachelor's and master's study programs for architecture, urban planning and landscaping, we can see how all over Europe the existing programs are being shaken at their foundations in connection with the role of the architect (how about a training for architectural haptonomists?) As a result symposia are being organized and publications with hundreds of quotes are appearing which amazingly enough all proclaim something different. But there is one thing they all have in common: the rock-solid conviction that the role of the architect is that of a hero. This is something architects love to hear – and so do soccer players, car mechanics and nurses. I assume that

Ayn Rand's novel <u>The Fountainhead</u> will see a number of re-editions. Something only has to happen be it with the weather, society, air traffic or the stock market for architects to fall back to the ancient ideal image of Howard Rourke, the great Ego who triumphs over all adversities to implement his ideas, overcomes collective stupidity and is able to translate his great vision into concrete, steel and glass. In the famous scene photo from <u>The Fountainhead</u> we see the final product: a bit too large, isolated, lost and standing out a bit strangely in the surroundings, but with the aura of the Pantheon or the radiator grill of a Rolls Royce. Interestingly, one notices how the actor who has taken on the role of the visionary victor exudes a bit of unease in this scene shot. At the same time this kind of architect seems to have time on his side at least for the moment, now that liberal individualism is experiencing a heyday and Alan Greenspan, the head of the US Federal Reserve, has subscribed to Ayn Rand's philosophy as a genuine utopia. Each ego is wooed by the press and can briefly imagine itself as being a visionary spearhead – until the audience grows tired of this. In Berlin I recently saw posters advertising the appearance of the Ten Tenors (or were they Twenty?) who seemed to want to fill the void of the Three Tenors and moreover with their young, Chippendale-like appearance looked much more attractive than the old, sweat-covered fatsos. As much as this system seems to place its trust in the original ego, what is decisive is that the younger ones reflect the older masters – who embody the centuries-old traditions and disciplines – and so the educational system that goes along with it is a reinterpretation of the old traditional master-class system.

Unlike what is generally assumed to be the case, the architect in this model is not the omnipotent ruler who makes the city compliant with a well-placed building, but a cultural entrepreneur who launches a product – and be it only a coffee pot for Alessi – and waits with steel nerves for it to be bought – or not. He, too, is turned out to burn since for marketing he is strangely enough just as little trained as Ronaldo.

In his essay <u>Approches du désarroi</u> (Approaches to distress), Michel Houellebecq does not just write about contemporary architecture as an accelerating factor for locomotion but also about *the world as a supermarket and derision*. Here, of course, he also paraphrases Arthur Schopenhauer who described *The World as Will and Representation*. The will, as a conscious or unconscious tendency towards a specific goal, was replaced here by the uninspiring, insipid process of selecting products in a supermarket. The representation of the totality was fragmented into many ironic references to past ideas of a totality which we have meanwhile discarded as something unusable, without even trying to replace it with something else – save for the latest models of vacuum cleaners, cars, nail scissors, bottle openers, buildings or whatever. Gizmos, as Bruce Sterling and long before him Reyner Banham referred to it. Translated into architecture it becomes clear that this stance has serious consequences for the city.

Contrary to what the current media infatuation with the individual object would lead one to believe, there is also a tradition in architecture in which the object is socially embedded in a different way. It is a tradition in which the public role of architecture is the focus and in which architecture has to assume a public responsibility. In this tradition architecture is not just something that appears in public space and thus has the task of mediating between the private and the public (instead of dominating the public sphere) but rather to deal also actively with collective interests, problems, risks and responsibilities. In this tradition city and urban planning are the points of departure. They define the general conditions of architecture. Here it is not about a non-committal theory of architecture but about an everyday practice which has largely become institutionalized over the past century in western European welfare nations – in legislature and regulations, property and real estate, monetary flows as well as generally speaking through democratically inspired and controlled inclusion of the authorities in planning and design. This practice is important not just because cities in general become more beautiful this way but mainly because they function better this way, guarantee legal security and it thus becomes possible to back and protect certain functions and groups – everything under the democratic control of society. As the ARCH+ edition on populism shows, it becomes clear that this tradition currently finds itself in a deep crisis for which there are many good and not so good reasons. Whatever the case may be, in architecture this can lead to an exceptionally unstable situation, in which much more is expected of architects than just design and technical skills. In the past decades it has become evident that it is not enough to invoke the historical continuity of the discipline alone. It is equally insufficient to teach the professionalism of Winston Wolfe ("Hi, I am Winston Wolfe. I solve problems") in Quentin Tarantino's Pulp Fiction, including sports' car, to get somewhere quickly and to be able to take off just as quickly. His qualities only unfold when he is able to act illegally. Today an architect must communicate with the affected parties – be it the building commissioner, the authorities, the future inhabitants or the users, neighbors, technical consultants or the press – and negotiate their needs and interests both on an organizational and also aesthetic level. For this it is necessary for the architect to analyze a complex situation and to be able to offer perspectives that are as far-reaching as possible and also back by society, and not just the pragmatic solution to an acute problem – and this especially when it has to do with urban planning. It is here that architectural theory can play an important role.

A number of universities and independent master's study programs already offer specialized top design courses run by the top league of the world of architecture. Yet as interesting and avantgardistic the work produced in these courses may appear, it simply fails to consider the fact that the role of the architect itself has changed dramatically and will continue to change. In the meantime we can see that the changes taking place in fields of forces, architecture and urban planning are much more far-reaching than we could have guessed five or ten years ago. A master's study training program in architecture and urban planning should thus primarily be conceived as a research institute. There is an enormous need for such an institution since the agendas of architecture and urban planning are increasingly informed by internationalization, deregulation and privatization. In the resulting polyarchy in which the various authorities have dramatically lost power, it is important to investigate what powers inform architecture and urban planning and what *behavior* or response the built environment develops to be able to anticipate and control this. In spite of the fact that the individual has become more and more politically mature and one can assume that the free market is able to solve everything *by itself*, there are still a number of collective risks, problems, wishes and needs that have to taken care of rights that have to be ensured. When the authorities lose power, the areas in which they exert their remaining power has to be strategically selected and efficiently administered. Now that an ever bigger part of the built environment is evading traditional methods of control, it is imperative to develop new dynamic and process-related mechanisms of control.

A new aesthetic discourse must also be introduced – one that allows today's disparate diversity of styles and idioms to be commented on again. A garden in which a thousand flowers bloom is beautiful but not all plants get along. Precisely here recourse to the historical roots of the discipline is no longer sufficient since the discipline has lost its natural authority as <u>high culture</u> in a society that is more geared to the individual. For the same reason it is no longer enough to assess architecture exclusively on the basis of a specific cosmology. How good and interesting this may be for architects, theoreticians and critics themselves, the reality of the historically grown city invariably deviates from this and within today's architectural production it no longer represents a <u>niche market</u> within many others. In order to develop a discourse for this, one has to take recourse to cultural studies in the development of theories on the one hand, and include the contemporary arts on the other.

A master's degree study program is the best place for this type of research, development and processing of architectural and urban design theories and strategies. In a PhD program, which is also becoming increasingly important for architects who ultimately aim at a career in teaching, this should take place on a higher, scientific level. Of course, all of this should stand in the service of design and it is thus important that students in such a master's degree program develop their own designs. But it is absolutely imperative that now more than ever that a distinction is drawn between pure design, exploratory design, design-backed research and actual research. Today one side dilutes the results of the other side as, for instance, when theory development is *adapted* to design and becomes degraded to a philosophy of design, which is solely geared to an individual's *branding*. Thus the knowledge acquired can no longer not only be tested, but also the design since a closed cycle emerges in which the designer formulates his/her own rules of the game. If an architect is still able to make a living this way, then it is unfortunate that the knowledge that has possibly been gained is no longer available to the public at large.

In an ideal case, such a master's study program consists half of research and half of design. Of course, this would offer the possibility of cross-fertilization – whether the design subjects use or interpret research because the research courses discuss or critically analyze the designs or whether this takes place on an unconscious level – simply given the proximity since students are able to see and hear what the others are doing.

A stricter delineation between design and research is also necessary to better prepare and select candidates for a PhD study program, i.e., to check whether the interested candidates actually have the potential for scientific and theoretical work.

A publication strategy is a fixed part of a master's study course. Not just to made publicity for the program itself but also to strengthen the position of the better design students for their further career and to initiate a discourse with third parties. This strategy helps all sides – the discourse with the bachelor's study programs, real-life work and scientific research.

The most important contribution that a master's program can make to the current architectural debate is providing the methods by means of which architecture, urban design and regional planning can once again create a continuum. It should be possible to work here from different perspectives, on different levels, in different contexts and scales – be it analytically and pragmatically or be it in a visionary and utopian way, but always in a respectful dialogue and in collaboration with other parties – politicians, experts or contractors. It is not just about "developing images of freedom" as Sanford Kwinter says, but also about examining what really needs to be done. It is about linking individual interests with larger common concerns and goals by continuing to show and juxtapose the spatial consequences of the needs of individual parties affected by a project. This way a dialogue on a solution taking all sides into account can be triggered. And for this we need a planner with analytic and synthetic skills and, so we hope, with more modesty and team spirit than some of today's stars show.

BACK MATTER

Van Toorn, Roemer. "Situated Knowledge." Published here for the first time.

"Architectural Theory." Published here for the first time.

"More Maastricht Bean Counting: Or: What might a modern European theory or architecture look like?" Originally published in *Architektur & Theorie: Produktion Und Reflexion = Architecture & Theory: Production and Reflection*, edited by Luise King. Hamburg: Junius, 2009.

"Body & Globe." Published here for the first time.

"Now switch off the sound and reverse the film. Koolhaas, Constant and Dutch culture in the 1960's." Originally published in *Hunch*, the Berlage Institute report, No. 1, 1999.

"Reality Bytes, The Meaning of Research in the Second Modernity." Originally published in *Daidalos* 69/70, 1999.

"The Style of Choice." Originally published in *Insiders*, edited by arc en rêve centre d'architecture, François Barré, Francine Fort and Michel Jacques, Dijon: Les presses du réel, 2010.

"Individualization." Originally published in German in *ARCH+* 158, 2001.

"The nth typology, the typology of the And, or the end of Typology?" Originally published in *Collectif. Nouvelles formes d'habitat collectif en Europe*, edited by François Barré, Francine Fort and Michel Jacques, Bordeaux: arc en rêve centre d'architecture, 2008.

"The new Landscape." Originally published in *Mutations*, edited by Stefano Boeri and Multiplicity, Rem Koolhaas and Harvard Design School Project on the City, Sanford Kwinter and Daniela Fabricius, Hans Ulrich Obrist and Nadia Tazi, Bordeaux; Barcelona: arc en rêve centre d'architecture; ACTAR, 2000.

"9 Points on Public Space." Originally published in *Daidalos* 67, 1998.

"Of Other Spaces, (re)vis(it)ed." Originally published in *Artificial Arcadias*, edited by Bas Princen, Rotterdam: 010 Publishers, 2004. Translation Victor Joseph.

"Black Holes in Megalopolis." Originally published in *Manifold* 4, 2010.

"Something's Missing." Originally published in *Latent Utopias*, edited by Zaha Hadid and Patrik Schumacher, Wien: Springer Verlag, 2002.

"The Paradoxes Of Contemporary Populism." Originally published in *The Populism Reader*, edited by Lars Bang Larsen, Cristina Ricupero and Nicolaus Schafhausen, New York; Berlin: Lukas & Sternberg, 2005.

"The Computer as Camera and Projector." Originally published in *ARCHIS* 11, 1998.

"The Diagram Debate, or the Schizoid Architect." Originally published in *ArchiLab Orléans 2001*, edited by Béatrice Simonot and Marie-Ange Brayer, Orléans: Mairie d'Orléans, 2001.

"Multiple Exposure, On Architecture, Artificial Light and Media." Originally published in *Lightopia Volume 1: Essays. On the Cultural History of Light*, edited by Mateo Kries and Jolanthe Kugler, Weil am Rhein: Vitra Design Museum, 2013.

"En Route to a New Tectonics." Originally published in *Daidalos* 68, 1998.

"Bodysnatchers." Originally published in *Forum* "Comfort", 38, 1/2, 1995. Translated by Vic Joseph.

"The Architect as a Mid-Field Strategist." Originally published in *ARCH+* 163, 2001. Translated by: Camilla Nielsen.

BIOGRAPHIES

Bart Lootsma (Amsterdam, 1957) is a historian, critic and curator in the fields of architecture, design and the visual arts. He is a Professor for Architectural Theory and Head of the Department for Architectural History and Theory at the University of Innsbruck. He was Guest Professor for Architecture, European Urbanity and Globalization at the University of Luxemburg; Head of Scientific Research at the ETH Zurich, Studio Basel; a Visiting Professor at the Academy of Visual Arts in Vienna; at the Academy of Visual Arts in Nurnberg; at the University of Applied Arts in Vienna; at the Berlage Institute in Rotterdam and Head of the Department of 3D-Design of the Academy of Arts in Arnhem. He held numerous seminars and lectured at different academies for architecture and art in the Netherlands. He is an External Examiner at the Bartlett School of Architecture in London since 2013.

Bart Lootsma is and was a member of several governmental, semi-governmental and municipal committees in different countries, such as the Amenities Committee in Arnhem, the Rotterdam Arts Council, the Dutch Fund for Arts, Design and Architecture, Member and Crown Member of the Dutch Culture Council, Member of the Expert Committee 11th International Architecture Biennale, Venice 2008, at the German Ministry for Building and Planning as well as reserve-member of the Council for Architectural Culture at the Cabinet of the Austrian Prime Minister in Vienna and curator of the Schneider Forberg Foundation in Munich. He is a member of the Advisory Council of the IBA Vienna 2016–2020.

Bart Lootsma published numerous articles in magazines and books. He was and is an editor of among others Forum, de Architect, ARCHIS, Yearbook Architecture in the Netherlands, ARCH+, l'Architecture d'Aujourd'hui, Daidalos, domus, GAM and L'Industria delle Costruzioni. Together with Dick Rijken he published the book "Media and Architecture" (VPRO/ Berlage Institute, 1998). "SuperDutch", on contemporary architecture in the Netherlands, was published by Thames & Hudson, Princeton Architectural Press, DVA and SUN in the year 2000. "ArchiLab 2004 The Naked City" was published by Editions Hyx, Orléans 2004.

Bart Lootsma was guest curator of ArchiLab 2004 "The Naked City" in Orléans.

Roemer van Toorn is Architectural Theory Professor at the Umeå School of Architecture, Sweden. From 1993 till 2010 he has been in charge of the History and Theory program and was Head of publications at the Berlage Institute, the Netherlands. He was a guest professor at the Delft School of Design (DSD) at the University of Technology Delft (TU Delft), and visiting professor at the Universität der Künste Berlin (UDK), while at the same time pursuing a career as an international lecturer and researcher. He has been the editor of several issues of the annual publication Architecture in the Netherlands, as well as an advisor of the magazine Archis (Volume), Hunch, domus and Abitare. As author and photographer he also contributes to many other publications.

Imprint

Bart Lootsma
Institute for Architectural Theory,
History and Heritage Preservation,
Faculty of Architecture, University of
Innsbruck.
office@architecturaltheory.eu

Printed with financial support of the
University of Innsbruck.

Copy editing:
Karin Huck, Franz Xaver Sitter, Kanokwan
Trakulyingcharoen,
Michael Walch
Layout und Coverdesign:
Mevis & van Deursen
Printing:
Holzhausen Druck GmbH

Library of Congress Cataloging-in-Publication
data:
A CIP catalog record for this book has been
applied for at the Library of Congress.

Bibliographic information published by
the German National Library:
The German National Library lists
this publication in the Deutsche
Nationalbibliografie; detailed bibliographic
data are available on the Internet at
http://dnb.dnb.de.

This publication is also available as an e-book
ISBN PDF 978-3-0356-0259-3
ISBN EPUB 978-3-0356-0282-1
and in a German language edition
ISBN 978-3-99043-355-3

© Bart Lootsma
© Roemer van Toorn
© 2016 Birkhäuser Verlag GmbH, Basel
P.O. Box 44, 4009 Basel, Switzerland
Part of Walter de Gruyter GmbH, Berlin/
Boston

Printed on acid-free paper produced
from chlorine-free pulp. TCF∞

Printed in Austria

ISBN 978-3-99043-366-9

9 8 7 6 5 4 3 2 1
www.birkhauser.com